W9-DEU-335

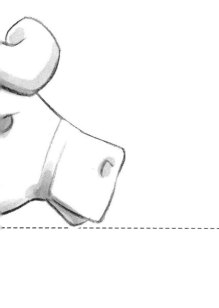

GAY

-2-

Zee

A Dictionary of Sex, Subtext, and the Sublime

DONALD F. REUTER

St. Martin's Griffin ⚓ New York

*To the thesaurian in
each of us,
who says things in
his own words—*

www.stmartins.com

Book design and illustrations by Donald F. Reuter

Library of Congress Cataloging-in-Publication Data

Reuter, Donald F.
    Gay-2-Zee/Donald F. Reuter.— 1st ed.
      p. cm.
    ISBN - 13: 978-0-312-35427-5
    ISBN - 10: 0-312-35427-4
1. Gays—Language—Dictionaries. 2. Gay Men—Language—Dictionaries.
3. Lesbians—Languages—Dictionaries. 4. English language—Slang—Dictionaries.
I. Title: Gay-to-Zee. II. Title.

PE3727.G39R48 2006
427'.09—dc22
                                    2006040191

First Edition: June 2006

10 9 8 7 6 5 4 3 2 1

contents

definitely **GAY**?

I was sure that putting together a dictionary of gay language was going to be a breeze. I mean, how hard could it be for a "minty" like me, who's published a few "fey" books already, to figure this one out? "Fairy"? "Homo"? "Fag"? All of them were just words at the tip of my pink-inked quill waiting to be written down.

But I was wrong to think I could just open and close the book on this golden-edged page-turner.

As I organized my thoughts before I began to type (no, I don't actually write with a pink-inked quill!), I had a startlingly queer revelation (the first of many): To make this a dictionary full of the usual "queer" suspects wasn't going to fly. Truthfully, how many needed to be told that a "pixie" is a "pansy" is a "poof," and so on? Such had all become well-known—and if I were to be true to my "gay sensibility" I couldn't allow this to be a plebeian undertaking (even if I used fancy words like "plebeian" to try to gussy things up). So I was persuaded to expand the contents of *Gay-2-Zee*. But to include what?

This was when my second revelation hit.

Though I had determined it would be expanded, I still had to gather together an "esthetic" core upon which to build outward. I was struck when I realized there was no longer any universal agreement on the definition of gay. You're probably saying right now, *But sweetie darling, of course there is!* However, before you go and tell me all about yours, *dearest*, consider what I found when trying to establish the fundamentals: that the meaning of "gay" had evolved greatly in the last couple of generations. (This became my third revelation.)

While I had never made it an actual study—I suspected just living "in the life" was schooling enough—I did have to do some serious reading (oh, bother!) about homosexuality for the sake of the book. This academic endeavor was what proved so eye-opening: It gave me a picture of the yellow brick road, from "Kansas" to "Oz," we've all traveled along in a not-so-long amount of time—and one I hadn't been as keenly aware of. I'd like to walk you through what I mean, but before I do, a warning: My summary severely edits what queerly happened, in order to show only how basic changes in our culture (and the culture at large) continually rewrote the script.

All That Preceded World War II

Gayness in some guise has existed since the beginning of mankind. Before Oscar Wilde. Before heretics were burned in the Middle Ages. Before "Greek" was not a type of diner, but of the kind of sublime "intergenerational relationship" that the men of ancient Greece were encouraged to have—*and, boys, that was a long time ago.* However, until we were classified as gay, we were just guys who had sex with guys. Really! (Keep in mind, men who had sex with women weren't called straight, they were just normal dudes who had sex with dames.) But without a label, groups like us were harder to identify. Consequently, our dialogue did not have the kind of structure that worked for my deconstructionist purposes—with the exception of words definably "that way."

Post–World War II to the Late Sixties

For my purposes, I read that it was right after the war's end that categories really started to show themselves, "traditional" and not so. As an example: A returning soldier was heralded as ideally "masculine" and given back his rightful kingdom, while his formerly working wife, Rosie (maybe a riveter?), resumed a suitably "feminine" job: keeping her man's castle. However, there were *the few and the proud* who did not easily fit into this blissfully domestic setup. But instead of trying to conform, badly, this occasional "misfit" made the wise decision to find for himself a more comfortable place to call home: often the port city where his boat had docked. (San Francisco? New York? Hmmm.) There, these men (and women) were able to continue the close bonds they had established in the service, and, in turn, forged our premier gay communities. These contained many of the institutions we take for granted, including a cant that could (and did) form the foundation for much of current gayspeak (and for *Gay-2-Zee*).

Notably, it seems also to be the last time that what was said among the "friendly" stayed there. Why? Because making it a "choice" to be gay back then meant that—for your own good—you automatically led a behavioral and verbal "double life." So, in public a gay man spoke as, well, *straight*forwardly as possible. Or he talked in code to avoid detection, at the same moment hoping his signals were heard by the rare sympathetic ear. But in private, it wasn't as necessary to "pervert" his speech. There it was expected that the things he said behind closed doors were being heard only by members of his own kind. But to a great degree, separation of a gay man's insider and outsider selves—along with how he articulated them—would soon enough end.

Stonewall

The importance of this moment as a turning point in gay history (and communications) cannot be doubted. Pre–June 28, 1969, thanks to mass urbanization, a gay man was recognizable (albeit within a very narrow range). "He" was presumably slim of build, affectedly mannered, possessing some wit and some style of person and place. "He" was thought to be cocktail-prone and "chem-friendly" (yes, even then we swallowed most everything placed before us), "queeny" (from a low-flame type to a total flamer), very sexual (but mainly "passive")—and, of course, not very manly. "He" also appeared to have a special affinity for sailors (owing to the harbor connection), and to having intimate relations with heterosexual males overall. Indeed, a "sissy" who wasn't busy thinking suicidal thoughts (sad, but true) seemed interested only in getting busy with a straight male, whom he felt far superior to both himself and the sexual company of a "sister" (even if the guy was no better than a "hustler," which he often was). Surprisingly, the "demimonde" found these "pay for play" types in the not-too-uncommon "degenerate bar," or in the most common grounds of all: public bathrooms ("tearooms" they were called). The lewd details of this constant, *errr*, blow-by-blow could be overheard anywhere we congregated, and they were written down quite often. Unfortunately, what was good for me and my *Gay-2-Zee* research may not be for those who bristle at reading about our unsavory past. Post–Stonewall, everything about who we were would change. By throwing open the doors to our clandestine existences, the aftereffect of Stonewall (actually five fateful days) forever threw into sharper focus what we looked like, how we acted, and turned up the volume on what we had to say—for everyone to hear.

The Seventies

The immense cultural growth that developed during our first decade of being officially "out" also gave the world what many believe is one of the defining words of the gay community today: "diversity." Queers were not just queens anymore. "Effies" could be he-men. Homos were women, too, and fairies danced in a rainbow of colors. But the spectrum wasn't the only thing uncovered. The newfound freedom to show our inclusivity also made visible what excluded "us" from "them" (or "you," if, *dear reader*, you happen to be one of "them") to begin with: our illicit homosexual acts. Many took this as necessary exposure. After all, a doubtful shadow is cast over things that are hidden—and same-sex relations no longer deserved the "shade." Inadvertently though, all the laying bare (or "bear," if you will) meant that by decade's end we would be nothing but slaves to our desires. Of course, we were then, as we are now, not all sexually inclined in any one direction. Nevertheless, carnality and gay became synonymous. It certainly appeared to be all that we read and talked about. This was a boon for the "linguist" like myself, in search of substantial evidence, with any number of gay novels from the seventies amply "endowed," with one "load" following another, so that an overflow was all too real a possibility. (Did it just get hot in here?)

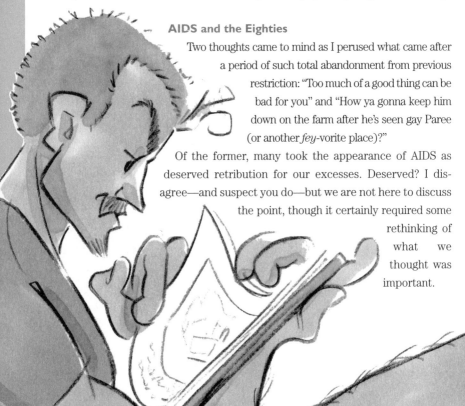

AIDS and the Eighties

Two thoughts came to mind as I perused what came after a period of such total abandonment from previous restriction: "Too much of a good thing can be bad for you" and "How ya gonna keep him down on the farm after he's seen gay Paree (or another *fey*-vorite place)?"

Of the former, many took the appearance of AIDS as deserved retribution for our excesses. Deserved? I disagree—and suspect you do—but we are not here to discuss the point, though it certainly required some rethinking of what we thought was important.

Of the latter, despite whatever fears and regrets we may have felt over our edginess, we had come too far to regress to the murky depths of our former selves. We were here; we were queer; and it was time to start getting used to it.

The opposing nature of these two sentiments caused an entire socio-political upheaval and a notably verbal one. Suddenly we were not only trying to articulate complicated medical conditions, we were learning that saying "healthy" or "positive" didn't simply mean you were feeling good. Conservative voices were raised in the hopes of placing us in the shadows again, and we spoke back in liberal tones. All the while, we were weaving ourselves tighter into the fabric of the mainstream.

The Gay Nineties

It could have to do with the sympathy generated by AIDS, which made the world wonder about the contributions we had made while so many were being taken away. Or it could just have been that our time had finally come. Whatever the reason, we were the darlings of the decade—especially if you were looking at fashion, beauty, and all the mass media. But there was also an indication that it was more than just what meets the eye. Maybe the whole world had gotten a bit gayer. Certainly there was something profound afoot. When one president (Clinton) names your group in his party's nomination acceptance speech and when another (of the NRA) uses the most famous dragspeak line of them all on film ("You go, girl," spoken by Charlton Heston, at the end of his introduction to the 1997 Disney animated feature, *Hercules*), you know you've made it.

But when you splash on an eau de toilette, while the smell may overwhelm for a time, won't it quickly begin to fade, leaving only traces of its original "flowery" notes?

Assimilation and the "Post-Gay" World

It was the very real possibility

that gayness (and the queer vernacular) could have been so influential that gave me a sense of its diffusion and demise. My feeling (as I continued my Homo 101 studies) was that a great deal of what defined being gay was, like a veneer, surface-oriented. By the time shows like *Queer as Folk* and *Queer Eye for the Straight Guy* hit in the 2000s, who we were had become obvious to the point of transparency. Not only that, we had entered into a new "beau monde" populated by the "metrosexual" and the "gay vague" male. Both of whom were/are being touted as fashionable, witty, and refined as any gay man. Goodness, if being a sissy didn't mean we were the most stylish, sly, and sartorial ones in the room, what did that leave us, uhmm, behind: having "mansex"? I should have been able to answer an unadulterated "yes" to that, until I remembered there are heterosexual males who enjoy having sexual contact with other men (a phenomenon that, for the uninitiated, would take a whole other book to suitably explain).

Now I hope you don't think I think being gay is just about façade and fornication. I know it is not. But the definition most of us are familiar with wasn't going much deeper. Curiously enough though, while assessing this "post-gay" era in my continuing search for a template, I had another revelation: If I had been putting together *Gay-2-Zee* a few years earlier, things would have been much "queerer" (if not clearer, factwise). But our rapid assimilation into the mainstream and the broadening in scope of ranks had made it more difficult for our individual language to stand out—and the sounds are growing harder to hear by the minute.

We seem to be revisiting the time when people weren't confined to a group that many belong to "in name only." This is a welcome emphasis on individuality—and on our acceptance into the greater population. But we should remember that it is natural to want to belong. It gives one strength, validation, and security. Belonging is also a particularly necessary thing for the disenfranchised. Unless we show our faces one way, we too easily become an invisible part of another chain.

After all I had read, I still felt as though I hadn't made much progress concerning my center for *Gay-2-Zee*. My mind just kept coming back to the same archetypical details. That's when another revelation dawned on me: The "queen" I had been avoiding, the prickly priss who made many recoil, was no bad guy. In fact, he had many, many good features. One that I could not deny was that he influenced all who had followed—and was a part of who we had all become. This made him very important—and essential. So, I made the decision to give him his due. But I still had a couple more things to work out before moving him in.

As informative as my resources were, I discovered they mainly presented gay language as something one used *after* "coming out." That is to say, words I would use as a queer but not while discovering my sexuality. However, as a kid, while I was expected to be straight (as, really, all children are), I was, as they say, "different." Therefore, my young life seemed rife with warnings about some impending doom. But these admonitions were never spoken that deliberately, nor spoken just to me. They were spat in the abstract, through questions about any skinny kid's manliness or lack thereof. This was really how I knew what being gay was—that it was about being unmanly and fearing it. But even when I was finally called a "fag" the first time, in junior high school, it wasn't because anyone thought I was—it had just (unfortunately) become a word to describe any young fellow who happened by who wasn't "normal" (as all of those straight boys felt they were). More than that, as far as they were concerned, real homosexuals didn't exist in the "heteronormative" city where I was raised. If something doesn't exist, what's there to say about it? But guys who were "cowards" and "pantywaists" did exist. Along with words that teased (and threatened), in their insidious, veiled way, conditions like "sensitive" and "temperamental," or worse, "deviant" or "perverted," were to be a avoided at all costs.

I also realized that the gay lexicon is as much about how we gay men say words. Take "fabulous" for example. Its definition is "astonishing, very pleasing." Kinda, but not really gay. However, our using it has forever affected how it is heard, making it sound pretty darned queer. This has to do with the context(s) in which the word is heard (at an "in crowd" cocktail party as opposed to a board meeting setting) and actual speech patterns (inflection, etc.) which, in our case, are rather well-known (though difficult to translate and excuse). Typical "gay" intonation can take any word and make it more "splendid" (if ya know what I mean, and I think you do). Old (and I do mean old) "fabulous" is, again, a perfect "gaily" spoken specimen. Said the regular way, it shines with only a dull sheen. But place an emphasis, say, on the first syllable and it can really bedazzle one's palaver. Try it with me: *FAB*-ulous. (Okay, if you're looking to be *au courant*, you can try: fe-*RO*-cious.) Simply, there are oodles of words that aren't gay but end up gay—or at least sounding gay. In fact, one of us could read a phonebook and make it sound like lines from *Boys in the Band*. (Neat effect, if you're so inclined.)

Basically, I surmised that our language is not just about words with a definite gay meaning. It is also about the implied, the alleged, and the just-maybe. So, while other dictionaries included largely the direct, I was compelled to wend my way indirectly, too.

Voilà, I had arrived at the end—of my beginning. . . .

DEFINING *GAY-2-ZEE*

With all my criteria finally(!) in place, I set about filling in the pages of *Gay-2-Zee*. I began by imagining who my leading man was in order to be able to better describe him. Doing that was easy: The poor thing fell to pieces at my touch. (In that way, my perception was much like the way the world judges us: as parts that break off easily but not the whole of an individual. Note to self: Save for another project.) As far as I could tell, he was all about just a few things: sex, appearance, attitude, awareness, and behavior. So, I gathered what would, could, and should put those aspects into words. Simultaneously, I envisioned him in a larger venue, where I was able to hear what was being said about him "in reference" (and jotted those things down). I also set him against his foe: the alpha male. This way I could experiment by envisioning every possible *Gay-2-Zee* word as it would sound if a gay man or a straight man used it. Thus, I was able to distinguish words that sounded "gayer" from those that sounded "straighter." (It would be a very good time to mention that *Gay-2-Zee*, while it is meant to be a pretty concise source on our verbology, is still the creation of one gay male person, whose judgment of what is a "dash of lavender" may—and will—smell slightly different to others.)

By now, the book's contents had grown to where cuts were in order. (Already, can you believe it?!) But to do that properly I would have to further home in on who resided inside *Gay-2-Zee*. And guess who I found? Me! Wait, not specifically myself (if you must know, a forty-ish, ethnically mixed, ex-fashionista urbanite male in a long-term relationship who's been out for a *loooong* time), but who I represented. (I figured: any mid-thirties-to-mid-forties man, ethnically variable, a snappy city-dweller who's relationship-inclined and has a clear sense of his sexuality.) This is what my editor would call clarifying the market for *Gay-2-Zee*, and doing so also enabled me to take what had become a large forest and focus on a few trees that would still cover the entirety of "twee" territory. I found them by dividing gay language into what I felt were its six categories:

1. The Gay Sex-icon
Bear in mind, we don't own the carnal acts we are so readily accused of committing, nor the words used to describe them. Therefore, only a smattering of "blue" language deemed most relevant, mainly the frequent wise "pearl" and recent hard-edged "mansex" terms, was included.

2. Man-dates for Boys
Ya know, all that blather about growing up to be man enough or not being unmanly.

3. Femininely, Ours
Since we are so often considered girlish, there's lots of "fluff" that fell in here.

4. Sissy-phean Notes
How we are described in a social, political, secular, and religious context, mainly by those looking at us from the outside—and thinking they know what's going on inside.

5. Collo-queer-isms
Words that make sense when one has a clear, though hardly "politically correct," comprehension of what it means to be a "queen" in the very royal and grand sense.

6. Per-sway-sive Arguments
Technically, these are almost all of the words in gay language, since it's a very sub-textual lingo to begin with and continues on its "merry" subversive way. But these are also those intentional well-meaning euphemisms, when they thought it was nicer to call us "odd" and "creepy"!

All of the words in *Gay-2-Zee* fall under at least one of these categories (and most under many more), which should help explain how some entries made it into the book. But they are still discretionary classifications, subject to my whims. (Another timely note: My pink may be paler or hotter than yours, but it is still pink.) The following more precisely illustrate each *Gay-2-Zee* entry:

☞ Each word (or phrase) contains a gay definition (well, yeah!). But very often more. Among other things, most include a non-gay meaning which will help show its link to our own. Without this our derivation can seem too, *well*, queer to fully comprehend. (If a word has more than a single traditional meaning, I chose the one most relatable.)

☞ Some words also have a "history" (Latin, Greek, French, etc.) and a backstory (or two) about their origins. But I included those only when they seemed relevant *and* interesting (as some old fairy tales can be). What I did not do—with any regularity— was call a word (and its use) outdated. Frankly, such a determination is best left to the reader. Besides, most "gay" words have really been around for quite some time (and new ones are being contrived every day). However, in keeping them, *Gay-2-Zee* ends up with a lot of words that are no longer usable (unless you like being slapped). But such is the inescapable truth of a *slang*-uage born out of some very dark places.

☞ Often each entry is followed by secondary listings. These italicized words are directly connected to the primary in meaning, spelling, or both. However, some step out of the alphabet when it seems appropriate. For example, a "polar bear" is placed under "bear" rather than under "P" because it is an understandable subcategory of that listing (at least to a follower of "bears"). A less significant related entry is shown, in italics, within the definition of the primary word. A grouping of connected words can also be preceded with a standard generic list-

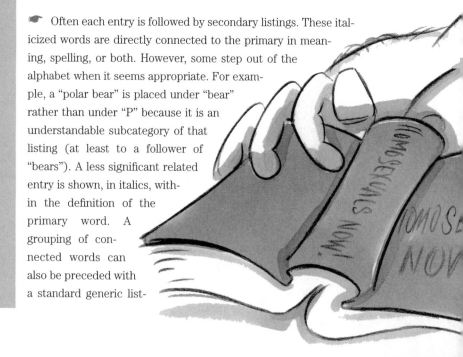

ing that isn't gay, but followed by many that are (example: "boot" before "bootlick," etc.). Still with me?

☞ Some entries are just for fun, and aren't really "gay" until you put them in context. For example, if one were to encounter the "delivery boy" noted inside *Gay-2-Zee* out in the world, most would see him as a roving naïf. But within these pages the lad moves in a much queerer direction because of the influence of his more festive surroundings. The same can be said of the animals and mythical beings that you'll find wandering about.

☞ Any entry explanation with a "-speak" in it (dragspeak, bearspeak, Britspeak, cyberspeak, etc.) is part of a subcategory language. In particular, our cyberspeak (Internet) communication is so big that it warrants its own dictionary. Be that as it may, I have chosen to list only a few representative expressions. Sometimes these are noted by the medium's well-known "abbreviations" (in parentheses) alongside a full-length non-Net entry or have their own listings.

☞ All entries are written with a gay male in mind. That should help you to understand the many points of reference which come up. (I also say this now, so that it won't be

necessary to write "gay male" two thousand more times!) Additionally, because I am what I am, the book can't help but be inclined in a specific gender and race direction. Under these circumstances, examples of lesbian, gay persons of color, bisexual, and transgender dialects, while earnestly explored, cannot be considered comprehensive. But no slur was intended by any omissions.

☞ Exemplary sentences frequently follow entries. These were given to help flesh out meaning. But they are written mainly in the droll, punny (I can only hope slightly funny) double-entendre style that was/is a hallmark of "coy" conversation. Be warned: Most are rather ribald (as was often the point of many of the things we had to say).

☞ Finally, a startling number of gay words are derogatory. What can you expect of a language largely based on a minority's state of oppression and hatred, both directed toward us and self-imposed? While we need to be reminded of our "delicate" condition, I avoided reiterating it at every turn. Just put the thought in the back of your mind. By the end, you may feel as I did: sad, angry, and emboldened to move "gaily forward."

Speaking of which . . .

THE LAST WORD (unless you count the thousands in the dictionary!)

When all was put in place, I had my final revelation (of what could have been a whole book of them). And it was a doozy. It was a conundrum that questioned the very existence of a gay language on two of its most basic levels: "What it meant" and "Is it relevant?"

Before I embarked on *Gay-2-Zee*, I had an inkling that our argot was not always very pleasant. But I had no idea that it would sound so melancholy overall. Aside from the frequent witty tones, most words had an oppressed and tainted edge. The general subversiveness made me feel I needed to come up for air. Often. However, at the moment I felt the most despair, I heard what our language was trying to say. Yes, it was rife with insult and innuendo. But it also spoke of the bitter plight of our community's struggles. And, while it may not make for an easy read, it says things with passion, humor, and perseverance. I hope *Gay-2-Zee* does justice to that noble cause.

But is the specificity of *Gay-2-Zee*'s content still relevant in this, the great age of merging cultures?

Well, if you're wondering if our language is like French and that when you're in Paris it's all you hear, then the answer is no. It is not used in that way. If you're considering it as just words used as a flavoring, then hell yes, it is! Even when it was queer chatter at its undiluted best, it was never all-or-nothing. At most it was used half the time: when twilighters were talking alone together in their hideaway haunts. In that way, what's represented in *Gay-2-Zee* makes it a historical reference. But is it necessary when most of us no longer need or want the protection and secrecy? It is if you read what's in *Gay-2-Zee* as what constitutes some common ground—before going your own way in search of an individual identity. While it may not totally define who you are (it shouldn't), it may help distinguish who you are not. We are just beginning to grasp that a person is not one thing, gay or straight, but many things—and occupies space alongside other multi-dimensional beings. So, use in *Gay-2-Zee* what helps put into words who you are—while others do the same, differently.

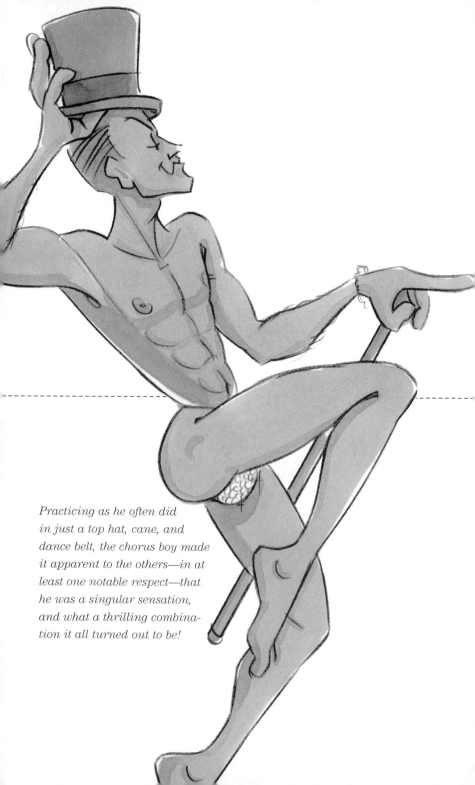

Practicing as he often did in just a top hat, cane, and dance belt, the chorus boy made it apparent to the others—in at least one notable respect—that he was a singular sensation, and what a thrilling combination it all turned out to be!

GAY
-2-
ZeE

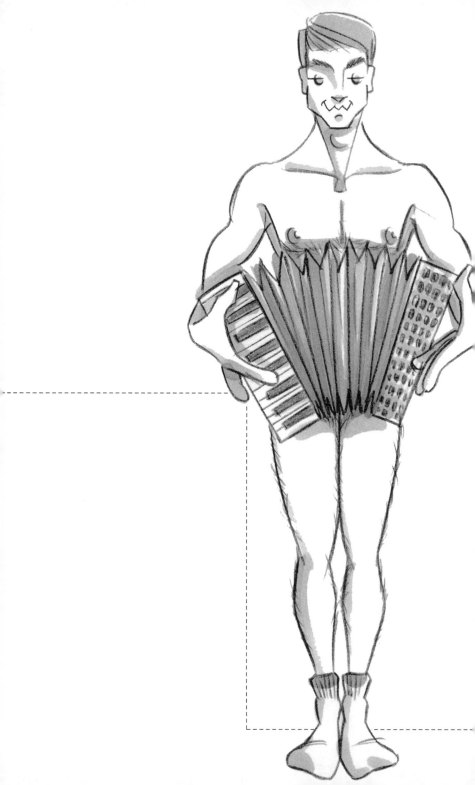

abdicate • When a "queen" is asked to leave a place where he is loitering. (AKA dethroned)

abnormal • Not usual, irregular, deviate. Latin: *ab*, away from; *normalis.*

abort • To abruptly end a process before its completion; when a passive partner (the "bottom") must, *ahem*, excuse himself, often with urgency, in the midst of anal sex.

abstinence • Refraining from a pleasure. Latin: *abstinentia*, holding back.
 Craig promised Daniel he would practice abstinence after his next number.

acceptance • The act of greeting with approval (and the kind of speech I'll make when I finally win that Golden Globe!). *Self-acceptance*: the individual approving of who he is as a person (and, if one wants the same from others, a necessity).

accordion • A musical instrument that folds in and out to produce sound; a flaccid penis.
 He loved to pump and play with his accordion in the nude.

AC-DC • Short for *alternating* and *direct* electrical current; bisexual since he (or she) can alternate between being gay and straight. (AKA acey-deucy; *futch*: one who mixes "femme" with "butch")
 Ya never know with an AC-DC until ya try pluggin' somethin' into one.

ACLU (American Civil Liberties Union) • A group founded in 1920, dedicated to preserving and enhancing the freedoms of *every* citizen.

acquaintance • A person one knows slightly, but is not necessarily intimate with. Latin: *accognoscere*, to recognize.

active • In motion; the "aggressive" sexual partner. Latin: *activus*, driving, doing.
active-passive split • The theory that in same-sex male relations only the passive partner is perverted while the active partner remains unbowed, and masculine, by being the perpetrator (and penetrator).
activist • One who is aggressively in support of or in opposition to a cause.
 I'm an activist—and my cause is me.

ACT-UP (AIDS Coalition To Unleash Power) • An organization founded in 1987, whose policy it is to take a firm approach in fighting the disease and discrimination against those who have it. Well-known for its mantra: Silence=Death.

"Adam and Eve, not Adam and Steve" • Phrase used to remind gays of the couple whom God originally created as opposed to the kind he most certainly did not.

The singer lost her fabulous legions the night she exclaimed that the Almighty made "Adam and Eve, not Adam and Steve."

adickted • A penis lover. From *addicted*: to be compulsively dependent.

Adonis • In Greek myth, a comely young man adored by Aphrodite, goddess of love and beauty; any gorgeous and youthful man.

He had the kind of body that would shame Adonis, and no shame showing it off while running along the beach in his barely adequate thong.

aesthete (esthete) • One who is aware of and appreciates beauty—in art and nature—but whose attentions can sometimes seem forced. Greek: *aisthetikos*, of perception.

You can tell the man's a true aesthete—by the way he studies every guy in a bar to see which one would most likely appreciate the piece that he, Art, has hung back in his bedroom.

affectation • A put-on rather than a natural condition. Latin: *affectare*, to strive for.
affected • When something (or someone) appears to be a self-conscious display.

The only thing more affected than the star's show was the affectation of her followers gathered at intermission.

affirmation • To proclaim in an unwaveringly positive manner. Latin: *firmare*, to strengthen.

You're fitting into this season's True Religions—what more affirmation do you need?

aflutter • Behaving with added excitement. No, this is not a "gay" word—but I venture it sounds gay (as noted in the introduction).

His heart was all aflutter upon learning that his pineapple cheesecake recipe had made the cook-off finals.

A-Gay • One who believes he is the embodiment of the gay ideal: well-connected, well-heeled, and good-looking. (AKA A-list Gay)

Yeah, he's an A-Gay—with a "Z" for personality.

ageism • To judge unfairly based on age.
Ageism in the gay community—is old news!

agent provocateur • One who is used to compel another to take action that will likely bring him punishment. French: agent; *provocateur*, instigator.

aggressive • Uncowed, often contentious and brazen action. Of the active sex partner (see *passive*). Latin: *aggredi*, to attack.

AIDS (Acquired Immune Deficiency Syndrome) • First called GRIDS, for Gay-Related Immuno-Deficiency Syndrome (when it was assumed that it affected only homosexuals), it then became known as AIDS, in 1982, when it was shown to affect everyone. The condition represents a body's compromised immune system when its T-cells are infected by HIV, leaving them highly vulnerable to other severe and unpredictable ailments (which is why it is called a *syndrome*: a successive cluster of sorts). (AKA the A-word)

AIDS terrorist • One who knowingly tries to pass on his HIV-positive status to others.

PWA/PLWA • Short for "person with AIDS" or "person living with AIDS" (which is preferred as it portends a livable condition).

allege(d) • To characterized harmfully, but without proof.
I got your alleged swingin'—right here!

alpha male • One considered the utmost embodiment of masculinity (virile, courageous, stalwart, etc.); in nature, the leader of his pack.

He was big, brawny, and brave, but one thing kept him from being an alpha male: He was also a bottom's bottom.

altar boy • One who attends the altar (an elevated place where religious ceremonies are undertaken) and the men of the clergy; a man (or boy) who gives an impression (false though it may be) of being well-behaved and free of sin.

The altar boy prayed that the father was impressed enough by his devotion to ask him back for some evening services.

alternative lifestyle • A way of life not considered the usual kind. Latin: *alter*, the other of two.

What alternative lifestyle could they be talking about: summer in the Pines or winter in Palm Springs?

ambiguous • Having a meaning that is not clear. Latin: *ambiguus*, uncertain.

How ambiguous can a man be with a statue of David in his vestibule, a bidet in his pissoir, and a sling in his boudoir?

amendment • A law presuming change for the better (from *amend*: to make good).

I have an amendment to propose: that we make it a rule not to sleep with a guy twice until we've all bedded him at least once.

amoral • Without good *or* bad consciousness. (See *morals*)

6

And the amoral of his story: He'll do any man any way he can.

amyl nitrate • A vaporous yellow liquid, first used medically, now as a mood stimulant. (See *poppers*)

anal • Of the anus (the open end of the rectum); of pyschosexuality involving sensations of same (*anal expulsive*: one with outgoing traits; *anal retentive*: one with withholding traits).
anal copulation • To sexually penetrate the rectum. (AKA anal sex; see also *fuck* and *fornication*)
analismus • A condition of the anus being too tight to penetrate.
anilingus • Sexual stimulation of the anus by mouth. (See *rim*)

androgyny • Not easily discernible as male or female; sexless (as an unmanly behaved young man might be perceived); to have both masculine and feminine characteristics at once. Greek: *andros*, man; and *gyn*, woman. "Androgyny" and "transgender" are often thought to describe the same condition, but their meanings differ slightly. The former implies an unrestricted fluidity between gender characteristics (and, as an older term, is considered somewhat subversive), while the latter usually describes a situation moving decidedly in one direction.

angel food • Men in the Air Force regarded as divine edibles.

anomaly • A peculiarity in an otherwise fully functional system.
One man's anomaly is another man's kinky plaything.

anonymous encounter • Two strangers together for consensual but impersonal sex. Greek: *anonumos*, nameless. (AKA anonymous sex)
The chairman's habit of anonymous encounters came to an abrupt end when he mistakenly had one with the company's whistleblower.

anti-gay • Having intense aversion toward gays individually and as a group.
I'm not anti-gay, just not into queers.

antique dealer • A young male gigolo type who prefers well-off mature types. (AKA *gold digger*) *Mantique*: a decidedly older gay male (but I leave it up to you to decide how old that may be).

The only thing the antique dealer disliked was having to oil the creaky merchandise in those hard-to-reach nooks and crannies.

APA (American Psychiatric Association) • The leading organization of psychiatrists who, in 1971, took homosexuality off their list of mental disorders.

Apollo • In Greek and Roman myth, the sun god of medicine, prophecy, poetry, and music (and lover of Hyacinthus, the sporting young male upon whose accidental death—watch out for those flying discuses—the flower was named); a young male of great beauty.

Aristotle • Greek philosopher, student of Plato, tutor of Alexander the Great, and advocate of intergenerational relationships involving the guiding influence of an older man over a younger male.

artificial insemination • A simple, non-sexual procedure where semen is injected into a woman's vagina in an attempt to achieve pregnancy. (Because "artificial" sounds cold, "alternative" is sometimes used in its place.)

artistic • Appreciative and capable of creating art (especially if a hot-glue gun and a bag of loose rhinestones are handy); one whose sensibilities incline him to be overly conscious and caring of that which is of the world of visual artistry. *Artiste*: a class-A fellator.

They're all so artistic.

assignation • A secret rendezvous with a lover.

Another loud moan like that and it won't be an assignation much longer.

assimilate • To become like or cause to take after. Latin: *assimulare*, to make similar. *Assimilationist*: anyone in the gay community who aggressively adheres to the standards of "traditional" society.

The only thing I'd be willing to assimilate for that straight man is my own ass in his bed.

assume(d) • To suppose or expect. Latin: *assumere*, to take.

You assumed that because I acted this way I must be . . .

assumption • That which may be wrongly taken for the truth. Latin: *assumptus*, to have taken.

Well, your assumption is incorrect.

"attaboy" • Said when a man (not always a boy) has successfully completed what is expected to have been a very manly undertaking (like winning the Mr. Universe bodybuilding title or pinning one's brief-clad opponent using an upper thigh hold in a wrestling match).

"attractive by default" • Said of one whose allure benefits greatly from his surroundings, like low light. (AKA CED, "cosmetic effect of distance;" DEB, "distance enhanced beauty.)

attitude • How one conducts one's self (often loftily, contentiously). (AKA 'tude)

That queen's attitude is so cold I'm surprised he doesn't have icicles as earrings.

auntie • A parent's sister or older woman held respectfully; an older, seemingly sexless, but caring gay male (see *nephew, uncle*).

autoerotic • Sexually self-satisfying. (See *masturbate*)

auto-fellatio • The "all-guys-wish-we-could" ability to perform fellatio on one's own penis. (AKA *self-suck*, *self-serve*)

If he had had just one more inch in either direction he was sure to have this auto-fellatio thing licked. So to speak. But that's what they all said.

avow • To claim without remorse. Latin: *advocare*, to summon.

"ayuga" • The sound made by a submerging submarine; of fellatio: when one is "going down" on another man's penis.

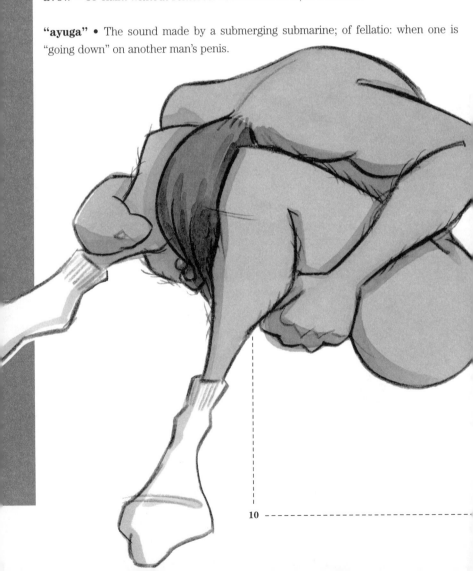

Babylonian • Regarded as extremely sinful. From ancient Babylon, a corrupt and crude Mesopotamian metropolis.

bachelor • One who is unmarried. A *confirmed bachelor* or *bachelor uncle*: a man who leaves little doubt as to his sexuality.
How can you be so handsome and still be a bachelor at forty-five?!

back • Behind; in retaliation.
"back door off its hinges" • Said of an anus (AKA back door) that is out of service.
backlash • Angry reaction to a movement, event; a snide comment.
I hear that makeup artist, Kevyn, was a master of the backlash.
backroom • Area in the rear of an establishment where persons can gather unnoticed (and where gay men do lots of naughty things). (AKA cafeteria, darkroom)
backstage • A brutally cutting attitude (as when one is shown everything behind the scenes).
When he gets goin' backstage like that, your best bet is escaping through the front lobby.
backyard • A gay man's play area: the rear and anus. (AKA back porch)
I left my boyfriend after I caught him in my best buddy's backyard.

bad boy • The one who is almost more trouble than he's worth. Almost.

ball(s) • The testicles; great nerve; events, like those given in high society circles, but held as creative competitions for select members of the gay community.
ball(ing) • Anal sex (as in: up to one's testicles inside another).
ballroom • Any room where one might have sex, but mainly the bedroom.
The ballroom was packed with dizzy queens taking turns spinning on each other.

Bambisexual • Said of one who only likes to cuddle and kiss, but not involve his genitalia. (From Bambi, the almost sexless deer at the center of author Felix Salten's story and Disney's film.)

banana • A notably long and arcing penis (reminiscent of the curvy, dangling fruit); one who fellates.
banana hammock • Revealingly cut men's underwear or swimwear (*hammock*: a

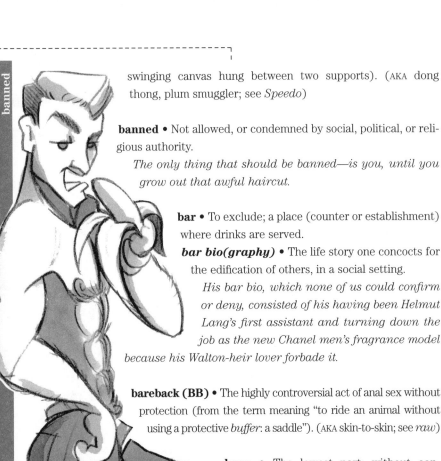

swinging canvas hung between two supports). (AKA dong thong, plum smuggler; see *Speedo*)

banned • Not allowed, or condemned by social, political, or religious authority.

The only thing that should be banned—is you, until you grow out that awful haircut.

bar • To exclude; a place (counter or establishment) where drinks are served.

bar bio(graphy) • The life story one concocts for the edification of others, in a social setting.

His bar bio, which none of us could confirm or deny, consisted of his having been Helmut Lang's first assistant and turning down the job as the new Chanel men's fragrance model because his Walton-heir lover forbade it.

bareback (BB) • The highly controversial act of anal sex without protection (from the term meaning "to ride an animal without using a protective *buffer*: a saddle"). (AKA skin-to-skin; see *raw*)

base • The lowest part; without conscience.

You can't get much more base than being on your knees in the bathroom—draining some dude's pipe.

basher • One who attacks another with violent intent and thoughtlessness. (See *gay bashing*)

basket • A man's crotch (as it appears contained in one, a basket, through his pants, underwear). (AKA box) *Lunchmeat*: What is found in one's "basket."

basket days • Warm weather that allows men to wear less (and/or more revealing) clothing.

The skies above are clear again, so let's sing a song of cheer again, basket days are here again!

basket shopping • "Cruising" with a focus on crotches.

basket weaver • One who plays with (or adjusts) his genitalia to get another's attention especially while wearing tight-fitting trousers, shorts, briefs, etc.

bat boy • The young lad who watches over the accouterment of baseball players; one fond of large penises.

Amazingly, the anxious-to-please bat boy was able to take care of the entire team's equipment without stopping for a single break and, it seemed, without taking a single breath!

baths, the • An establishment outfitted with therapeutic water features; a place containing same, but intended mainly for gay sexual encounters. (AKA the tubs, gay sauna)

Bathsheba • He who often indulges in the bathhouse scene.

bath sign language • Basically, where a "bottom" in a room displays his backside and a "top" shows off his penis.

Batman and Robin • A couple where one is either bigger, older, and/or more in authority than the other, who is smaller, younger, and/or less in control.

Just promise me that when Batman and Robin get here, no jokes about sliding down his pole or if the boy really is a wonder!

"bats for the other team" • Phrase denoting whether one is gay or straight (dependent on the "otherness" of who is making the mention).

beach bitch • A gay male who loves the shore.

bead-reader • One who thinks he knows everything about other people's business (taken from the notion that gay men wear imaginary "beads" like gossipy matrons). (See *"drop a hairpin [bead/pearl]"* and *"read your beads"*)

One day that bead-reader is gonna be strung up by his own cheap strand.

bean queen • A white guy attracted mainly to Latino men. (See *cha-cha queen*) *Rice and beans*: a white-Latino couple.

bear • Gayspeak for a hairy, hefty man, often attracted to or social with those of similar physicality and furriness.

bear code • A system that allows one bear to determine the looks and manner of another, by interpreting a series of combined numbers and letters.

bearotica • Pornography made specifically for bear lovers (and the complete visual opposite of the once preponderant hairless, buffed-up, clean-cut gay pornographic norm).

big bear • An extra heavy-set bear. (As if you couldn't have guessed that!)

black bear • A bear of color.

daddy bear • One whose hair isn't the only thing that comes out on top. (Note: A daddy doesn't have to be hirsute, and a bear isn't always a daddy, but most often, for fans, the two conditions go happily hand-in-hand.)

koala bear • A blond one (or one from Down Under).

polar bear • An older, typically white-haired bear.

Teddy bear • A big, fuzzy, and particularly cuddly bear of a man (or something stuffed one might have atop his bedsheets before he "stuffs" you).

beard • A person used to take the focus away from another (specifically a woman who would be used by a gay man in the hopes that her presence would vanquish doubts about his heterosexuality—as a

beard would cover his face while at the same time leave no doubt as to his masculinity).
bearded lady • A queen with facial hair.

"beat your face" • Dragspeak for applying makeup (with a heavy hand). (AKA "slap up;" see *drag*)

> *You can beat your face with a broom full of foundation, but you'll never look as flawless as me.*

beau • French for masculine beauty; a dandy; a genteel description of one's partner (*His new beau is très bon!*). Others: *beau geste:* a courteous move; *beau idéal:* a supreme example; and *beau monde:* the realm of the fashionable.

bedazzle • That which blinds with its sparkling display. Like "aflutter," bedazzle is another non-gay but very per-*sway*-sive sounding word. It also does what a lot of gay speech does: It overstates things. In other words, we often bedazzle when dazzle will do just fine.

bedbug • Small biting insect that dwells in bedding; a gay guy who just can't get enough sex.

> *I think that bedbug tried takin' a bite out of every-one at the party.*

bedwetter • One who pees while sleeping. Although bedwetting is involuntary, it is still thought to show a lack of self-control. Hence, it is considered a very unmanly thing for a boy to do.

> *I bet Tinky-Winky's a bedwetter, too.*

beef(y) • "Meaty" men. *Beef gravy*: semen.
beefcake • One who is of great sexual attraction and in great physical con-dition. (*Cake* can mean muscles in general or the buttocks in particular.) *Calfcake*: a well-built younger (pre-adult) male.
beefcake magazines • Periodicals devoted to the male physique, featuring artfully done photography of superlatively muscled men. Though this is descriptive of the content in today's bodybuilding

magazines, true beefcake magazines were far more prevalent during the golden age of the sport (roughly the mid-forties to mid-sixties). At the time, they were also important to "our" experience. Though never queerly marketed—such wasn't in the sphere of possibility—it was still obvious, even under cover of a brown wrapper, who the intended viewer was.

before shot • A guy who could use a makeover (turning him into an "after shot").

behavior modification • Therapy causing one to feel aversion to one's previous or current actions. (AKA conversion/reparative therapy)
The only behavior modification you'll learn in that place is going from "standing up" to "on your back."

behr • Bearspeak for one who is clean-shaven or has a mustache, but not a full beard.

beige • A neutral color; to be lacking in "color."
You could dress him in head-to-toe hot pink and that old queen would still leave a beige impression.

bellboy • One who assists hotel guests with bags to their rooms.
The bellboy was hoping to get more than a tip from this latest check-in.

belle of the ball • Said of one who is or likes to be the focus (for example, at the center of an orgy).
He'd like to be the belle of the ball, but isn't ringin' anybody's chimes.

bender • A gay man—and likely a passive one, in that he is "bent" over, under, or into a pretzel shape for anal sex. But it works for the active male as well, who loves "bending" his partners.

Ben Dover • A punny name for gay men which presumes their willingness to "bend over" for both oral and anal sex. (Many of these plays on words are used sarcastically, in queer conversation. Look for them. Signed, Phil McCracken.)
Ben Dover and I will try to see how well it fits.

bent • Not straight; "gay" in the deviated sense, and in the literal, pliable-for-all-sex-activities sense. (Note: "Bent"—and "bender"—are most often considered gay Britspeak terms.)

bent wrist • An obviously effeminate man. (AKA *limp wrist*)

How does a bent wrist drink without spilling on his pants?

"get bent" • The more polite way to say "get fucked" or "suck my dick."

Benzadrina • One who is a habitual user of amphetamines. From the trademarked drug name, Benzadrine.

Looks like Benzadrina is up early tonight.

berdache • A seventeenth-century term (from Italian slang: *bardascia*, for transvestite) to describe Native American men who dressed and functioned as women, and who, rather than be despised, were revered for embodying the spirit and wisdom of both sexes. These persons still exist today in rare, far-flung places, and the term can be heard in crossdressing circles.

"beyond the pale" • Someone (or something) morally or socially unwelcome—and no, not someone who needs to spend about a month sunning in South Beach. Historic origin: The Pale was a part of Ireland under English rule. Anyone living inside the boundary was thought to be more civilized than those outside. A pale was also the first stake in a fence.

Bible, the • The Good Book, set down under God's spiritual direction over a period of about 1,500 years (from the time of Moses, 1200 B.C., to about a hundred years after Jesus' death).

I never leave home without the Bible: You don't know when a seat might need a booster.

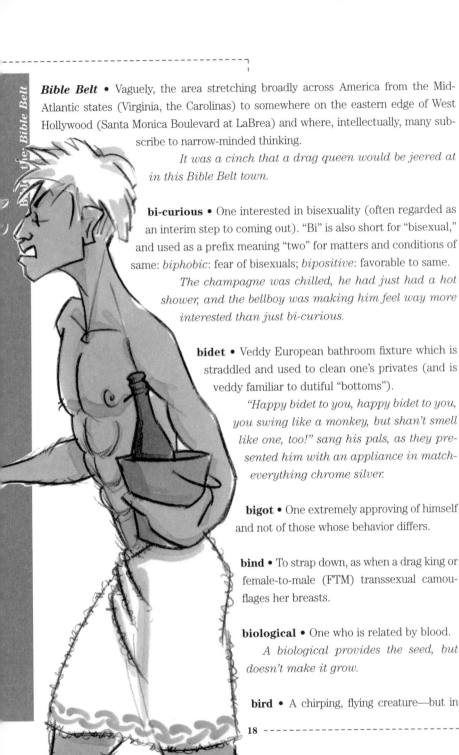

Bible Belt • Vaguely, the area stretching broadly across America from the Mid-Atlantic states (Virginia, the Carolinas) to somewhere on the eastern edge of West Hollywood (Santa Monica Boulevard at LaBrea) and where, intellectually, many subscribe to narrow-minded thinking.

It was a cinch that a drag queen would be jeered at in this Bible Belt town.

bi-curious • One interested in bisexuality (often regarded as an interim step to coming out). "Bi" is also short for "bisexual," and used as a prefix meaning "two" for matters and conditions of same: *biphobic*: fear of bisexuals; *bipositive*: favorable to same.

The champagne was chilled, he had just had a hot shower, and the bellboy was making him feel way more interested than just bi-curious.

bidet • Veddy European bathroom fixture which is straddled and used to clean one's privates (and is veddy familiar to dutiful "bottoms").

"Happy bidet to you, happy bidet to you, you swing like a monkey, but shan't smell like one, too!" sang his pals, as they presented him with an appliance in match-everything chrome silver.

bigot • One extremely approving of himself and not of those whose behavior differs.

bind • To strap down, as when a drag king or female-to-male (FTM) transsexual camouflages her breasts.

biological • One who is related by blood.

A biological provides the seed, but doesn't make it grow.

bird • A chirping, flying creature—but in

this instance: the penis (especially during the advent of gayspeak: the fifties onward).

birdcage • A man's underwear (where his "bird" is kept); a room used temporarily for sex; the anus.

Before I roost, I just want to be sure you've had time to clean out your birdcage.

bird circuit, the • When visiting gay bars to be better acquainted with each establishment's clientele. (Specifically, the term comes from the New York City gay scene in the fifties, when a number of bars along Third Avenue had "bird" names, like The Blue Parrot, the Yellow Cockatoo, and the Swan, among others.)

bird in a gilded cage • A man's crotch in fancy trousers.

bird's nest • Hair on a man, from his navel to his genitals (specifically, his pubic hair).

He's hopin' to find a coupla big eggs to keep warm in that one's bird's nest.

early bird • One who manages to find the best spots in a bar (where he's more likely to catch something before his friends arrive).

You could get your fill of worms if you were an early bird like him.

bisexual • One who is drawn (emotionally, sexually) to members of both sexes. Note: This does not mean equal attraction, merely its dual presence. Also, bisexual attraction extends to transgendered persons, who sometimes refer to themselves as "bi" during transitional stages.

bitch • A female dog; to complain; prisonspeak for one's controlled, passive sexual partner; a "queen" with a snarky attitude. *Bitchy*: Having a spiteful sense of humor.

hateful bitch • What one gay man can be called by another, often in a playful manner.

You hateful bitch, how dare you look better in that Paul Smith than me?!

bite • To tighten and release the sphincter muscle during anal sex.

I like a guy with bite, but that one almost bit my candy cane in half!

"Bite me" • A disparaging phrase, similar to "suck my dick."

bitter • A sharp, unpleasant taste; a disappointed mood; resentment (as when your so-called best friend ends up boinking the boy you had planned to boff).

black jack • A man of color's penis. (AKA licorice stick, dark meat) His semen: cocoa butter. Note: These are some of those un-PC terms, from our past, mentioned in the intro.

blackmail • Wresting gain from another by threatening to lay bare his shameful actions. From sinister (dark) messages coming via the post.

Finding the nude picture of himself among his daily e-mails, the senator sensed that blackmail had finally come to him—the modern way.

black party • Notorious gay social event where the general dress is dark—if one wears much of anything—and so are the general proceedings. (See *circuit party*, *white party*)

black sheep • Member of a family or group who, because of untoward behavior, is no longer wanted among them. From herds where only a sheep's white coat is of use and a black one is not.

It isn't so bad being a black sheep, because you know your coat goes with more things.

blade • A long, sharp-edged object; a dashing, slender—and gay—man.
That blade will cut you down to size, but with his wit, not his wallop.

Blanche • A woman's name used often to address a gay man. Notably, "Blanche" is the name of three gay-beloved female characters: Blanche DuBois ("I have always depended on the kindness of strangers"), played by Vivien Leigh in the film adaptation of Tennessee Williams's *A Streetcar Named Desire*; Blanche Hudson, played by Joan Crawford in the film *Whatever Happened to Baby Jane?*; and Blanche Devereux ("This brings out the artist in me"), played by Rue McClanahan on television's *Golden Girls*.

blasphemer • One who speaks disrespectfully of God and his teachings. Greek: *blasphemos*, evil-speaking.
You're a blasphemer—for saying Tiffany's and Zale's in the same sentence!

blatant • To be disagreeably obvious. Latin: *blatire*, to blab.

    He couldn't be any more blatant if he ran through Times Square in a scarlet Speedo and purple Pumas.

blind • Said of an uncircumsised penis (because the "head is covered"); *blinds*: the foreskin (AKA *curtains*, *drapes*). To "make the blind see" means to have sex with a guy who has an uncut penis.

blow, to • To fellate, because one seems to be "blowing" into the penis. (Although, ahem, as I'm sure you already know, this is not what's really going on: See *cocksuck*). (AKA deep throat, brush the teeth, gobble the goop)

blowjob (BJ) • The act of fellating, given the name of an occupation (and, for some, it truly feels like work).

    A blowjob is no way to make a living, but lots of guys try.

blown • Post-fellated (and a wonderful state of mind and body it is indeed).

blue • Color equated with the unseemly (although it's unclear why, except that when poorly made "adult" films were played, a cold light was cast upon darkened surroundings and viewers—among them gay men, who have themselves been referred to as "blue"; also, "blue laws" were those, from the late 1700s, which regulated social activity, such as when liquor could be sold).

body • One's entire physical structure.

body image, gay • The gay male's awareness of his own physicality as it relates to one of those designated for the group: the 98-pound weakling; the over-ripped smooth boy-man; or the pumped-up hairy-daddy type.

body language, gay • Anything from a limp wrist to emphatically showing off one's rear (if you're a bottom) and grabbing at your crotch (if you're a top).

body rub • A stimulation of the muscles, not always done in a professional manner. (See *massage*)

body service • Another way of presenting these options to a customer, but with more sexual implications. Specifically, a bottom who takes care of the hygienic (and erotic) needs of a top.

body work • Services offered to a man ranging from massages to grooming. However, the offering is made under this legitimate guise with the understanding that, in some cases, more personal attention may be paid to the client.

body worship • Slavish attention given to another's body, but usually not returned. (The expectation is that the body being so attended is in peak physical condition, but this is not always the case.)

bohemian • One thought to be unorthodox (at best) or bound for Hell (at worst), but whose creative and fertile mind attracts like types. From Bohemia—a historical Czech state—where Gypsies supposedly lived a wild life.

bona • Gayspeak to mean "good." Latin: *bona*, the female of *bonus*, good. The word is also one of the few to remain in some use from "polari." (See *polari*)

bondage • Restraint of the body (for sexual pleasure).
B&D • Familiar pairing of "bondage" and "discipline." Of the four activities in the following description, these two, often paired, are considered the milder, less painful, and less definably controlled. (See *discipline*)
BDS&M • Four psychosexual activities—bondage, discipline, sadism, and masochism— usually linked together and sometimes considered mental disorders. Being queer was also once thought to be a defect of the brain. This is a key to why these acts are so often connected to gay men. But keep in mind, a great many BDS&M practitioners are heterosexual. (See *discipline, masochism, sadism*)

bone • Penis; intercourse (anal copulation). Referring to sex this way has become common gayspeak, as it makes such activities sound dispassionate, and precisely how "men" should regard such actions. (See *load, plow*)
bone queen • One who loves to fellate.
bone smuggler • A drag queen.
boner • An erection.
"bury the bone" • To, *uhmm*, fuck.

bookworm • One who studies (reads) excessively—and keeps very much to himself.

boonies • From "boondocks" (the backwoods), and the place where it is presumed the unenlightened dwell—and where gay men avoid visiting or deny coming from.

boot • Protective footgear (that may make the wearer feel more "masculine").
boot boy • One who tends and fetches these items for his owner's pleasure (as well as his own).
We all agreed that the boot boy worked best on his bare knees and bootless.
bootblack • One who cleans and polishes these items for his owner's pleasure (as well as his own).
bootlick • One who is expected to salivate all over these items for his owner's pleasure (as well as his own). (See *boot boy*)

booty bump • A measure of drug (bump) forced directly into the anus (booty), where it quickly enters the bloodstream, "hastening its effects" (which is also known as a bump). This practice is hardly gay, but straight guys are loath to admit they enjoy shoving things up their kazoos (though more do than you know) as much as they like passing things out of them.

bo-peeps • One's eyes, especially when they're on the lookout. Taken from the nursery rhyme about the little girl who has "lost her sheep."
I'd keep my bo-peeps on that little lamb; I hear he strays easily.

Boswell • One who is extremely attentive to another of greater authority. From James Boswell, noted 1700s diarist and biographer of Samuel Johnson, a dictionary writer!
The professor was quite happy to have found a Boswell who kept him company as well as kept his papers in order.

bottom • The lowest point, opposite the highest (see *top*); the passive sex partner (to one who is active); generally speaking, submissive behavior (as it is expected that one is likely to be the less aggressive and possibly more effeminate); the anus.
big ol' bottom • Qualification of one who thinks he is masculine, but who is, in reality, quite the opposite.
He may top out at 6'4", but it's as close as that big ol' bottom will get to bein' one himself.
bossy bottom • One whose dominating demeanor contrasts with his "low" position. (AKA control bottom)

The easiest way to stop a bossy bottom from bossing you around is to stay on top of him.

bottom boy • Redundant but oft-used reference for one who is undoubtedly passive.

bottomless (pit) • A passive partner whose sex drive appears to be without end.

I hear it's bottomless, so I suggest you take a few friends in to help pull you out when you're done.

"bottom's up" • The position the passive partner takes to show he's ready for action: on his stomach, with his buttocks raised. (AKA sunnyside up)

"boxers or briefs?" • A paradoxical question, whose answer, in theory, can determine either one's modest yet manly tendencies (boxers) or his more brazen and, *maybe*, more fey interests (briefs).

boy • A young male; one, of any age, with a boyish mien; a bottom; a younger gay man in a relationship with an older daddy male. (Note: Specific age is not necessary when being a boy. But one should be the more passive, owing to "youthful" inexperience and immaturity, while an older mate should be the active, knowledgeable, mature one.) "Boys" are an indelible part of gay culture. But why? Well, a coupla reasons: 1) We are a community that appears to give greater value to youth (expecting he also has beauty); and 2) According to straight men—who can act like boys, but grow up to be men—we gay guys can never be man *enough*. Therefore, we are caught in an arrested state of perpetual boyhood. It also doesn't help that so many of us live like Peter Pan. In any case, the gay boy is everywhere—and everywhere in *Gay-2-Zee*, too. So, please keep your eyes out for them—they get to rambling off when your back is turned. (AKA boi)

boy butter • A sexual lubricant.

boy Friday • One who is paid to serve an older man (taken from *girl Friday*: an efficient female assistant, which came from the "man Friday" character in *Robinson Crusoe*). (AKA kept boy)

I hear his boy Friday works weekends and holidays!

boy pussy • The anus of a passive male (a "pussy boy") fondly regarded as like the genitalia of a woman. (See *mangina*)

boy soup • Any sizable gathering of males in a pool or hot tub.

boy toy • A young male as a total plaything; a penis.

boy-chick • One who is transgendered; a younger, effeminate male (or masculine female).

boyish • One with the good/bad attitude of a boy; one with a likably immature manner.

boy-next-door (BND) • One with unintimidating and accessible looks and manners.

How can I ignore the boy-next-door?

boys' club • Any establishment that counts gay men as their main or entire clientele.

boycott • To avoid, refuse to patronize, or not use as a point of protest (as when things gay men favor are purposely avoided by others and vice versa).

He thought boycott meant catching a young trick for the night.

boyfriend (BF) • Reference to one's male lover or companion (but often considered adolescent-sounding).

bracelet • One's lover (implying that he is someone whom one keeps close at hand).

charm bracelet • An address book where a gay man lists names of lovers (and tricks, too).

Sister, you've filled enough charm bracelets to use 'em as dumbbells.

breakthrough • Rather indelicate (but accidental) flatulence while having sex, especially anal intercourse.

Yeah, his breakthrough was outstanding—as was I after fleeing the bedroom to breathe.

breed • To procreate; sexual intercourse; gayspeak for "raw" anal copulation (often with the expectation that actual insemination may occur).

breeder(s) • A heterosexual; all heterosexuals (but specifically those who gloat over their procreative ways).

breeder boy • A young, straight male; a gay man, always a bottom but not always younger, who, often by enthusiastic choice, allows himself to be inseminated anally.

"bring out" • To escort into the "scene" or seduce a newly acknowledged gay man.

broiler • A young gay man (see *chicken*) with way too much experience for his years; one who worships the sun—to the point of a burning obsession.
I think it's time to turn the broiler over and cook his other side.

bronco • An untamed horse; a young gay male (in need of breaking in).
bronco buster • The active male who breaks in wild broncos.

brown family • Said of all gays. The name is an allusion to the color of fecal matter often present in anal copulation (unless you're the type who strives to be "as clean as a floor you could eat off of"—and many tops thank you for that).
browner • An active gay male.
brownie • The anus; a passive gay male.
I'm hungry for a brownie.
browning • The act of anal copulation.

Brucie • Nickname for Bruce, but also somewhat mocking of its implied masculinity (as would be, in some contexts, Donnie for Donald or Robbie for Robert). As a result, it has been used to address those—not even named Bruce—who don't seem very manly. (And what would you say are the odds that many of us are really named Bruce? Pretty slim, Slim.)

bruin • A bear who is into sports.

bubble • A perfectly round and highly *prick*-able object.
bubble butt • Exceptionally well-rounded and attractive buttocks (coveted by both bearer and viewer).
He possessed a bubble butt that was in serious danger of bein' popped constantly.

bubble gun machine • A condom dispenser.

bubble yum • One who has the aforementioned *ass*-et (and of the trademarked gum name).

buddy • A friend; a generic, genial, nonsexual address for men; one who voluntarily helps and offers companionship to a person with AIDS.

buddy booth • A small room, usually within the confines of a sex-shop, for viewing pornographic films, where it is possible to fellate another (a "buddy") through a common partition.

fuck buddy • One with whom sex occurs semi-regularly, but casually and, most important, without romantic attachment.

good buddy • Euphemism for one's sex mate.

buff • Naked; to be remarkably muscular (but usually hairless to the point where the body shines as though it had been "buffed").

buff puff • A muscular but fey man. (AKA *Muscle Mary*)

buffet • A gathering where guests serve themselves; the main attraction (most desirable male) at a sex party.

bug • A disease-bearing micro-organism; the HIV. *Superbug*: An as-yet undiscovered strain of HIV that would be so powerful as to be uncontrollable under current medical treatments.

bug chaser • One who is not yet, but wishes to be, HIV-positive (and therefore has unprotected sex with known-infected partners).

bug parties • Sex gatherings where it is known that all or some of the participants are HIV-positive, and those who are negative are not given to caution. (See *positive: poz-4-poz*)

bugger • From the Turkish (*bulghar*: promiscuous) and the French (*bougre*: heretic, originally from Bulgaria). One who practices anal copulation. (AKA sodomite)

buggery • The act of sodomy. (Note: America's sodomy laws directly descended from England, where such transgressions went on the books after the Buggery Law of 1533, during the reign of Henry VIII, and were punishable by death. It was only in 1861 that sentencing for such a crime was reduced to the more lenient ten years to life.)

bugle boy • The guy who likes to blow as much as he likes to have his blown.

The bugle boy carries a horn with him I'd love to put my lips around.

bukkake • A sex act of symbolic servility, where one man is ejaculated upon by a group of others. The term comes from the Japanese, meaning "douse," but many dispute that the practice originated there, as it only appeared in Japanese adult films in the late 1990s.

bull • A large, often clumsy animal; a large, often clumsy man.

bull pen • A gathering place for "he-man" types (taken from a holding place for male prisoners, *not* where baseball pitchers practice).

bull ring • The anus of an active partner.

Only the toughest matadors can be allowed into that bull ring.

bull's balls • Unusually large testicles (considered a sign of virility).

bull's-eye • The anus, as a target for a he-man's penis.

The second he saw the bull's-eye he was ready to take a shot at it.

"ride a bull" • To anal-copulate a masculine bottom.

bully • One who is frequently combative toward another whom he believes is weaker (from the notion that to behave as such makes that person like a bull: rough, uncaring).

bum • Mainly Britspeak for the buttocks.

bum boy • A passive gay male.

bum chums • All gay men.

bummer • The active gay male.

He can be such a bummer—but that's what all the bottoms love about him!

"bump and twirl" • To take drugs (bump) and dance (twirl).

"bumping pussy" • Two passive males (or drag queens) trying, with scant success, to have sex.

Those two cats, Jason and Reese, will be bored to death bumping pussy until that top dog, Meyer, shows up.

bungee boy • A straight-acting gay (or bisexual) young man. From the extreme sport of "bungee jumping," where one stretches dangerously in one direction, then recoils back to safety in another.

Ya never know with that bungee boy if he's coming or going— until after he comes and goes.

bunker • From *bunk*: to "bed" down; an active sex partner.

bunker-shy • One who is afraid of anal sex. From nineteenth-century prison-speak, for a man fearful of entering a *bunker*: a prison's sleeping quarters, where he may be sexually violated.

bunkie (bunkee) • The passive partner of a bunker.

butch • One who is active and aggressive; a gay form of address (*"Hey, butch, how's it hangin'?"*); an impression of real or affected masculinity (as when a bottom wears butch clothes hoping to take on that persona).

Cassidy was hot, but unfortunately not very butch.

butcher • To make one into a man (make him butch-*er*) mainly by submitting him to anal sex.

butchilinity • The measure of a gay man's masculinity.

"butch it up" • To affect masculine mannerisms often to offset indications of effeminacy.

butt • The end of something (example: a cigarette's butt); short for one's *buttocks*: the rear pelvic area (from Old English: *buttuc*, end).

butt floss • A thong or bikini (so skimpy as to slide right in between one's cheeks); hair around the anus.

butt fucker • A derogatory way (but hell, aren't they all?) to say gay man, and not necessarily describing the more active participant.

butt munch • To perform analingus with glee, as though snacking on a well-deserved treat.

butt pirate • How to say gay dude pillages and plunders for with imagination: This precious *booty* (treasure).

29

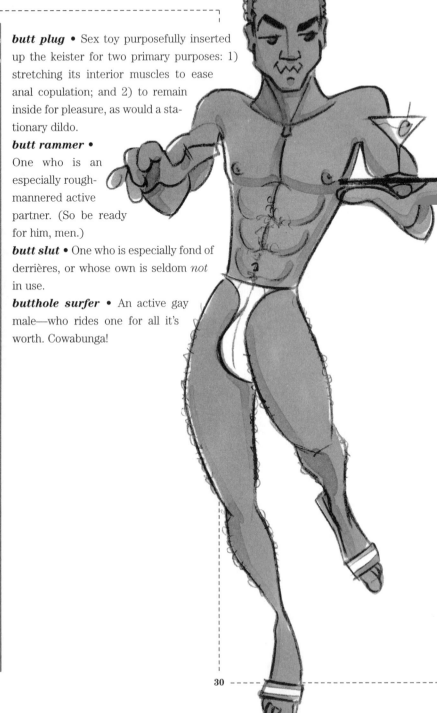

butt plug • Sex toy purposefully inserted up the keister for two primary purposes: 1) stretching its interior muscles to ease anal copulation; and 2) to remain inside for pleasure, as would a stationary dildo.

butt rammer • One who is an especially rough-mannered active partner. (So be ready for him, men.)

butt slut • One who is especially fond of derrières, or whose own is seldom *not* in use.

butthole surfer • An active gay male—who rides one for all it's worth. Cowabunga!

cabana boy • The tanned poolside or beach attendant who serves cocktails—or both his cock and his tail. His cousin? The pool boy.

That cabana boy could be served to me on a tray—any way he wants.

cabin boy • The young ruffian who serves *under* all the men onboard ship.

cabin fever • Said of a straight man in close quarters (ex: barracks) who ends up having homosexual relations. (AKA lost at sea [specifically a malady for straight sailors on a ship])

cackle • To talk shrilly (from the sound a hen makes after laying an egg).

One chicken cackled to another, "I guess that rooster's cock-a-doodle didn't do it for you?"

cafeteria • A place where food is served; a sex club or backroom.

Just consider me the cafeteria's blew plate special.

cake boy • He who is regarded as something sweet and confectionary, like, *well*, a cake. (Note that "cake" frequently implies the buttocks in gayspeak.)

call boy • A for-hire male whose sexual services can be discreetly secured over the telephone or over the Internet. (AKA COD boy, which stands for "cock on delivery")

To be hung up over a call boy was a bad connection.

"Call wardrobe" • Phrase for when a gay man has a complaint to make. From the theater (and our perpetual link to it), where problems are often encountered with costumes (see *theatrical*).

Calvins • Men's underwear made with homoerotic sex appeal (originally from designer, Calvin Klein, who marketed his with a tangible amount). (antonym: BVDs)

Camille • A gay man who overdramatizes everything in his life, especially his love affairs (from the theater piece where the heroine dies tragically in her lover's arms).
"pull a Camille" • To use a dramatic excuse to get out of one's obligations.

camp • Appreciation of the put-on, crude, or trivial in behavior and style; one whose company is highly amusing. (*He's such a camp, it's like going out with the circus.*) "Camp" is a hard thing to explain, but let me try: It is basically something that was originally serious, that can now be made fun out of. For example, the masculine iconography used by the notorious gay-conceit musical act The Village People. Such hilarious calamity occurs mainly by accident or over time; the deliberate creation of "camp" is not (as) credible. The origin of the word is even harder to explain. But let me try here, too: Supposedly, "camping" was what it was called when men wore dresses in sixteenth-century English theatrical productions; and *campagne* is the French word for "countryside," where wandering troupes of mimes performed. (See, neither explanation really helps, does it?)

"camp it up" • To heighten or add absurdity to an ordinary endeavor or one that may already have a sense of crudity.

camp name • A gay alias, often a feminized version of a masculine original (ex: Alana for Alan; or the Weeping Willow, for a guy who complains a lot).

camp(y) • Someone (or something) full of preposterousness. Examples of things that are campy: the film *Showgirls*, lawn decorations, most '80s pop stars.

    He's a mess in a dress, but a campy hoot in a three-piece suit.

candy ass • A guy who is breakable (and lickable) like a sweet. (AKA candy pants)

candy maker • One who masturbates another to ejaculation (candy), then often ingests it. A *candy boy* is a young gay male who is prone to sexual activity where semen is freely (and unsafely) exchanged.

canned goods • A virgin (unopened) gay male.

    Last time my opener was handy there were no canned goods to be found.

"No canned goods allowed" • A rule in BDS&M sexual activity, where no one without experience is admitted into a scene.

capon • An extremely effeminate and/or attractive young male (taken from the name for a male chicken that has been castrated to enhance its flavor). (See *chicken*)

    You need only partake of a soupçon of capon in order to appreciate the unique taste of one.

card, the • The "proof of membership" that all gay men supposedly carry with them (but few seem able to find when asked for identification). Also, many are threatened with having their privileges revoked if they don't queerly get with the program. (AKA the gay card)

If you didn't know Bette said that in All About Eve, *you should have your card taken away.*

carpet munch(er) • To perform cunnilingus; one into same (often used by gays to describe lesbians and heterosexual males).

castrate • To render a male *sexless*: without virility, unmanly. From the operation where a man's testicles are cut away for purposes of sterility—*youch!*—or, as was the case with the Italian castrato singers, to enable his singing voice to remain high past the age of puberty.

Castro, The • The most famous gay neighborhood in all the world began as a nondescript immigrant community in San Francisco. But in an act of early queer gentrification, great numbers of us (who had settled in the city after service in World War II) moved over the hill from the Haight-Ashbury district in the late sixties, owing to that neighborhood's increase in drug use and violence. By the seventies, they had turned this once Irish enclave into what became known as the "Gay Mecca." Today, the immediacy of the place is not as rarified as it once was. Nor is the idea of a gay area, away from a straight one, nearly as necessary. But the place still has a vibrancy all its own that queerly shines through. (Of particular note, the unofficial "Mayor of Castro Street," Harvey Milk, opened his camera shop there in 1975, drawing more gay men to the area in the process. Significantly, Milk went on to become the city's first openly gay elected official. But in 1978, he and Mayor George Moscone were assassinated by fellow city supervisor Dan White.)

catamite • Historic term meaning a young gay male in a servile relationship with an older male (see *pederast*). From the Latin: *catamitus*, a derivation of the Greek: *Ganymede*, the beautiful boy of myth who was carried off by Zeus to serve as his cupbearer—and you can be sure daddy's cup was a mouthful! (Note: "Catamite" was also shortened to "cat" and took on a meaning only slightly less "gay.") (See *Ganymede*)

catcher • "Playful" term for a passive sex partner

(named for the crouching baseball player at home base who catches the ball thrown by the pitcher). (See *pitcher*)

As dangerous as it was to do so, the catcher preferred playing without a mitt.

catty • An attitude of deliberate hurtfulness, as from a cat's way of seeming to be uncaring. (Question: Can straight men act "catty" or just women and, of course, gay men?)

You know if I didn't shave my whiskers every morning I'd be even more catty.

celibate • Abstaining from sex for religious reasons ("vows of celibacy"). (Note: "Celibacy," from the Latin, *caelibatus*, means an "unmarried state" and, therefore, is not really the condition of sexual abstinence.)

Joining meant he'd have to be celibate, but the priest knew that wouldn't be a problem in the monastery's secluded quarters among the other men.

censor • To repress what appears objectionable. Latin: *censor*, to assess.

The censor left the gore in, but cut the two men kissing out.

centaur • Greek myth. Race of half men (upper), half horse (lower).

Having all the physical attributes of one, he was sure to be the centaur of attraction at the pool party.

cha-cha queen • Derogatory gayspeak for an effeminate Latino male, or for a non-Latino male attracted to Latino men. (AKA *bean queen*)

charge • An unsafe-sex term implying that semen (HIV-negative or HIV-positive) has the ability to energize (charge) another. Note: It is always the passive partner who is *charged*, and is *supercharged* when he and/or his active partner is HIV-positive.

chaser • One in fast pursuit of another. (See *bug chaser*, *chubby chaser*, and *tranny chaser*)

chat room • A "place" online where gay men converse in "real time."

It's called a chat room, but no one here is ever interested in talking.

chatterbox • One who talks (and talks) of trivial things.

Your son is quite a chatterbox with the girls, but is mum around the boys.

Chelsea boy • Named for the New York City neighborhood this rascal populates, he is perceived (at least by himself) as the quintessential queer: well-built, well-groomed, well-connected.

chem-friendly • To find acceptable the company of someone who takes drugs and/or taking them yourself. (This is an instance of a word that comes up often in our vocabulary, but incorrectly implies that gay men are more inclined than straight guys to take drugs. We are not. However, our lifestyles—childlike and child-free—supposedly afford us greater opportunity, perhaps, to indulge.) (See *drugs*)

cherry • A virgin gay male. (Note: To "pop a cherry" is a term specifically descriptive of tearing a virgin female's hymen, which causes bleeding. This does not usually occur when copulating with a novice male—unless you're really rough on him.)

cherry on top • A young male (possibly under age or a virgin) who seduces older men. *He went in for some plain vanilla, but came out with a cherry on top.*

cherry-picker • A man who seeks out males who have not yet enjoyed anal copulation.

chic • Fashionable, but often illusory (from the French, for elegance). *Chichi*: style seen as intentional and artificial (as the word is, itself, an unnecessary doubling of "chic").

chicken • One who is fearful; a young gay male. (Both derive their meanings from the actual birds who are easily frightened, caught, and handled.)

chicken coop • Any place where young gays flock—and can be snatched.

chicken dinner • Sex with a young gay man.

chicken hawk • An older man whose prurient interests are best satisfied by "chicken." Named for the bird of prey who hunts down such fowl. (AKA chicken plucker)

He was a skilled chicken hawk, who deftly circled the room until he found his victim: an unwary, squawking chicken who sat cross-legged on a stool in the front bar.

chicken pox • (To be stricken with) an attraction to younger men.

Never worry, once he gets over his chicken pox, I'm sure he'll be up to his old tricks.

broiled chicken • One who is a bit long in the feather, overdone (past the age of true chickendom). (See *turkey*)

fried chicken • Young and (overly) tanned. (AKA roasted chicken)

chickenshit • A coward (from how excrement of this low and common bird would be regarded).

chick-with-dick • A man who appears outwardly as a woman, but keeps his penis and uses it sexually. (AKA Venus with a penis) (ant: guy with pie)

children, the • Mainly dragspeak (African-American) for all gay people. *Child* (*chil'*): one gay individual.

choice • An option.

Mother, don't you think if I had a choice—I'd take the Mercedes?

choir, the • An organized group of singers; euphemism for all gay men.

If ya wanna be in this choir, ya have to sing high and be ready to go down when I wave my baton.

choir boy • One who appears to have heavenly virtues.

"sings in the same choir" • Phrase which designates one's gayness. (Because singing is considered *unmanly*?)

choker • A penis so large in length and girth that it's able to cause, *well*, choking (at least to those with little experience handling such big deals).

chorus boy • One of the many males who dance in theatrical productions (and, because he is not a chorus "man," the implication should be obvious).

chub • Short for *chubby*: one who is, *uhmm*, portly—and of gay men whose ample presence makes them easy targets of the slim and buff who view their own physiognymy as the more suitable image of gaydom. (Note: A bear can also be a chub, as many are noted for their girth. But a chub technically only qualifies as a bear if he's hairy. See *bear*.) Also, an erect and usually thick penis.
chubby chaser • A customarily thin male attracted to men of much heavier builds than his own.

Cinderella • One who does not keep the usual late-night gay hours.
Don't bother asking Cinderella to join: He needs to be home, in his bunny slippers, by midnight.

circle jerk • A group of men gathered "in-the-round," each masturbating himself or another man.

circuit • A "line" that encloses an area. Latin: *circuitus*, that which goes around.
circuit, the • A group of interconnected parties as definable now by its followers—well-heeled, well-built, drug-friendly gay men—as was their original raison d'être: AIDS benefits; a series of gay bars often patronized in one evening.
circuit boy • A notable attendee of the above who is said to embody, attitude included, the essences once (and forever?) coveted by our culture: youth, beauty, and pleasure-seeking.
circuit party • An individual "charity event" accounting for one link in "the circuit." (See *black party*, *white party*)

civil • Of the people. Latin: *civilis*, citizen.
civil disobedience • When people disobey laws hoping to change them.
civil liberties • One's basic freedoms.
civil rights • One's freedoms made official.
civil union • Legal term for a same-sex relationship, but (at this time) of less

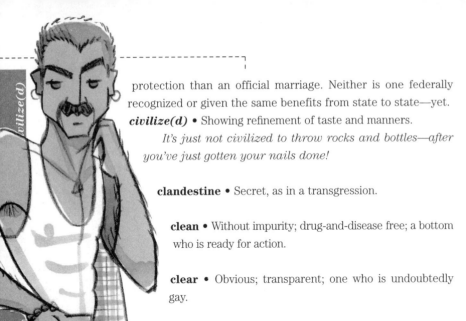

protection than an official marriage. Neither is one federally recognized or given the same benefits from state to state—yet.

civilize(d) • Showing refinement of taste and manners.

It's just not civilized to throw rocks and bottles—after you've just gotten your nails done!

clandestine • Secret, as in a transgression.

clean • Without impurity; drug-and-disease free; a bottom who is ready for action.

clear • Obvious; transparent; one who is undoubtedly gay.

cliché • That which is overused. French: *clicher*, to stereotype. *Yeah, this damned book is full of clichés, but where there's smoke there's sure to be flamers.*

"click" • Said (silently) when one hears and understands that an insult has been spoken (imitative of angrily hanging up a telephone in mid-conversation). (See *"ping"*)

clock • To take specific note (as when a timepiece chimes at a particular moment); to mark the second when one notices someone is gay, a drag queen, or transsexual.

I can clock a queen in the time it takes him to waltz from the "ten 'til" to the "ten past" position.

clone • To copy identically; a gay man in the exact same style as another. Popularized in the early seventies, the infamous "gay clone" was our community's way of trying to vanquish the idea that all queers looked effeminate. How they acted is another story. This was done by appearing with the same masculine affectations: short-cropped hair, a hairy chest (if possible), a mustache, a plaid flannel shirt—topped with a leather jacket—worn (button-fly) 501s, construction boots, thick socks, and underneath the jeans, a jockstrap.

clone zone • From the Castro (past and present) to Chelsea, Weho, and more, the areas where gay men—many resembling each other—congregate in pronounced numbers.

closet, the • A "symbolic place" in the mind to hold things that one believes are best kept out of sight—like homosexuality. Notably, being "in the closet" is a mental state of both punishment, because one's nature is condemned by outsiders, and protection, as in doing so one fears less personal harm.

closet case • One who hides his homosexuality and affects "heterosexuality" (hoping to enjoy its privileges).

closeted • Actively keeping secret a part of one's identity (sexual or otherwise).

glass closet • Thinking one's secret is safely stored away, but—*surprise!*—is clearly seen by others.

> *He was living in a glass closet if he thought his fondness for rhinestone-studded tops had gone unnoticed.*

matrimonial closet • When a gay person uses the specific "structure" of heterosexual marriage to keep his homosexual orientation hidden.

"club, in the" • Code phrase for being gay (a member of the community; see *card, the*). (AKA member of the club)

"clutch the pearls" • Dragspeak for when one has an aghast reaction to something seen or heard (from the matron's gesture of involuntarily touching her valuables when taken aback). (See *bead-reader*, *"read your beads"*)

coach • One who trains "players" in sports (and the dominant partner in a coach-player "role play" setting). (See *role play*)

> *Coach, I could use some personal training after school—if you're game.*

cock • Yet another way to say penis (but I've spared you most of them), rumored to have come from *watercock*, the Middle English term for "faucet."

cock and ball torture (CBT) • A form of BDS&M sex where a man's genitals are either bound, tugged, slapped (ouch!), and/or hit (again, ouch!).

cock fight(ing) • A competition of sorts, where men compare penis sizes and use them to play against each other.

cock ring • Device made of metal, leather, rubber, or string and worn (or wound) around the base of the penis to enhance erections (and orgasms, by constricting blood flow). And yes, they're worn just for looks, too.

cockaholic • One addicted to penises (as if it could possibly mean anything else!).

cocklover • Said of all gay men—and pretty apt.

cockpit • A guy's privates in his underwear; the anus of a gay man.

Son, have you ever seen the inside of a pilot's cockpit?

cocksuck(er) • To fellate; a fellator; all gay men. Though an accurate description of the act, when it is spoken as an insult, as it often is, something more than just the obvious is said. Which is: Fellating another man's penis supposedly denigrates the fellator. So, basically the slur attacks a major part of homosexual behavior. More troubling, its original offensiveness has been neutralized by overuse, allowing us to forget who's always being hurt the most.

cocktail • A for-hire male (who, like the drink, is easily had at a bar); a regimen of medications (usually taken by those with HIV).

You think that cocktail is 2-for-1 during happy hour, too?

cocktease • A guy who dangles it, but does not give it up.

stunt cock • From pornography: one man's erect, large, or climaxing penis that is filmed in place of another one deemed inadequate (awww!) for the desired effect.

I think by now we can make your stunt cock the star of the picture.

code(d) • When something (a word) is used in the place of another to secretly convey meaning.

coexist • To live well together, dissimilarities notwithstanding.

We can coexist with straight guys, just so long as we're willing to bend a little.

cognoscenti • Italian for those in the know (and we all know who they are, don't we?).

cohabit(ate) • To have an intimate living arrangement between two unmarried persons.

collar(ed) • To indicate possession (or inferiority) by taking control or by actually banding around the neck (as a "dominant" would do to his "submissive"). (AKA leash[ed])

Rail loved his new collar, but wondered if his owner, Spike, would approve?

color • Readers, a spectral interlude. Color isn't queer—except for when one spells it with a "u" and, *maybe*, pink, lavender, and, *oh yeah*, chartreuse, mauve, and puce are awfully gay. But I venture the sound of some others (again, this is a book on "gayspeak") is delightfully homo. Here's what I mean: Who would most likely utter *cerise, clementine, persimmon, scarlet,* or *vermilion* when a nice, simple, and regular *red* would do?

"color in the coloring book" • To masturbate while looking through a pornographic magazine.

No hurry, I'll just color in the coloring book while you color your hair.

Comanche • A man who obviously wears makeup (implying that he is like an American Indian who paints his face, warstyle). (Note: I put this term in deliberately to make a curious point. It was typical of the racially insulting verbology of the post–World War II pre-'70s gay male, who was likely white—and therefore predisposed to be almost as, if not more, racist as a typical bigoted straight male.)

come • Semen. *Coming*: climaxing. This word's original meanings of "to coax forward" and "that which is due" make it a logical choice for ejaculation. But some think it's confusing to read, and why we also use "cum."

"come clean" • Said of one who is HIV-negative (in that he ejaculates contaminant-free semen).

I'll admit it, if you come clean.

cometosis • One's breath after fellatio (blending "come" with *halitosis*: chronic bad breath).

When Listerine makes a pocket-pack for cometosis, that sucker should buy stock in the company!

come out, to • To declare embracingly; to admit openly—and, one hopes, affirmatively—to being gay.

"Come out, come out, wherever you are," said the reverend, liltingly, during the close of his speech on expanding congregations, without realizing the gathered clergy were not amused by the comment.

coming out story • From birth everyone assumes you are straight, until found otherwise. So, *all* gay people have some tale of disclosure, be it as benign as "everyone already knew" to the tragic "everyone disowned me."

commitment ceremony • An observance formalizing (but not legalizing) the union of two intimate gay persons.

companion • One in the frequent company of another (and how some, fearful of repercussions, used to refer to lovers in order that their presence could be read as platonic).

condom • A stretchy sheath worn over the penis to prevent insemination that might cause impregnation and to protect both the active and passive partner from transmittable disease. (It is believed the name comes from Cundum, a doctor during the reign of Charles II. However, this is hearsay.)

conform • To follow the measures of others, usually with some remorse.

The most I'm willing to conform to is my new Ben Sherman slim-fit shirt.

confused • Unsure of self or action.

He surely won't be confused if that guy gets his hands on him.

consensual • Requiring the voluntary sexual involvement of both parties. Latin: *consensus*, to be in agreement.

consent, the age of • When one is considered able and responsible by law to give agreement (to sexual intercourse).

consenting adults • Persons beyond the age of consent and in accord with one another (often over an "adult" act).

Despite their being consenting adults, the judge could still bring them up on public decency laws.

conservative • One inclined to traditional values. From *conserve*: to protect, preserve. An *archconservative* is highly rightist, especially in political matters (usually set against an *archliberal*).

He's conservative during the day, but really lets his resources flow at night.

contact sport • Athletic activity requiring bodily interaction (said of sex that lacks intimacy).

contagion (contagious) • Something causing a transmittable disease.

They make me sick thinking we're all a contagion.

conversion • Change from one known status to another (as when an HIV-negative person becomes HIV-positive).

convertible • That which can change from one form to another; a bisexual.
convertible top • An active partner who can bottom (when it rains?).

cornflake(s) • A gay guy from the country (AKA cream of the crop; see *flake*); robust (and rube-ish) queers from the heartland.

You bring the cornflakes, I'll supply the bowl, the milk, and the kitchen counter.

cornhole • One's anus; the act of anal copulation (no doubt enacted upon a "cornfed" lad, who, raised on the Midwestern staple crop, would be fit and full of vitality—and soon, some guy's corncob). (Note: "Cornhole" actually comes from the time when toilet paper wasn't available to farmers, who then used real cobs to clean up. Clever!)

corrupt • Depraved, deceitful, impure: Latin: *corrumpere*, to destroy.
I was corrupt even before you came . . . inside.

cottage • A small home, usually in a forested setting—and of city park public restrooms that resemble them, where men have gone (and still go) looking for sex. (Note: A "cottage tour" and "cottaging" are terms for when one visits a series of these places.)

You're right, Michael, it does look just like the type of storybook cottage that would inspire a lot of George's fairy tales.

cover boy • One whose looks make him quite suitable to appear on the front of a magazine (and who, hopefully, will grow into a catalog man).

It's such a shame that cover boy thinks he still has to hold his up to keep his true you-know-what from being shown.

covert • Not out in the open. Old French: *coverir*, to cover.

Any queer who still thinks he has to act covert today is living in the Dark Ages.

coward • One who is debilitated (and demoralized) with the fear of any great or small danger. Old French: *coe*, tail; *ard*: of something (in other words: one who "turns tail and runs").

You can run your life like a man would, or run like a coward.

coy • Shy and uncommitted, often teasingly so. (See *decoy*)

cream puff • A weakling (or rather, one who is as substantial as a fluffy baked good).

That cream puff is about ready to have some of his filling knocked out.

creep • One who is repulsive; to make another uneasy or fearful.

crêpe Suzette • A French dessert delicacy; an old gay man who's particularly weathered (as in *crepy*: a crinkled surface).

"crime against nature" • A legal phrase from the nineteenth century, still used in religious contexts today, that equates homosexuality (then "sodomitic" behavior) with being unnatural. Therefore, it was deemed punishable.

crossdresser • One who, for effect or pleasure, wears the garb typical of that person's opposite sex. (Note: These are more typically heterosexual than gay males, and female crossdressers are rare.) (See *drag queen, transvestite*)

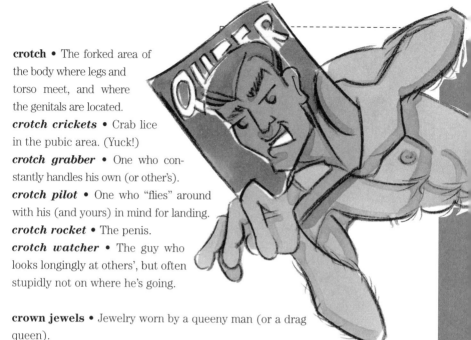

crotch • The forked area of the body where legs and torso meet, and where the genitals are located.

crotch crickets • Crab lice in the pubic area. (Yuck!)

crotch grabber • One who constantly handles his own (or other's).

crotch pilot • One who "flies" around with his (and yours) in mind for landing.

crotch rocket • The penis.

crotch watcher • The guy who looks longingly at others', but often stupidly not on where he's going.

crown jewels • Jewelry worn by a queeny man (or a drag queen).

I'm not big on queens, but I'd be his king if he gives crown jewels as gifts.

cruise • To move around at leisure (for pleasure, discovery, or specifically to find sex). Dutch: *kruisen*, to make the sign of a cross.

cruiser • One quite fond of roving about for (sexual) encounters.

cruisewear • Clothing meant to facilitate the actual physical act of cruising and to attract attention. (AKA work clothes)

I brought very little cruisewear to put on for this trip, but that isn't really such a bad thing.

cruising • Staring with sexual interest, among those largely unknown to each other. (*Heavy cruising*: to look for sex without question; *light cruising*: just browsing)

cruisy • The tangible mood of sex about a person or place.

For a straight guy, Tom was acting mighty cruisy.

crybaby • One who cries a great deal, owing to oversensitivity; one who complains with little justification.

crystal dick • Said of a penis that is nonfunctional, due to aggressive cocaine intake, or one over-functioning (that is to say, its owner is unstoppable) due to aggressive crystal meth(amphetamine) intake. (See *drugs*)

cub • Bearspeak for a mainly "passive," often smaller, younger, inexperienced, but no less hairy member of their clan.
cubbyhole • The dwelling of a cub, or his butt.
    Boo-Boo's cubbyhole was available, but the twist was that he much pre-ferred holing up in Yogi's den.

culture, gay • The collective behaviors, arts, and beliefs of our community. *Cultured*: learned, fine, and accomplished. But wait, is "gay culture" really definable? Most would say yes. Yet, can we confirm the unequivocal correlation between being queer and any of our so-called contributions? Talk amongst yourselves.

cum • Semen. *Cumming*: climaxing. (See *come*)
cum dump • One who wants only to be the vessel for receiving other's ejaculate. (AKA cum bucket)
cum freak • One who cannot get enough (but who is not of the same receivership setup as the man previous). (AKA cum junkie, cum whore, etc.)
cum rag • The clean-up cloth, and one that should never be farther than arm's reach.
pre-cum • Seminal fluid that oozes out of the penis before orgasm.

cunt • A most unpleasant word for a woman's vagina that is too often used by gay men to address and speak about one another—sometimes in seemingly pleasant terms(!). However, it is usually used to mean one is ill-mannered or bitchy (or in a *cunty* mood, similar to a woman—or sissy—being "on the rag," a term for a female's time of menstruation known to put her in a foul frame of mind). (AKA the c-word)

cupcakes • One who likely has a tasty set of bitesize buttocks. (AKA sugar cookies, bon-bons) (A set of bigger buttocks are called "cookie jars.")
    I hear cupcakes over there has difficulty keepin' his wrapper on.

curb service • One who can be picked up while walking a sidewalk (but not a hustler).
    Dude, I'm offering you curb service and a free, warm, and cozy place to park your stretch limo for the night.

curious • Interested in.

After hearing about his roommate's exploits, he was rather curious if that kind of sex could be as great as it sounded.

curtain call • A return sexual visit.

One more curtain call and the two of you should be in for an extended run.

cut • A penis where the foreskin has been removed by circumcision (see *uncut*); well-defined musculature (where it looks like your muscles have been sliced into shape).

cuteness • An extension of "cute" (daintily attractive) into a gayspeak noun for a guy who is.

Be still, my heart, cuteness just walked in.

cybersex • Erotic "chat" over the Internet, which often leads to masturbation and nothing more meaningful.

D

daddy • Informal for "father" (from baby talk); a male who exudes an attractive air of authority and undeniable presence (and often used by gay men to remark about obviously alluring and definitely procreatively inclined straight men); an older, aggressive, and experienced gay male—usually paired with one with the opposite qualities (a "boy"). (Since being a daddy can also be a role, it is possible for the man in question to be young, as long as he has the proper looks—being hairy helps—and demeanor. However, many believe that to be the "real deal," reaching a certain age is required. But when a man hits that milestone of maturity is always a point of contention.)

cigar daddy • One whose phallic fixation can quite often be refocused on you, boy.

daddy-boy • Of the intergenerational relationship between an older and a younger male. While this is quite a common pairing in the gay community, it is also, dynamically, one of the most complex and troubling. At issue is the appropriateness of the age differentiation, which, to some, calls to mind pedophilia, and the familial aspect, which conjures thoughts of, *yup*, incest. However, it should be noted that the vast majority of these couplings are wholly appropriate.

daddy's boy • The "young" lad who is special to his dad (and is expected to do *anything* for him).

leather daddy • One whose masculinity is strappingly enhanced with animal skin accouterments: harnesses, chaps, belts, boots, etc.

muscle daddy • One who expands his already hard-to-dispute dominance to Herculean proportions.

sugar daddy • One who is financially supportive of those younger (and poorer) than he.

daffodil • A brilliant yellow, frilly-edged flower; said of one who is especially frilly.

dainty • Delicate and fine, picky and easily piqued. *Dainties*: underwear.
   That guy's a little too dainty to handle the heavy stuff.

dairy queen • A non-white male who is attracted to white men; a guy with a nipple fetish.

daisy • An especially "sunny" flower; a noticeably "radiant" man.

daisy chain • Flowers linked for ceremonial purposes; a group of gay men linked sexually via genital (anal-oral) connections. (AKA floral arrangement, link-sausages)

damned • Cursed and condemned to eternal punishment.

Well, if that's all it takes, I'll be damned, damned, and damned.

dance belt • Worn by male dancers to protect and cover their genitals during performance. These differ from athletic supporters in that they do not have straps under the buttocks—which would spoil the visual line in tight clothes. (AKA gaff)

dandelion • A small yellow flower; and, yet again, another "flower" in our garden. Anglo-French: *dent de lion*, lion's tooth.

You've got an unexpectedly big roar for such a dandelion.

dandy • A man of extreme stylishness, elegance of person, and humor, whose interests make it likely that he is you-know-what. (See *fop*, *gay vague*, and *metrosexual*)

He's just dandy—and that's fine with me!

dapper • Descriptive used mainly for an elegantly, trimly attired male. (AKA natty)

darling • One who is well liked; something that is charming; gayspeak that can be read both seriously and sarcastically. Old English: *deore*, dear. (See *dear*)

Yes, it would be darling if all the guys brought their own whipped cream and nuts this time.

dash • A small amount; one who shows apparent signs of gayness.

I'd say he's more like a dollop than a dash.

date • To go out "romantically" with another; a guy with whom

date

another goes out "romantically" (with the expectation that their pairing is more substantial than that of a one-night stand). (See *one: one-night stand, trick*)

daughter • A female child; a young (feminine-behaved) male often watched over by an older gay man. (See *house mother, mother*)

Daughters of Bilitis • The country's first national lesbian organization, founded in 1955, in San Francisco, by a gathering of four female couples. The group took their name from the "Songs of Bilitis" sequence of Sapphic poems. Their mission: gay integration into and acceptance by the mainstream.

dawdler • One who wastes time unnecessarily (and, *perhaps*, the way a frivolous woman might behave, but not the way any serious-minded, real man would). (AKA dilly-dallier)

dear • Like "darling," one who is well liked, something that is charming, and gayspeak that can be read both seriously and sarcastically. (AKA dearie, dearest)
Be a dear, and don't mention that you saw me at the club tonight.

debauchery • Overindulgence in erotic activity. French: *debaucher*, to lead astray.

debut • When one "comes out"; the introduction of a gay man into the life. (See *scene, the*).
debutante • He who is "coming out"; one who is in drag for the first time.
He works his skirt too well to be a debutante.

decadent • Indulgently immoral. Latin: *decadentia*, decay, decline.
I go down every time I think about how decadent we all are.

decent • Moral; obliging. (ant: indecent)
I'm being decent every time I get off another frustrated married man in the steam room.

decoy • That which is used as a lure in place of the real thing; a charmingly "coy" and attractive young male used by police, criminals, and bashers to induce a gay man to: 1) commit a sexual crime; 2) become the victim of an extortive act; or 3) become the victim of an assault (when the "decoy" is used in an ambush). A "decoy" is also what a dildo is when worn under the pants to falsely attract attention.

The whole gang thought it was an interesting idea for the decoy to wear feathers, but they decided a boa might be carrying things too far.

de-fag • To rid one's surroundings of homosexual signs.

Joaquin had one week to de-fag his apartment before his fundamentalist relatives arrived from Phoenix.

defame • To tear down someone's character.

Oh, de fortune and defame that singer has to endure whenever he comes out with another CD but refuses to come out.

Defense Of Marriage Act (DOMA) • Legislation passed by Congress in 1996 that defines "marriage" as between a man and a woman, and "spouse" as one of the opposite sex of a husband or wife.

degenerate • One without any morally redeeming qualities. A "degenerate bar" was how a drinking establishment patronized by gay men was often referred to in the fifties. Isn't that sweet?!

delectable • Very satisfying and delightful. Latin: *delectare*, to please.

Yeah, he's a tart—and quite a delectable one at that!

delicate • Easily broken or harmed; dainty. Latin: *delicatus*, pleasing.

I may be delicate, but, as you can plainly see for yourself, my bone structure is quite resilient.

delish • Gayspeak short for *delicious*: quite agreeable in taste. Latin: *delicia*, pleasure.

delivery boy • One who transports things from one place to another.

He was sure the delivery boy was willing to receive, just as he was planning to make a drop-off.

demimonde • A group on society's margins. French: *demi*, half; *monde*, world. (See *twilighter*)

I know part of Ashton does the demimonde more than you can imagine.

democrat • One who ascribes to government by the people, through elected representatives; one who practices social equality. Greek: *demos*: people; *kratos*: power.

He's the usual gay democrat: He'll make room for any man who wants to come in and join his party.

demonize • To (unfairly) make something diabolic, as though of a *demon*: an evil being.

I wouldn't say demonize, but he sure has a mean look.

demystify • To make a situation clear.

There'd be nothing to demystify if we were all out in the open.

denial • Not accepting reality.

He floats along in denial, while the rest of us watch him gaily pass by.

dental dam • Piece of latex placed over the anus to protect against the spread of disease.

depraved • Perverted. Latin: *depravare*, to corrupt.

De more depraved, de more fun.

designer • One who conceives of something in an artistic way; something created by a designer or status manufacturer. Latin: *designare*, to mark out.

There's that designer whose stuff looks so good on the rack.

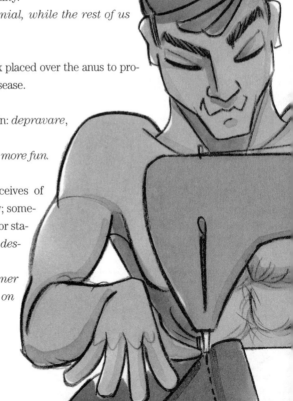

deviant • One who is different from the norm; a low-life. (See *deviate*)

deviate • To stray from the straight course. (See *deviant*)
Deviant. Deviate. Go in any direction you want. They're all queer.

dick • Penis; to fornicate. Perhaps from the Old English: *derrick*, an erect gallows named for its maker, a hangman. But more likely its use as another name for a penis comes from its being a frequent nickname for the common Richard (as would be a "willie" for Will, "peter" for Peter, and so forth). A "dick" is also a name for a loathsome man, rumored to derive from the impression that a penis can get one into trouble. Well, no kidding!

dicklicker • A gay man (only minutely less offensive than being called a cocksucker). (AKA peter-eater)
Not only was he a dicklicker, but of Tom's and Harry's, too.

different • Unlike that which is normal.
Uhmm, your son is different from the rest of the men . . .

diffident • Timid, without confidence. Latin: *diffidere*, to mistrust.
. . . and, not surprisingly, quite diffident.

dignity • Respect for one's self. Latin: *dignus*, worthy.
At least the big guy still had his dignity—well in hand.

dildo • A penis-shaped object used for sexual activity (possibly from the Italian: *diletto*, little darling).

"dine in/dine out" • To have sex at home; to have sex somewhere other than your own place.
Dine in or dine out, I still eat the same ol' thing.

diners' shore • A beach popular with gay men (and a

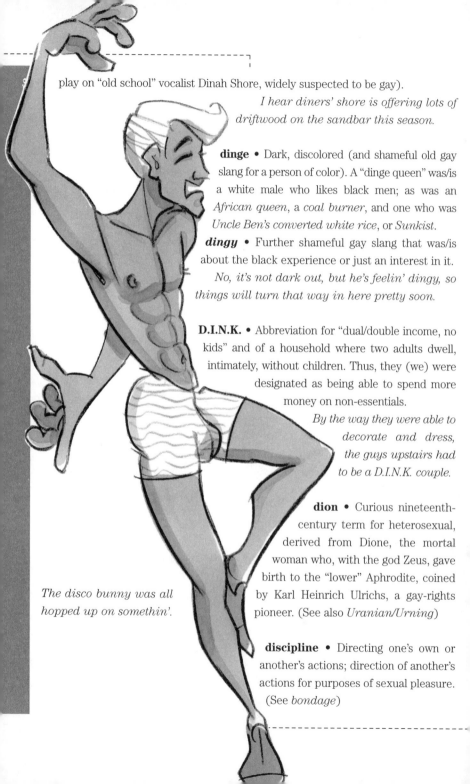

play on "old school" vocalist Dinah Shore, widely suspected to be gay).

I hear diners' shore is offering lots of driftwood on the sandbar this season.

dinge • Dark, discolored (and shameful old gay slang for a person of color). A "dinge queen" was/is a white male who likes black men; as was an *African queen*, a *coal burner*, and one who was *Uncle Ben's converted white rice*, or *Sunkist*.

dingy • Further shameful gay slang that was/is about the black experience or just an interest in it.

No, it's not dark out, but he's feelin' dingy, so things will turn that way in here pretty soon.

D.I.N.K. • Abbreviation for "dual/double income, no kids" and of a household where two adults dwell, intimately, without children. Thus, they (we) were designated as being able to spend more money on non-essentials.

By the way they were able to decorate and dress, the guys upstairs had to be a D.I.N.K. couple.

dion • Curious nineteenth-century term for heterosexual, derived from Dione, the mortal woman who, with the god Zeus, gave birth to the "lower" Aphrodite, coined by Karl Heinrich Ulrichs, a gay-rights pioneer. (See also *Uranian/Urning*)

The disco bunny was all hopped up on somethin'.

discipline • Directing one's own or another's actions; direction of another's actions for purposes of sexual pleasure. (See *bondage*)

disco • Short for *discothèque*: French for a "place where records are played"; dance-oriented music; a scene vital to gay history and the gay experience because it came out about the same time and from the same underground places as we did. (But not, *sweetie*, because we're all such great dancers.)

disco bunny • One who is cute and constantly dancing or hopping from club to club (and could copulate like a bunny, if you were able to bounce him around in one place long enough). (Cousin of the "gym bunny.")

disco diva • Said of the many female recording artists whose dance hits were/are anthemic of the nightlife and, consequently, the gay experience (especially of a certain gay-relevant time period, the '70s).

disco nap • A short rest taken before one goes out for the night.

disco tits • The expected well-defined chest of the guy who feels it's his duty to show them off on the dance floor.

disco-lovin' • Said of a doubtless fan, who leaves little doubt as to his sexuality.

discreet • Prudently self-editing.
> *He's about as discreet as blowing a dog whistle in a kennel.*

discretion • Using caution.
> *I used discretion: I looked around before entering and wore my towel.*

discriminate • To remove from; to assess the value of. Latin: *discriminare*, to distinguish.
> *I don't discriminate, I just edit tastefully.*

diseased • To be of a harmful condition.
> *How can we all look so darn good and still be diseased at the same time?*

disenfranchised • Deprived of the rights and privileges given to others.
> *No, actually, the last time I felt disenfranchised was when that guy passed me with supreme attitude in Jack-in-the-Box.*

disguise • To elude notice by altering appearance; to mislead.
> *I guess if he's planning on dressing as Lucy in disguise—with diamonds—I'll have to go as one of the Fab Four.*

dish • To serve spoonfuls of appetizing food; to divulge ("dish it out"); to gossip ("dish the dirt"). A *dish queen*: A queer gossip.

There they sat, getting a dish in for each of the others foolish enough not to show for dinner.

dishonorable discharge • To have to masturbate at home, alone, after not being able to find someone for sex.

One more dishonorable discharge, and I'll have to enlist to get some action!

disorder • An abnormal, unhealthy condition.

"Mrs Gullable, your son's homosexuality is a treatable disorder," said Doctor Fabul.

ditz(y) • One who is silly, scattered. From blending "dotty" and "dizzy."

One more ditz in this bar and you might as well put the DJ on the roof—cuz soon the whole place'll start spinning.

diva • A person whose behavior is arrogant, volatile, and/or grand. Latin for *goddess*, Italian for leading lady of the opera.

The diva does everything over-sized, so I'm sure he'll be happy to accept all that you have to offer him.

diversity • Variety. Latin: *divertere*, to turn aside.

Diversity in numbers does not mean sleeping with an Asian guy one week and a white guy the next.

divine • Gayspeak for something "out of this world."

do • To perform; to fellate.

"do for trade" • To fellate someone in exchange for money (or just for the honor of it). Disturbingly, these interactions, gay men paying straight men, were once as prevalent as they were demeaning. (See *trade*)

He'd rather do for trade—than do without.

"get done" • To be fellated.

The best thing about a queer is that you get done in a jiffy, or can pop him from behind if you're so inclined.

dock(ing) • To couple together; to arrive at a place for unloading; a sex act where one uncut male enfolds the head of another's penis with his foreskin.

doggy style • The ever popular anal-sex position where a passive partner is bent forward (on all fours, like a dog) and the active partner penetrates from behind—at a more elevated stance (but still mimicking a hound).

dollhouse • A place popular with drag queens.
Barbie loved that Ken was so nice to her friends in the dollhouse, but worried that he liked spending so much time there without her.

do-me • A gay guy only interested in being sexually satisfied (and not in returning the favor).
As far as I'm concerned, that jerk's a do-me don't.

domestic partner(ship) • Legal-sounding term for one (gay or straight) person in a committed but unmarried relationship; of those residing in the same home, who are granted some privileges of marriage—insurance/work benefits, visitation rights, etc.—but not on a nationwide basis.

dominant • The more powerful and in charge. Latin: *dominare*, to rule; *dominus*, lord. (AKA dom)
He may be shorter, but I'd say Napoleon is the dominant one, while his partner, Joe, is definitely his Josephine.

_D&S_ • Of dominant and submissive couplings. (AKA power exchange)

"Don't ask, don't tell (don't pursue)" • Controversial Armed Services policy (put into effect in 1993, during the Clinton administration), which sidestepped the issue of openly admitting gays into the military by making it unlawful to inquire about sexual orientation and a dischargeable offense to "come out" of one's own accord.

"Don't get up in my world" • Dragspeak for when something is not your business.

"Don't go there" • Originally dragspeak (but now, anybody's speak) for when you should change the subject of a conversation because it is not your business or is a topic with details you will likely not want to hear.

Ya wanna know how I lost the hottest man in town? Don't go there!

Dorothy and Toto • A gay man and his dog; an effeminate man who's in control in a relationship with a masculine partner.

If Dorothy and Toto come over, I can have one watch the soufflé while the other helps me move the couch.

double • Two.

double bagger • A guy so unappealing that "two containers" must be worn over his head for another to entertain the idea of intimate contact; the wearing of two condoms for added protection.

double feature • From film terminology when one movie is followed by another; to have sex twice in one day—with different men.

I did a double feature last week where both had screwy endings.

double header • From baseball terminology for back-to-back games; mutual fellatio (see *sixty-nine*); to have sex twice with one person in the same day; a two-ended dildo.

So, how many times is he up at bat during your usual double header?

double life • A life existing on two levels: one usually proper and public; the other not so proper and far more private.

He was prepared to tell his childhood sweetheart that he was leading a double life, and his childish boyfriend that he had a wife.

double penetration • An extreme sex act where one anus is simultaneously entered by two penises (OWWW!). (AKA double entry)

double standard • A system by which one group (or person) is given rights, benefits, or privileges denied to others. or the assumption that one standard of behavior is acceptable within one group, but not within another. (This term first appeared in the fifties, when it was found that white men were afforded greater standards in all matters of life over women. It has since come to include that being gay also comes with less than being straight.)

douche • To cleanse the rectum (of a bottom). French for shower. (See *bidet*)

"down low, on the" (DL) • African-American jargon for a black male who has secret sexual relations with another male while still in an intimate relationship with a woman (usually unaware of her mate's actions). For the most part, these men do not consider themselves gay or bisexual. The term comes from being hidden "down low" to avoid capture or view.

He may be on the down low, but surely his thing sticks up too high to hide!

drab • Ordinary clothes (not what "drag" is supposed to be). *En drabbe*: said of a drag queen in regular clothes.

drag • Attire associated with one sex worn by the opposite gender. Drag can also be any clothes worn for effect, great or small, like leather or office clothes. Rumor has it that the term was first used in late-1800s theater (where else?!) to describe how a female *or* male, thusly attired, had to "drag" the cumbersome, trailing long skirts of the day across and behind the stage.

drag bag • A portable container for transportable articles such as wigs, makeup, heels, boa, and minidresses—or just a guy's regular clothes.

drag king • A woman dressing deliberately as a man for entertainment value and/or to show that gender identification is something that can be "put on" (like a lesbian wearing butch clothes), but not like a heterosexual female who wears her boyfriend's tee.

drag name • Name chosen for one's "female" persona. (Drag "actors," as many like to be regarded, prefer to use their female drag names only when in costume, and use their real male names when not working.)

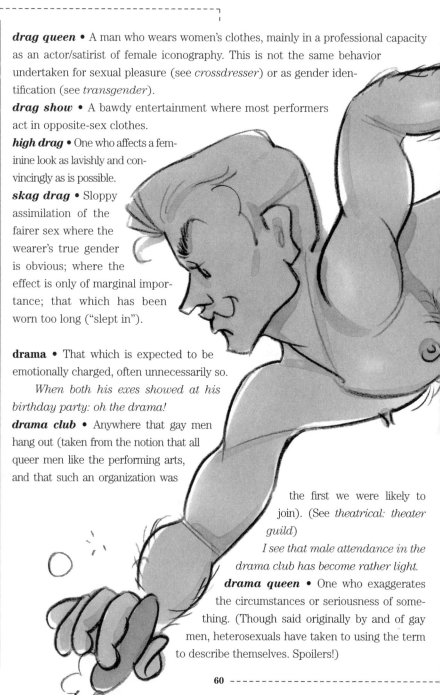

drag queen • A man who wears women's clothes, mainly in a professional capacity as an actor/satirist of female iconography. This is not the same behavior undertaken for sexual pleasure (see *crossdresser*) or as gender identification (see *transgender*).

drag show • A bawdy entertainment where most performers act in opposite-sex clothes.

high drag • One who affects a feminine look as lavishly and convincingly as is possible.

skag drag • Sloppy assimilation of the fairer sex where the wearer's true gender is obvious; where the effect is only of marginal importance; that which has been worn too long ("slept in").

drama • That which is expected to be emotionally charged, often unnecessarily so.

When both his exes showed at his birthday party: oh the drama!

drama club • Anywhere that gay men hang out (taken from the notion that all queer men like the performing arts, and that such an organization was the first we were likely to join). (See *theatrical: theater guild*)

I see that male attendance in the drama club has become rather light.

drama queen • One who exaggerates the circumstances or seriousness of something. (Though said originally by and of gay men, heterosexuals have taken to using the term to describe themselves. Spoilers!)

drooly • Extremely attractive (so as to cause another to salivate in anticipation of a taste); one who is so alluring.

I suggest you wear a bib next time you hear drooly will be out.

"drop a hairpin (bead/pearl)" • Phrase for an instance when someone's gayness has been (or could be) revealed. This is typical of a term that makes sense only if you equate our behavior with being womanly, since gay men don't really wear hairpins! (Unless their mane is getting in the way of a home spa treatment.) (See *"let one's hair down"*)

"drop one's petals" • Phrase for taking off one's pants to expose the penis (as a flower dropping its petals would expose the stamen within).

"drop the soap" • Said of "accidentally" losing grip on your cleanser, but gaining something in the end.

He's never clumsy outside one, but he's always the one to drop the soap in the men's shower.

"drop your camera" • To get a guy to place his focused attention somewhere more important. (Today it may be more apt to "drop your cell.")

Dude, drop your camera and take a look at the hunk who just walked into frame.

drugs • Chemical substances that alter behavior or perceptions. Supposedly, our lifestyle means we are more likely to partake of drugs, which is why drug-related terms pop up everywhere in gay language studies. But as I take umbrage at that, I have chosen only to list those items *assumed* to be favored by us here (and not elsewhere, with the exception of a couple of related terms): cocaine, crystal meth, Ecstasy, Quaalude, Special K(etamine), and Viagra. (See *amyl nitrate, 420, k-hole, poppers, tweak*)

D-n-D (drug and disease free) • How those who do not "party" and are healthy make it known. This term informs and appears, frequently, in personal ads (see *profile*). However, saying that you are not pharmaceutically inclined is a good thing, but saying that you are "without illness" is another. It has the unfortunate effect of making those who are ill (in general, with HIV) feel even more stricken and cast aside. (See *UB2*)

duchess • A female of high birth (and wife of a duke); one who puts on airs; a passive male (along with countess, empress, etc.).

dude • A man of friendly aspect (popular nonsexual address to any man from another); a young man with a casual air. Before the "dude" became identified with the California surf, he had a rather "gay" history. First, he was a "dandy" who went to a "dude ranch" (there to live life, temporarily, like a "real man"). Oscar Wilde reportedly came up with the name by combining "duds" (clothing) and "attitude," but then there's the queer connection to a *doodle* (as in *Yankee*), an unassuming chap who, after sticking a feather in his cap and calling it *macaroni* (an Italian fop), came to be known as all men who care too much about appearances.

dungeon • A dark, often underground, chamber where persons are kept under constraint; where BDS&M sex often occurs.

It was upstairs in the second bedroom, but I knew, regardless, when I saw the rope and chains, that it was his dungeon.

Dutch boy • Any man, gay or straight, who likes to hang out with a dyke (a lesbian, but also variant on *dike*: a floodwall found often in Holland [AKA Dutch country]).

I hear Dutch boy spreads evenly across most any surface.

dyke • A lesbian. While this book focuses on gay men, a few "sisterly" terms are so prevalent, like dyke, that they cannot be overlooked. Oddly, this one has very unclear origins—despite its popular usage. One version says it was a term for men's clothing. Some believe the word came from Boudicca, the name of a Celtic queen known for her warrior ways. While many question the claim's authenticity, its phonetic similarity to two oft-heard yet also hard-to-pin terms—bull dagger and bull dyke—makes for a compelling argument.

dykedar • The lesbian version of gaydar.

dykon • A lesbian icon (Zena, Warrior Princess; Ellen DeGeneres; Rosie O'Donnell; Marlene Dietrich, et al.).

dyksicle • "Dyke" plus "icicle" equals a particularly icily mannered lesbian.

earring code • From the scandalous seventies, when wearing a single earring in your right ear (or one in each) meant you were gay (and passively so), and, in just your left ear, straight or *actively* queer. Nowadays it means naught.

eat • To consume; to perform fellatio or anilingus.
"Eat me" • Similar in meaning to "suck my dick" (both of which imply that the one doing the eating is performing a demeaning act).

eccentric • One who engages in peculiar or abnormal behavior.

edge play • Sex that takes both (or more) parties to harmful extremes.

edging • Taking oneself almost to the point of orgasm, then leveling off, then returning again. (This is often done numerous times, with the expectation that the more it is done the bigger one's orgasm will be. Verdict? 'Tis true.)
We were edging for close to an hour, when he fell right off the side of the bed.

effeminate • Having qualities associated more with women than with men; of one who is weak and excessively refined. Latin: *effeminare*, to make feminine.
That one is so effeminate already, a sex change might just make him more like a man!
effie • A passive male (short for "effeminate").

effete • Overly refined or lacking in influence.
He was an effete esthete with little effect.

emasculate • To take away a man's manliness.
Can one emasculate he who has no masculinity to start?

embellish • To add details without need. ("Embellish" is not a gay word, but it is something we are accused of doing. So much so, that the language of it—gewgaw, folly, folderol, frippery, glitz, festoon, passementerie, pailettes, razzle-dazzle, baubles, sequins, and rhinestones—can sound excessively like our own.)

empower • To give or enable strength or ability.
I'll feel empowered when they are out of power.

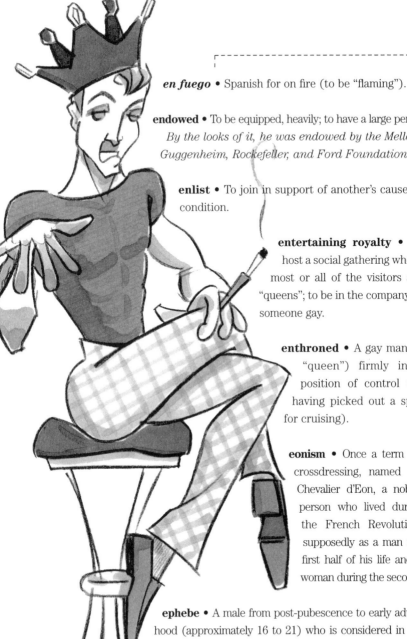

en fuego • Spanish for on fire (to be "flaming").

endowed • To be equipped, heavily; to have a large penis. *By the looks of it, he was endowed by the Mellon, Guggenheim, Rockefeller, and Ford Foundations.*

enlist • To join in support of another's cause or condition.

entertaining royalty • To host a social gathering where most or all of the visitors are "queens"; to be in the company of someone gay.

enthroned • A gay man (a "queen") firmly in a position of control (or having picked out a spot for cruising).

eonism • Once a term for crossdressing, named for Chevalier d'Eon, a noble-person who lived during the French Revolution, supposedly as a man the first half of his life and a woman during the second.

ephebe • A male from post-pubescence to early adulthood (approximately 16 to 21) who is considered in his sexual prime. *Ephebophilia* is a desire to have relations with a man of that age. (This is a gray area in terms of behavioral appropriateness. However, there is a great difference between its legality and the illegality of pedophilia.)

epicene • Having both masculine and feminine qualities; of effeminacy; a name that is both male and female (ex.: Pat). Greek: *epikounos*, common.

Are you talking about last night's epicene where the hero wasn't sure he saved a boy or a girl?

epidemic • A harmful condition spreading rapidly and extensively.

The only epidemic I'm aware of is that too many people are wearing ugly clothes.

equality • Having the same value as another. Latin: *aequus*, even.

I'll believe there's equality—when he starts paying for his half of the drinks.

escort • One who accompanies another; one who is hired as a social companion or secured under such pretext for sexual purposes.

I was hoping my escort would take me to some wild places, but he was only taking me to the letter "F."

eunuch • A castrated male; a man who is without power. Greek: *eune*, bed; *ekhein*, to keep (of men entrusted with watching over a woman's bedchamber).

Just because we don't sleep with women doesn't mean we're eunuchs—assuredly.

everyman • One who is ordinary.

When they're looking for everywoman and not everyman—I've got your number.

exclusive • Not accepting of (that which is thought to be lower than). Latin: *excludere*, to shut.

But reverse psychology tells us that no one will want to join in, if we're not exclusive ourselves.

ex-gay • One who was, but is no more. This type of transformation is made possible, but not always credible, through the convictions of those who believe homosexuality is learned behavior or the kind of activities which can be placed away in a "no access" zone.

experiment • To determine the efficiency or depth of what was previously untested. Latin: *experimentum*, an attempt.

Didn't everyone experiment with it in college?

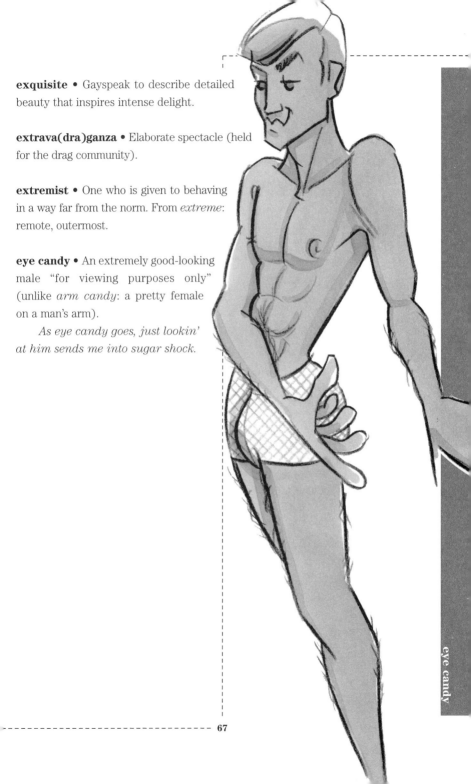

exquisite • Gayspeak to describe detailed beauty that inspires intense delight.

extrava(dra)ganza • Elaborate spectacle (held for the drag community).

extremist • One who is given to behaving in a way far from the norm. From *extreme*: remote, outermost.

eye candy • An extremely good-looking male "for viewing purposes only" (unlike *arm candy*: a pretty female on a man's arm).

As eye candy goes, just lookin' at him sends me into sugar shock.

fabulous • Extremely pleasing, celebrated; hard to believe. Latin: *fabula*, fable. The most well-known of gayspeak words purloined from the mainstream, that we use as a catch-all punctuate. Curiously, its popularity has come into question, as it is now rather ironically considered "too gay" for many to use. (AKA fab, fabu)

Nothing in this life's as fabulous as it once was.

facial • Semen shot upon another's face. To "give a facial," by intentionally ejaculating on a man's face, is a sex act unto itself. (AKA face cream)

No, two in the morning is not too late for a facial—believe me.

factory-equipped • Transspeak for one who has all his (or her) necessary parts from the point of manufacture (birth).

You came factory-equipped, but I have to go in and remake this whole chassis.

fade • A male person of color who prefers the company of whites.

He's so fade now he's more like cream with coffee flavor than coffee black.

fag(got) • Any and all gay men—implicitly as inferior to straight males. So, before going into its complex origins, something more must be said of its use: While our reclamation of the word has lessened its negative impact, try never to forget its original intention to demean us. Now, to its intricate beginnings. Supposedly, the first real "fag" was any British underclass student sent "fagging" (fetching) by upperclassmen. Notably, he was sent for cigarettes, which were also nicknamed "fags." This came from "faggot," a term for kindling. Incidentally, there is a legend that these firestarters were gathered by heretics—who ended up burning alive on the very pyres they built. Well, maybe not too incidental after all, because these heretics were sometimes said to be called faggots, too. Were these the original "flamers"? I know, it's a bad pun, but you should get the idea that others have tried to link this all together. However, if none of this is perfectly clear, don't fret. No one is certain of the exact moment we became "fags." But, in the sense that the word has always meant something, or someone, easily and deliberately disposed of, you can't miss the "smoke equals fire" connection. One last relatable thought: Of all the tobacco-related habits, cigarette smoking has always been regarded as the queerest. Put that one in your pipe, Mr. Upperclassman.

fag bag • A straight woman married to a gay man.

fag bangle • A gay man regarded as an "accessory" to a straight female.

That stylist is just another fag bangle on her bottle-tanned arm.

fag hag • A straight female extremely fond of the company of gay men.(AKA *queen bee, fruit fly*, ribbon clerk)

fag magnet • An event or a celebrity drawing the rapt attention of gay men.

If she were any more a fag magnet, my Rolex would shatter!

fag stag • The odd straight guy attracted to and comfortable around gay men. (See *stag*)

fagatini • A young queer; a straight man with queer edges; the latest beverage in a gay bar. (AKA fagateeny)

faggot in training • Term for any young male showing signs that he is working his way from apprentice to a full position in fairydom (often said of those in school for fashion, retail, or interior design—and especially ones who attend New York City's Fashion Institute of Technology [AKA FIT]).

faggoty • Behaving queerly. (AKA faggy)

If you didn't do such faggoty things—like carry your books like a girl or take yoga class—no one would think you were queer.

hag-fag • A gay man doting on straight women.

Stepford fag • A gay man who behaves in the "traditional" mode of heterosexual society: one who, like a "clone," looks, acts, and behaves almost exactly like his brethren. Taken from the Ira Levin novel *The Stepford Wives*, wherein all the women are turned into robots that adhere to the same values and actions for their men.

faint-hearted • Of little surety, cowardly. The classic phrase "faint heart ne'er won fair lady" means that if a man behaves unmanly he can't expect to get the attention of a beautiful woman. *And that's something all brave men want, right, guys?*

fairy • A tiny, spritely, often winged, imaginary being with a clever mind and powers to do good *and* bad; a queer.

He was so good at playing a fairy he didn't need the suspension wire to fly.

fairy dust • Any sparkly substance (glitter) sprinkled about that leaves a magical effect (like to fly, as when Mary Martin did it while playing the title role in *Peter Pan*, the first televised musical, in 1955); cocaine (when it was the popular drug of choice for gay men from say the late '70s to the late '80s).

fairy godmother • A gay mentor of a gay man.

fairy-go-round • Any area cruised by gay men.

Like so many of us, he could spend most of the night on the fairy-go-round, but go for a spin with the right man, no matter how late the guy appeared.

fairyland • A place where gays congregate happily.

I remember when this used to be such a fairyland—then the mayor cleaned it up and kicked us all out!

flip-collar fairy • A gay clergyman. (Note: His penis is a *steeple*; "Is the congregation aware of how many altar boys the father had serving under his steeple?")

grimm's fairy • An older gay guy with a somber attitude. From the famed Brothers Grimm, who wrote many German fairy tales, which became *Sleeping Beauty*, *Snow White*, *Tom Thumb*, and more.

radical faeries • Gay persons who eschew traditional (homo)sexual role behavior by reveling in their unique queerness. (See *pagan*)

falsetto • A man's voice talking or singing at a higher level than is normal. Latin: *falsus*, false.

You have a wonderful falsetto, Sylvester,

No matter where he went, Cecil always brought along what was in fashion.

but unless you plan on dressing as a woman, what good do you think it'll do your singing career?

family • A basic societal unit made up of, traditionally, a pair of parents (one male, one female) and children. (We know that such can be defined as two who share each other's lives, or a group sharing commonalities, not just physical structure); the unit in which one was born and raised ("family of origin"), and opposite of a "chosen family." Also, family can be a way to announce if someone is gay: *Honey, with that walk you can bet he's family!*

chosen family • Unit to whom one goes for love and support voluntarily and/or as an alternative to a family of origin.

His chosen family made him feel more welcome than his own ever did.

family values • Moral and social standards maintained and affirmed by "tradition."

nuclear family • A legally married man and woman, raising children in a single-family dwelling, regarded as the perfect foundation for a righteous society to build upon. A *nuclear family meltdown* is when an element of this veers ideologically from the core and its entire ideological structure collapses.

fanboy • One passionately devoted (from *fanatic*: of unreasonable ardor).
You can call him a fanboy, but, as per usual with that actress's groupies, he's about fifty.

fancy-pants • One who is not expected to engage in anything that may disturb his appearance (or, specifically, soil his precious trousers).

fantabulous • Wondrously splendid (a blend of fantastic and fabulous).

fashion • The prevalent style (usually of clothing). Old French: *façon*, appearance.
fashion designer • One who creates clothes; a gay man (because a straight guy isn't supposed to know what "blouson" or "diaphanous" means, or know what "charmeuse," "pongee," or "tulle" is).

fashion plate • One who wears the latest glad rags; a clotheshorse; a queer? (Well, for sure we are the "fashion customer," no?)

fashion police • One who always knows what's right to wear and cites those wearing what's wrong. (Us?!)

fashion victim • One who is wearing the wrong thing (never a gay man! I don't care what you say!).

fashionista • One who cares about style with militant ardor. (He has to be gay, right?!)

father • The man who begets (and raises) a child; an older male whom we regard as an authoritarian role model, but from whom we still expect a little tender, loving care.

father figure • One who substitutes for a biological father, but provokes the same emotions.

While he personally adored older men, he did not believe the theory that all gay men were looking for a father figure.

fatherfucker • A young male attracted sexually to older men.

"fats, femmes, and/or flamers" • A trio of gay "types," owing to body shape or personality, that far too often hears a "no"—as in "not welcome" or "not interested"—from the slim, butch, conservative types who believe they more suitably represent the community.

faun • Naughty creature, of Roman myth, with the body of a man, and the legs, tail, and horns of a goat. (See *goatee*, *Pan*)

Since he was already poured into the faun costume, Vassie figured he might as well make a night of it.

faunlet • A young male of extreme wantonness (and boy version of a *nymphet*).

faygeleh • Yiddish for "little bird"—and for "faggot"!

featherdusters • A gay man's flailing hands.

Why not take your featherdusters over to the vitrine and clean my tchotchkes while you kvetch?

Federal Marriage Amendment (FMA) • Recently introduced Constitutional amendment proposal that defines marriage solely as the "union of a man and a woman"—when before such could be determined by each state. Its power would also enable the government to override current anti-discrimination and domestic partnership rights.

felch(ing) • The sexual act of exchanging semen from one mouth to another. An extreme version involves sucking semen first—*hold on*—from another's anus.

feline • Of a cat's smooth and stealthy ways. Latin: *feles*, cat. (See *catty*)

He's so feline that you can get a hairball from licking him.

fellatio • The act of orally stimulating the penis (and the refined word to describe it). Latin: *fellare*, to suck. Again, this is hardly something only gay men do. But the impression that no straight guy entertains the thought—without being paid—makes it seem gayer. It's also why so many demeaning terms relate to it: "suck my dick," "eat me," and so on.

Felicia • Gayspeak nickname for a frequent fellator.

fellate • To engage in fellatio.

fellatee • The lucky guy getting fellated.

fellator • A guy who does it. (A woman who does it is actually called a fellatrice).

female • The gender that produces eggs and bears young; what is characteristic of this sex; "feminine." Latin: *femina*, woman.

He's more female than all the Rockettes combined!

female female impersonator • A gal who works mimicking gals, exaggeratedly.

female impersonator • A man who works mimicking the looks and mannerisms of women. (See *drag queen*)

F-T-M • Abbreviation for a "female-to-male" transsexual.

feminine • Of the actions and manners generally given to women, girls (and, when said of a man, he who is "effeminate"). Latin: *femina*, woman.

feminine side • Of any emotionally sensitive aspects of a man's personality, usually thought of as female in orientation.

I hear that's what being gay is all about: guys with nothing but a feminine side.

femininity • The mark of being "feminine."

Your son behaves with such grace and femininity—it's like having the daughter you always wanted.

femme • Showing usual or heightened "feminine" traits (used of gay men being very *so*, and of lesbians conforming to typical expectations of their gender). French: *femme*, woman.

He's so femme, ya have to wonder if he hasn't already been to Copenhagen and back.

en femme • Said of a drag queen wearing "his" preferred clothes (that of a female).

high femme • Showing extreme femininity in looks and actions.

Any more high femme, and his wig wouldn't fit under the doorway.

ferocious • Gayspeak for that which is wildly in fashion. (See *fierce*)

festive • Of a festival or that which is joyous; gayspeak to describe anything that is merry or gay (or not, as when we use it sarcastically).

My, how festive he is in that pretty frock—not!

fetishist • One who has a *fetish* (an irrational focus on something, often not part of the body, that gives sexual pleasure). Latin: *facticius*, artificial.

You're gay, so you must be a fetishist for something: leather, rubber, latex, socks, panties!

fey • Fairylike. (AKA fay)

As fey would have it, he was destined to be a flight attendant.

fierce • Gayspeak for that which is "ferocious." (Often gaily pronounced as though it had two syllables: fee-*urss*.)

fifth wheel • Unnecessary; a straight man accidentally finding himself in a "gay" way.

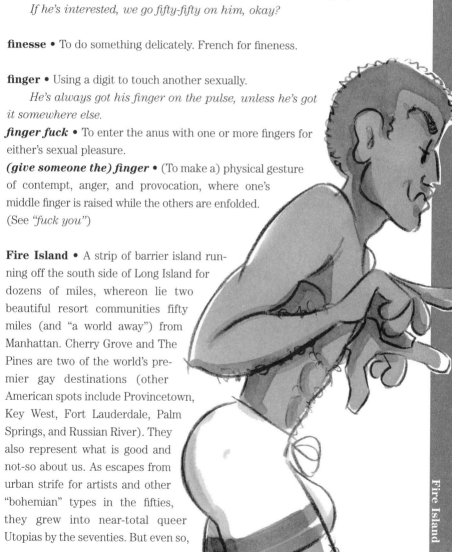

After they all chuckled at the strange Lindsay Lohan reference, he suddenly felt like a fifth wheel standing there with all the other guys from Pilates class.

fifty-fifty • Being just as probable or improbable; exact halves; a questionable situation; a bisexual; engaging in oral and anal sex; two aggressive men sharing a passive third.
If he's interested, we go fifty-fifty on him, okay?

finesse • To do something delicately. French for fineness.

finger • Using a digit to touch another sexually.
He's always got his finger on the pulse, unless he's got it somewhere else.
finger fuck • To enter the anus with one or more fingers for either's sexual pleasure.
(give someone the) finger • (To make a) physical gesture of contempt, anger, and provocation, where one's middle finger is raised while the others are enfolded. (See *"fuck you"*)

Fire Island • A strip of barrier island running off the south side of Long Island for dozens of miles, whereon lie two beautiful resort communities fifty miles (and "a world away") from Manhattan. Cherry Grove and The Pines are two of the world's premier gay destinations (other American spots include Provincetown, Key West, Fort Lauderdale, Palm Springs, and Russian River). They also represent what is good and not-so about us. As escapes from urban strife for artists and other "bohemian" types in the fifties, they grew into near-total queer Utopias by the seventies. But even so,

Cherry Grove, the older community of the pair, began taking on trashier tones, while its close-by "sister," The Pines, took on tonier aspects. That both places harbor many of the same underlying (often oversexualized) attributes has not stopped them from acquiring separate identities. In doing so, they mirror the philosophic dichotomy that one might say describes the whole "face" of the gay community—and each queer individually and internally.

fish • An insulting term—said too often by gay men—for a woman (in that her genitalia have a "fishy" odor).

fish and chips • The wife and kids of a man who has gay sex or is gay.

He left the fish and chips at home and went out for beef tips and gravy.

fishpond • The vagina. (AKA fishtank)

fishwife • The female heterosexual spouse of a gay man.

fishy • Said of a place crowded with women. (AKA *aquarium*: a container full of fish)

kissing fish • Lesbians.

fist(ing) • To penetrate a man's anus using part or all of one's hand, which, when inside, is to be folded into a "fist." Though this is a BDS&M sex act, it's arguably "safe." As such, it has become more widely practiced outside of that scene.

flagging • Identifying with a flag; for a gay man to wear a hanky in his back pocket indicating his sexual interest(s). (See *hanky code*)

I shoulda realized he had a head cold and wasn't flagging, when I noticed his monogram.

flagrant • Conspicuously censurable.

No, my flagrant is not available in a room deodorizer, bitch!

flagrante delicto, in • In the very midst of an offense, especially of sex. Latin for "while the crime is blazing."

Giving head to your professor behind a home game pep rally bonfire is a sure-fire way to be caught in flagrante delicto.

flail • To flap about erratically. Latin: *flagellum*, whip.

The way they flail about, I'm shocked that more don't get their eyes poked out.

flake • A small, fluttering piece; that which has broken off; one who is slightly off.
flakey • Peculiar.

He's as flakey as a damned blizzard of queerness.

flamboyant • Deeply colored; brazen and showy. Old French: *flamboyer*, to blaze.

If flamboyant meant that, he'd have floated halfway to the moon by now.

flame(r) • To blaze brightly, flash suddenly; a gay man with flashy ("flaming") behavior. (To be *flaming* is to be very effeminate, especially as seen by others.)

You could set yourself on fire and not be any more of a flamer than you already are, dearest.

flamingo • A brilliantly colored bird; one who dresses "flamboyantly" (see *peacock*).

It was queer enough that he stood on one foot at the bar, but pink made that flamingo really stand out.

flash in the pan • One who ejaculates quickly (especially while having anal sex) or "quickie" sex.

He was a flash in the pan, but at least I caught it!

flashlight • One so obviously "gay" that he is surely whom to ask where to go in a new town. (AKA pushbutton)

That flashlight gets around in the dark better than anybody I know.

flaunt • To make an unabashed or pretentious show.

He can flaunt it, cuz he's sure got it—enough to make copies of himself.

fleece market • A place where almost anything, but especially antiques and collectables, is sold at too high a price.

flighty • Dizzying behavior.

When he gets that flighty, he's apt to land upside down in any guy's bed.

flip • To behave with a casual lack of interest; to go from an active to a passive sexual position or vice versa.

flip-flop • To assume one position and then return, or two guys going back and forth.
There was no tellin' whose end was up with all the flip-flop going on.

flipper • One who switches his sexual position or physically "flips" another.
One night with the flipper and Nicholson'll feel like a flapped Jack.

flipping • Changing one's usual sexual position.
When I heard you yell, I was sure you were flipping for the first time.

flit(ting) • A ditzy, often straying person; darting about.

flounce/flouncy • A length of pleated, ornamental fabric; to move bouncily about or with extremely artificial gestures.
He's so flouncy, you could get motion-sickness just watching him walk.

flower • Something pretty, delicate; one as fragile.
I nipped that flower right in his bud.

flowery • Of flowers; grandly made impressions.
One almost expected a flowery aroma whenever he broke wind.

fluff • Of little value; of pale, frothy appearance; to inflate, give rise to (see *fluffer*); an effeminate male.
Time to pick off a bit of fluff?

fluffer • One who stimulates porn actors between shots.
Today, Dick Everhard was shooting, and Avery Day, the best fluffer in the biz, couldn't wait to do his stuff.

fluffy • Giddy, silly, and gay.

flutter(er) •
To make quick, excited actions; one who behaves in such a manner.
Another flutterer and his pool deck crowd would look less like a cocktail party and more like a tropical bird sanctuary.

fluter • A gay man (taken from playing a flute, a long, thin instrument). (AKA piccolo player) *Skin flute*: the instrument (penis) a "fluter" plays.
   He was the symphony's best fluter, and arguably a better one in the bedroom.

fly-fishing • Fondling the genitals (combining fly, the opening in a man's trousers or underwear, with the sport of fishing, where the idea is to hook something).
   Fly-fishing with that one is only gonna get ya a sardine at best.

folderol • Extraneous detail; to act in a nonsensical way.
   Books like these are full of folderol.

foofy • To act like a *foof*: a derivation of poof. (See *poof*)
   Sending readers elsewhere is such a foofy thing to do for such a silly word.

foot play • Fetishist behavior involving the feet. (See *shrimping*)

fop • A man who spends an inordinate amount of time thinking about his dress and behavior. (AKA dandy)
foppery • Silliness; the affects of a fop.
   Such foppery is not fond of a man.
foppish • Acting dandily.
   With foppish glee, he dashed down the escalator, two steps at a time, and out of Saks, his bags overflowing with sartorial splendor.

"for days" • Gayspeak for when something (or someone) possesses a great deal (sometimes too much) of something else.
   He's not my fave person, but, admittedly, the little prick has style for days.

forbidden • Something not allowed.

fornication • Sexual intercourse between unmarrieds. From the Latin: *fornix*, a vaulted ceiling over a cellar room where prostitutes plied their trade (the act was called *fornicatio*). Heterosexuals are only supposed to engage in sexual intercourse to procreate. *Pardon my stifling a laugh.* But those who fornicate do so without this justification. This is why anyone doing so, gay guys included, is considered irredeemably wanton.

Note to self: Contemplate whether to mate with Nate right after lunch date or fornicate late, say, post-dinner at eight.

420 (4:20) • Cyberspeak for marijuana-friendly. (Rumors abound to where this term got started. Of them one, from the early '70s, has it as a specific time right after high school classes when a group of students met to smoke. Another attributes it to a line from one of sci-fi writer H. P. Lovecraft's stories from 1939, wherein the tale's protagonist is coming out of a plant-induced hallucination to find that the time is, you guessed it, 4:20. Note that the proper way to say it is as a time, and not as four hundred and twenty.

fourgy • Two couples or just four men having sex. (AKA foursome)

fox • A male (often older) who, taking his behavior from the furry predatory mammal, hunts for younger men. **silver fox** • A slim, sexy, older man—often with salt-and-pepper hair.

'fraidy cat • One who is shy or easily frightened.

frail • Delicate. Latin: *frangere*, to break.
He's too frail for combat duty, but might work very well in the entertainment division.

fraternity • A social group composed solely of men. *Confraternity*: a group of men together for a common goal (from *confrère*: colleague, brother).

What fraternity is he in, Cumma Cumma Gain?

> **frat boy** • A fraternity member who's known to behave with acute abandon.
>
> *I bet that frat boy gets into lots of sticky messes with his brothers.*

> **freak** • One who is gay (a "freak" of nature).

> **free-living** • Existing indulgently.
>
> *Anyone who says we are free-living has never seen my bills for back and butt hair waxing and undereye creams!*

French • To be sexually oral (attributed to the French, who were known historically to be more orally permissive in matters of the flesh, as opposed to "Greek," which is to be sexually anal); open-mouthed kissing.

French active • Meaning one is a fellator.

French dressing • Semen.

I hear he tosses a zesty-tasting French dressing.

French embassy • Any location where large numbers of men congregate, like a gym, and gay sex activity, most easily fellatio, is bound to be found.

French passive • Meaning one who is fellated.

friend • One who is known and liked; euphemistic introduction for an intimate without specifying level of closeness. A *special friend*: One with whom another is particularly personal, but a relationship not yet made official.

There he is, over there with his special *friend.*

friendly • Amiable, allowing.

After what we did, I can guarantee you he's friendly.

"friend of Dorothy, a" • Phrase meaning someone is gay, and rooted in: 1) our fondness for Judy Garland, the iconic entertainer who played Dorothy Gale in the classic film musical *The Wizard of Oz* with her trio of sexless male buddies; 2) our association to and admiration for sharp-tongued writer Dorothy Parker, whose famed "vicious circle" of pals included gay men; and 3) the need for gay men, during much of the twentieth century, to speak in code (for fear of being found out).

friends with benefits • Those to whom you are close and with whom you can partake of sexual relations.

"frighten the horses" • Britspeak meaning something that startles animals in their stalls (as would noisy sex acts in the hay loft). In other words, overt sexuality (in this case, being obviously, noisily gay) that spooks the prudish.

frilly • Supercilious (from *frill*: a want but not a need).

fringe • The "frilly" end of a fabric; those whose views place them at the edge of their group.
   As long as we're on the fringe we might as well be frilly.

frolic • To move about gaily.
   They romp, we frolic.

froth(y) • Something puffed up, without substance; of giddy character.
   If we were drinks, I'd be a whiskey sour, you'd be tonic water, and our frothy friend here would be a whipped Frappacino.

frottage • The sexually gratifying act of rubbing against another person, often through clothing, in a crowd. French: *frotter*, to rub. (See *Princeton rub*)

frou-frou • An addition to something that might already be *too* gay.
   This is all a bunch of frou-frou.

fruit • An edible of nature; all gay men (implying that we are sweet, tart, colorful, and succulent). And who could argue with that?
   Dig the fruit carrying the fruit!
fruit boots • A gay man's shoes.

fruitcake • Someone gay, or nutty, like the holiday treat.

fruit cup • A jockstrap.

> *Dude, why bother going out for dessert when you've got a packed fruit cup right here?!*

fruit fly • A straight woman who favors the company of gay men. (AKA *fag hag*)

fruit juice • Semen.

> *Just activate this spigot and you can have fruit juice all night!*

fruit loop • An area known for its gay establishments; a gay man's anus.

fruit picker • A straight male who occasionally chooses to have gay sex.

fruit salad • A group of gay men.

> *Their fruit salad always has too much underripe melon and sour grapes.*

fruitstand • A gay hangout (AKA fruit bowl); a place where gay magazines are sold (AKA library).

fruity • Showing signs of gayness, craziness.

bruised fruit • One who was assaulted—or got bumped around in bed.

> *With all this bruised fruit, I'd say last night's party was a success.*

canned fruit • A closeted gay man; a virgin gay; one who does not like anal sex. (AKA cedar chest cissy; *cedar chest*: where one stores valuables under lock and key)

crushed fruit • One whose companionship has been rejected; one who's been denied something by the mainstream; one who's been assaulted.

> *You see a depressed lover; I see a crushed fruit.*

forbidden fruit • One below the age of consent.

fresh fruit • A gay guy new on the scene.

frozen fruit • A gay man abstaining from sex.

> *I have just the place to thaw out that frozen fruit.*

overripe fruit • A gay elder. (AKA dried fruit)

passionfruit • One of great masculine appeal to both sexes, but definitely gay.

> *They can try to get 'em all to bite, but a piece of passionfruit like that tastes better to those with discerning palates.*

ripe fruit • A male on the verge of "coming out"; a gay man in his prime.

> *You know, hon, ya get the most and sweetest juice from a ripe fruit.*

stewed fruit • One who is drunk (or one who's been at the baths for too long).

wax fruit • A queer who doesn't want to be bothered.

fuck • To have sexual intercourse; a sexual object. Possible origins: Nineteenth-century naval officers were said to have written in logs "F-or U-nlawful C-arnal K-nowledge" whenever certain trespasses were made; and the Dutch word *fokken* means "to breed cattle." But whatever its beginnings, it's what gay men do "in the end." This is why, since such an act is considered "sodomy," we are the ones most *accused* of committing it. (Heterosexual couples do it, too. But they are much better at keeping things focused, *err*, up front.) It's also why when a guy (rarely a gal) is told they are a "fucker" or to "go fuck" themselves, or just plain "fuck you," the insult makes all of us queers the butt, literally, of a very nasty joke—twice: 1) It is based on the notion that this kind of intercourse (same-sex anal) is something no man in his right mind engages in; and 2) It disparages a big part of the gay lifestyle. Oh well, what the fuck, right?!

fuckable • A man worthy of sexual intercourse; one who is not in a relationship. (AKA haveable)

fuck buddy (FB) • (See *buddy*)

fuck date • Two guys who've arranged to get together for one thing only—and it ain't to exchange recipes.

"fuck me raw" • Figuratively: expressing shock at hearing something; literally: to engage in unprotected anal sex.

fuck toy • One definitely passive guy who's played with, quite enthusiastically, by one who is definitely active.

fuck train • Technically, since two's a couple and three's a sandwich, it takes at least four guys hitched together to get one of these running. Incidentally, whoever is on the "tail" end, unpenetrated, is the "caboose." (See *"pull[ing] the train"*)

"fuck you" • The classic threat and insult that forever cast anal copulation (especially involving a man's anus) as the ultimate lowly act.

cluster fuck • An orgy. (AKA a fuck-n-suck)

dry fuck • To penetrate one's buns without butter (well, to try anyway); to rub one's penis against another's body.

face fuck • When a fellator's mug is forcefully used.

spit fuck • For a top to anal copulate using nothing more than his own saliva.

status fuck • To sleep with a coveted male in order to "pump up" one's place in a group.

fucking • Engaged in anal copulation. While there are practically a million ways you can say this, I wanted neither to bore nor mislead you into thinking such terms were all gay. In fact, most are not. However, there are a number which sound undeniably mansex-oriented. They describe the act without a touch of intimacy (which can be read as feminine), and go as far as to make it seem like totally brutal (that is, masculine) behavior. Here are "butt" a few examples: *cork; doughnut-hole; drill; gore;*

hammer; harpoon; nail; pile drive; pin; plow; plug (a hole); plunge; poke; pop (a cork); pork (a pig); pound; pump; ram; ride; rear end; roger; rut; shishkebab; skewer; slam (it home); spear; spike; spoke; stick; and *stuff.*

fudge packer • Said of any gay men, who "packs" (fucks) the "fudge" (feces).
He felt quite lucky to have found a fudge packer who came in milk chocolate.

full frontal • Nude images showing male genitalia.
If it's not full frontal there is no point.

full house • When a guy has more than one sexually transmitted affliction at a time.

funch • Quickie gay sex during the day (basically meaning to have a fag/fairy for lunch). (AKA nooner)

funny • A bit off; euphemism for gay.
That he suddenly seemed funny was no joke for his bride-to-be.

fussbudget • One who worries over trivial matters.

fussy • Quick to upset and lose temper; one who pays superfluous attention to particulars.

futzer • One who spends valuable time on silly things; a fool. (The word might be a combination of "fuck around" and "putz around.")

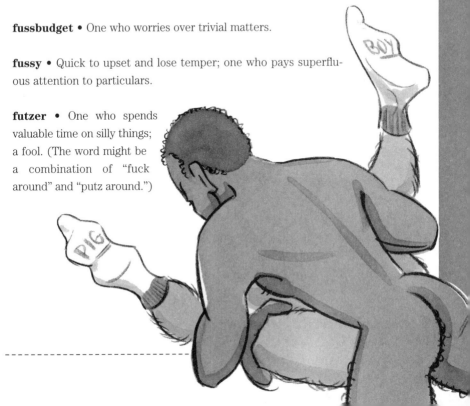

gadfly • A constant biting insect; an annoying critic.

Even after the gadfly wrote bitchily about his last collection, he had no choice but to have him buzzing around the front row at his next show.

Gaelick • Gayspeak for an Irish sissy.

ga-ga • Silly or overly excited; a young gay man anxious to be part of the community; someone obviously queer (*g*-ay *a*-cting, *g*-ay *a*-ppearing).

gag reflex • Involuntary choking, set off by something touching the back of the throat or tongue (often during fellatio).

It wasn't his gag reflex, he was just choked up over being with his ex again.

gaily • In a gay way. *Gaily forward*: queer for straight ahead.

gal pal • The female friend of a gay man.

gander • An "active" gay male. (See *goose*)

gangbang • Intense sexual activity where one passive male is assailed by a group of active males.

Ganymede • A young gay male. From Ganymede, the youth who was abducted by Zeus to serve him and other gods, with the implication that he tended to their sexual needs as well. Incidentally, his name means "joy" and "intelligence." (See *catamite*)

garage door • A man's pant fly. (AKA shop door)

Since you've already got the garage door open, ya wanna pull your car out so I can give it a shine?

gardening • Said of one looking for sex in a park setting.

That hoe is always out gardening.

gauntlet • Assault from both sides; a tight passage between two larger spaces (and where, within a sex club, men stand along the walls and grope others passing through). (AKA gangway)

gay • Originally meaning "full of cheer," but now used as an adjective to show positive conditions of "it" (many examples follow), as well as negative (*Why do you have to be so gay?*). Sometimes gay is used as a noun, but this is frowned upon, as many see being gay as only one aspect of who they are—not the totality. Also, in youth circles, gay has come to be known, of all things, as something that is passé. *Mais non!* In any case, the queer meaning of gay can be traced back at least to Victorian England, when both female and male prostitutes dressed *gaily* to attract attention, and where the young men of the trade were soon called "gay boys." Thereafter, the first undisputed "homosexual" link is attributed to our Noel Coward, who used it in his 1929 tune "Green Carnation." (A "green carnation," invented by Oscar Wilde, was supposedly a secret sign of gayness.) However, some trace back its gay use only to New York's Greenwich Village in the forties, the then-beating-heart of the "bohemian" community.

gay adoption • Where a male couple adopts because neither can beget a child or is not interested in being biologically linked with their offspring.

gay agenda, the • Alleged course of action that has us planning to defile all traditional and moral institutions and those who support them. (AKA the homosexual agenda)

Gay & Lesbian Alliance Against Defamation (GLAAD) • A non-profit watchdog group, formed in 1985, whose mission is to view our mass-media portrayals, while pushing for more positive representations.

gay bashing • Any physical assault (although socio-political ones are also possible) induced by homophobia and committed against any GLBTQ person. (See *hate: hate crime*) A gay bashers' phrase coined in the '90s: "Silly Faggot, Dicks are for Chicks." To which we replied: "Ditch the Bitch and Switch."

gay boy • Term used derogatorily to label a person by his condition (and redundant if you consider gay men "boyish" already).

gay business, a • Any professional endeavor which actively and (one hopes) respectfully serves our particular needs—and desires. A gay business should not be confused with one that is gay-owned. The former can belong to straight proprietors (and quite often is), while the latter is possessed wholly by the "pink dollar."

gay cancer, the • What AIDS was called early on (and still is, in backward circles), because it appeared to be a disease affecting only gay men. Thereafter, the battle against the illness had to be waged on two fronts: 1) to find a cure; and 2) to show this was a sickness that afflicted more than a single minority group.

gay community, the • The collective of GLBTQ persons. (Just saying gay is problematic in that it seems to favor and focus on homosexual males.)

gay conspiracy, the • Like our agenda, but framed more deliberately as us gath-

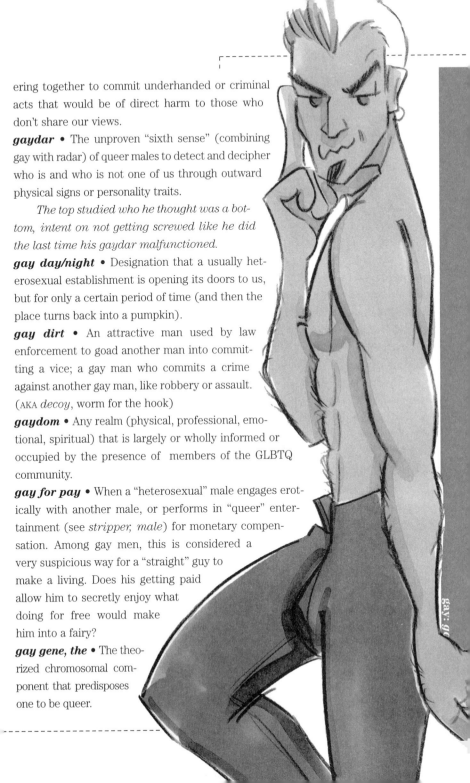

ering together to commit underhanded or criminal acts that would be of direct harm to those who don't share our views.

gaydar • The unproven "sixth sense" (combining gay with radar) of queer males to detect and decipher who is and who is not one of us through outward physical signs or personality traits.

The top studied who he thought was a bottom, intent on not getting screwed like he did the last time his gaydar malfunctioned.

gay day/night • Designation that a usually heterosexual establishment is opening its doors to us, but for only a certain period of time (and then the place turns back into a pumpkin).

gay dirt • An attractive man used by law enforcement to goad another man into committing a vice; a gay man who commits a crime against another gay man, like robbery or assault. (AKA *decoy*, worm for the hook)

gaydom • Any realm (physical, professional, emotional, spiritual) that is largely or wholly informed or occupied by the presence of members of the GLBTQ community.

gay for pay • When a "heterosexual" male engages erotically with another male, or performs in "queer" entertainment (see *stripper, male*) for monetary compensation. Among gay men, this is considered a very suspicious way for a "straight" guy to make a living. Does his getting paid allow him to secretly enjoy what doing for free would make him into a fairy?

gay gene, the • The theorized chromosomal component that predisposes one to be queer.

gay: go

gay ghetto • An area within a larger metropolitan setting, where we make up a noticeable part of the population. (Note: The negative connotation of "ghetto" has sometimes led to its being replaced by the more benign "gay village" and "gayborhood.")

gay icon • One who is beloved and admired by us. Because we are such art devotees(!), many gay icons are entertainers, largely female. But which ones they are depends on whom you ask and how old they are. It seems as our community matures and grows ever younger, so, too, does the scope of our iconography.

gay identity • What it means to be queer. (Is *Gay-2-Zee* making that any clearer?)

gay liberation • The "freedom" of all queers (from the tradition-based structure of the nation then and now), which began in the late '60s, alongside the emancipation efforts of women, persons of color, and the countercultural New Left. (See *stonewall*)

gaylights • "Highlighted" streaks in a man's hair.

gay mafia, the • Any group of queers who, relative to their small numbers, appear to run or hold enormous sway over entire businesses—notably entertainment, fashion, interior design, and retail—and in a somewhat covert manner. (See *velvet mafia, the*)

gay marriage • The union between two gay persons ceremonialized in a religious setting; a wedded state for gays with the same legal rights and privileges as that of a heterosexual married couple (where it is available).

Gay Men's Health Crisis (GMHC) • A not-for-profit, volunteer-supported, community-based organization founded in early response to AIDS, while we were under the impression that it was a "gay" health crisis. In recent years, attention has been given to other health aspects of the entire GLBTQ community.

gay movement • The ongoing cultural changes relatable directly (and hopefully positively) to gays.

gayola • Money paid out (as a bribe or extorted) in order to prevent a negative action that could be taken against a gay person or establishment. (From *payola*: money illegally exchanged for influence.)

gay positive • Supportive of gays and/or firmly against homophobia and heterosexism (AKA gay friendly).

gay pride • Personal feelings of esteem about one's homosexuality—often shown in a public context.

gay rag • One of the many printed and disposable materials with information about queer happenings. (*Rag*: items of little value post-use; to tease or complain.) (AKA fag rag)

gay sensibility • That which appeals to our tastes, or seems created by someone gay.

gayspeak • Language and speech for, from, and specific to GLBTQ persons, and expected to be without the usual negativity associated with words "about us" spoken by heterosexuals. (AKA gaylese, gaylish)

gay spray • The imaginary aerosol we own which magically transforms what we spritz from the dowdy to the divine.

gay time • Meaning never being the first to arrive anywhere; otherwise known as running fashionably late.

gaytriarchy • An as-yet-unrealized socio-political condition—that runs counter to the mainstream's long association with patriarchy-based authority—wherein the GLBTQ community holds all the power.

Everything in a gaytriarchy would look good, but would it run well?

gay vague • A man who has both gay and straight traits, whose sexuality therefore cannot be easily determined. This man's sexual ambiguity is supposed to be innate, not a willful act of assimilating the affectations of gay men. (AKA gayish) (See *metrosexual*)

If you can get very, very close to one, I can assure you they are no longer as gay vague as they think.

gay widower • The lonely husband of a woman who likes to socialize with queer men. (See *fag hag*)

gay youth • An important classification for adolescence. In times past, talk of a young person's sexuality was frowned upon. If it was addressed, it was usually assumed to be heterosexual in orientation.

gender • The determination of whether one is of the male or female sex by using masculine (for males) and feminine (for females) characteristics. What reads as simply defined is not. While humans are seen as one sex or the other, their gender is a condition of perception that can alter the awareness of others as much as it, itself, can be altered. (Whoa!)

gender bender • One whose gender is not readily apparent; one who deliberately manipulates gender characteristics to provoke; anything that calls into question one's precepts of gender.

gender confusion • When gender is not at all clear.

When the coach accidentally overlapped the end of the girl's hockey team practice with the start of the boy's figure skating club, the gender confusion was apparent to all in the rink.

gender fuck • Like a gender bender, but even more deliberate.

gender identity • Conditions of or used to determine one's gender.

gender identity disorder (GID) • Psychiatric term for when one's present gender feels incorrect. (Note: Many dislike this condition being classified as a "disorder," because it unfairly labels those affected as mentally ill.)

gender outlaw • One who purposefully ventures "outside" traditional masculine and feminine boundaries to benefit all those who do not fit neatly within any category.

genderqueer • Considered the entire spectrum of gays, lesbians, bisexuals, transgendered, questioning, et al. But not heterosexuals, and specifically not using a word that connotes "male" or female."

gender reassignment surgery • Medical procedure for changing a person's sex from what is felt to be wrongly shown on the outside to what is felt on the inside.

gender variant • One whose sexuality is in development (usually the state of someone young; see *questioning*).

"discover gender" • Phrase for when a person accepts his homosexuality.

That one'll discover gender the night he ends up on his ass!

genQ • Short for "generation" combined with "Q" (for "queer"), and of the world of GLBTQ youths, adolescents, and early twenty-somethings.

genteel • Of polite manner.

Ya think one is bowing to be genteel, 'til ya realize he's only gettin' bent.

gentry • A group of men who are well-bred (*deeply* and *frequently* so).

The gentry have arrived in time for the fine foie gras, dry martinis, and droll banter.

gerbil-jamming • Highly controversial, possibly apocryphal, sex act where a live rodent is shoved into one's anus.

> *The closest he ever got to gerbil-jamming was bein' poked by that ferret-faced guy with the ratty hair.*

"Get her" • Expression by which one gay guy wonders where another one got his (or "her") nerve.

GIB • Said for when a guy is "good in bed."

gift-giver • An HIV-positive gay man—or one with any other sexually transmittable disease—who deliberately passes his infection on to others who may or may not be aware of his condition. A "gift" is the infection one receives. (See *bug chaser*)

gigolo • A man paid for his companionship services, usually for an extended period of time, usually by a woman (which means he can often be gay, so is "straight for pay"). French: *gigolette*, girl dancer, prostitute. (See *escort*)

girl • A young woman; an effeminate young man; affectionate address between gays. Since queer males are thought, by some, to be pretty close to being women, we are often then characterized as being like "girls" (those girls who are pretty close to women).
big girl • One who is obviously a "sissy" (or one who is just, *well*, big!). (AKA big Mary, big woman)
girl stuff • Anything particular to a young female's fancy (ex: adoration of male pop stars). Consequently, that which is expected to be of interest to gay men. (See also *woman's work*)
girlfriend • One's female friend or lover; a gay man (especially one who acts with extreme girlishness); an affectionate form of gay address.
girlish/girly • Befitting of a young woman.
girly man • An adult male whose behavior seems better suited to a young woman. (Note: These "men" were made famous on *Saturday*

Night Live, in a parody of then-actor Arnold Schwarzenegger, who, upon election to California's governorship, added notoriety to its use by insulting his state's vacillating male Democrats with it. While the implication of its "gayness"—and sexism—has been repudiated, the slur's dual effects remain.)

"... like a girl" • Partial phrase usually preceded by a "throws," "walks," or "talks" and an insult to the female sex—and the gay men to whom it is often applied—in that it equates being girlish with inferiority.

old girl • Said affectionately of an elderly woman; not so sweetly for an elderly, queeny gay man.

giveaway • Something that belies true identity.
At first I wasn't sure, but his Adam's apple was a giveaway.

glam • Gayspeak short for *glamour*: to be compelling, exciting, romantic.
"glam it up" • To make something even more dazzling.

glamazon • An imposing woman (or man in drag) whose extreme physical presence is tempered by an extreme show of femininity.

"glazing the doughnut" • When one ejaculates semen on or around the anus.
After dunkin' a particularly sweet one, he loves glazin' the doughnut, too.

GLBTQ • Abbreviation for the "gay, lesbian, bisexual, transsexual, and questioning" community. (Even though it is meant to be all-inclusive, some feel it still places gay men "first" and others after. So, very often one sees it as LGBTQ.)

glitch • A momentary technical problem; a gay person.
Things are pretty normal here, but once in a while you do run into a glitch.

glitterati • A sparklingly sophisticated set of people (combining "glitter" with *literati*: the urbane and enlightened).
Who do you think puts the glitter in glitterati?

glory hole • An opening cut in a partition, usually between bathroom stalls, into which one male inserts his penis to have it fellated by another.
When he got me at the glory hole, I wanted to sing out Hallelujah in excelsis!

glut • Combining *glutton* (one who gorges on food) with "slut," to become a guy with an unstoppable appetite for fellating.

He was a glut, but no punishment for me!

goatee (go-T) • A small chin beard (from *goaty*: resembling a goat). Some claim goats are somewhat Satanic, and a person who chooses to look like one of questionable morality. Coincidentally, when goatees were most fashionable, in the early '90s, they were signs of gayness. Lately, sporting straight men have shifted the focus, while bunches of daddies, to balance their thinning pates, are tipping the scales back in our favor. (AKA prison pussy; see *Pan*)

go-go boy • One who is paid to dance, scantily clad.

The go-go boy got me going so bad I was a goner when he said "yes" to gettin' laid.

"going down" • The sexual act of (lowering one's self to perform) fellatio.

He's going down, but I can assure you it's not for the last time.

gold digger • One who is in an intimate relationship with another (usually older) for monetary support or personal gain.

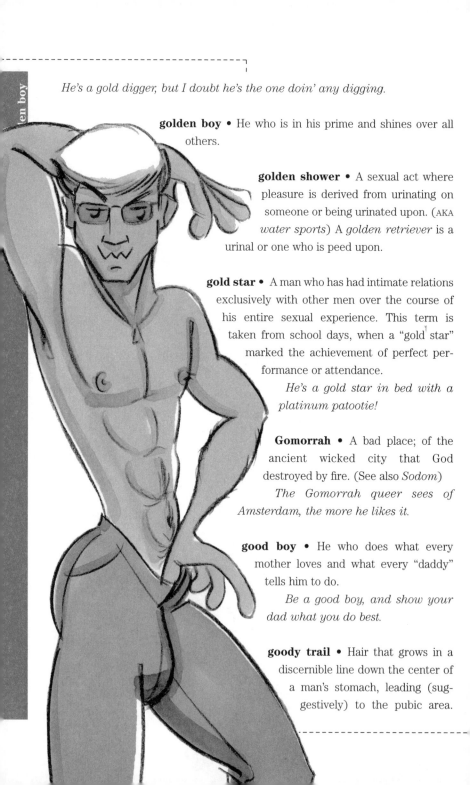

He's a gold digger, but I doubt he's the one doin' any digging.

golden boy • He who is in his prime and shines over all others.

golden shower • A sexual act where pleasure is derived from urinating on someone or being urinated upon. (AKA *water sports*) A *golden retriever* is a urinal or one who is peed upon.

gold star • A man who has had intimate relations exclusively with other men over the course of his entire sexual experience. This term is taken from school days, when a "gold star" marked the achievement of perfect performance or attendance.

He's a gold star in bed with a platinum patootie!

Gomorrah • A bad place; of the ancient wicked city that God destroyed by fire. (See also *Sodom*)

The Gomorrah queer sees of Amsterdam, the more he likes it.

good boy • He who does what every mother loves and what every "daddy" tells him to do.

Be a good boy, and show your dad what you do best.

goody trail • Hair that grows in a discernible line down the center of a man's stomach, leading (suggestively) to the pubic area.

From childhood tales, where candy is often left upon a path to entice one to move in a certain direction. (AKA treasure trail)

He was plannin' on followin' the golden boy's goody trail all the way—even if it meant walking through a golden shower.

goody-goody • One who is upstanding and/or doubly or artificially nice. From the nursery tale "The History of Little Goody Two Shoes."

He's the goody-goody man at work, but a baddie-baddie boy in bed.

goose • To prod, poke, or pinch the buttocks—and in penetrative anal sex. Taken from the habit of a goose to thrust his beak forward (and because they have cute, wiggling round rears).

"gay as a goose" • You might think this phrase means to compare us to *geese*: fowls who run afoul, squawk, shake their tail feathers, or constantly peck at one another. But not so. The popular term actually comes from "gay as a grig," which somehow got lost in the translation (from the British no less!). A "grig" is/was a bright and buoyant person. But these sprites seem no longer to exist—or, *ahem*, do they?

gooser • A pederast.

loosey-goosey • Post anal-sex condition, wherein the passive partner is visibly (maybe too) relaxed. The term is derived from *"loose as a goose,"* meaning "out of control."

gossip • Talk of a personal, sensitive nature; one who habitually spreads talk.

He's such a gossip, but you should hear what they say about him.

government-inspected meat • Any man in any branch of the military. Taken from the notion that anything our leaders test can be consumed without worry or guilt—and that everyone in the armed services will have been duly vetted.

He thought so long as it was government-inspected meat, it couldn't hurt to nibble.

Grand Canyon • A spectacular chasm in Arizona; a busy passive male's well-used anus (as a wide-open space). (AKA Lincoln Tunnel, broom in a cave)

grand(e) • Gayspeak French for when something is puffed up.

What a pity that he acts like a grande dame but looks like a great Dane.

greased • Lubricated to ease mobility; of anal sex and the passive male in anticipation of the act. (AKA PGE, pre-greased and eager)

He's so greased you'll need a banister around the bed to hold for safety.

Greek • An active gay male; anal copulation (taken from the legend that men of Ancient
Greece openly and enthusiastically participated in anal sex). (See *French, Turk*)

group • A gathering of at least four individuals.

group grope • Non-invasive sex activity where a number of clothed individuals
fondle and embrace each other. (AKA reading Braille)

group marriage • Union, without any legality, in which involved persons regard
themselves as wedded to and intimate with each other.

group sex • Intimate physical interaction, usually involving insertive sex, between
a usually substantial number of people. (AKA group therapy, mass lay)

"grow wings" • To go from placid to flamboyant behavior.

That one will grow wings the second a Cher song comes on.

"grower (not a shower)" • A flaccid penis that looks very small when compared
to its unexpectedly larger size in full erection.

Dude, you'll have plenty of ground to cover: It's a grower, not a shower.

"grrrr" • Bearspeak address of affection and sexual attraction for another man.
(See *"woof"*)

guest star • A gay guy who shows up late, grabs the spotlight, then leaves early
(AKA leading role); the invited third in a "threeway" (see *Lucky Pierre*).

guppy • Amalgamation of "gay urban professional" (and queer version of the '80s
"yuppy": a young urban professional). (Note: A "luppy" is the lesbian version and a
"buppy" the bisexual one. No word on whether there exists a "tuppy" or "quppy.")

gush(y) • To make an excessive display of sentiment or enthusiasm; excessively
sentimental or enthusiastic.

If he gets any more gushy, you're gonna need a mop and bucket.

guy thing, a • Something that would prove of great interest to a heterosexual male (ex: fishing at dawn) and, arguably, of far less to a heterosexual woman or a gay man. (Lesbian curiosity is still being weighed.)

gym • Short for *gymnasium*: a room equipped for sports. From the Greek: *gumnazein*, all-male exercise done in the nude (no wonder we love these places!).
  I'm sure it was some Woody talkin' who said, "Any gym where he's a member is one I'd like to join."
gym body • A gorgeous physique, obviously not something the guy was born with.
gym bunny • One who is there constantly, usually attractive and groomed, very social, bounces between old and new friends, and equipment. ("Sister" of a "disco bunny.") (AKA Muscle Mary)
gym queen • One whose reign revolves around the place.
gym rat • Obviously a club frequentor, but maybe, unfortunately, of its damp, dark, nether regions too.
gym tits • Enormous, exercise-enhanced pectoral muscles (considered a bit much, even by us connoisseurs).
gymbot • A guy mechanically precise in his workout routine.

hairdresser • The outmoded term for *hairstylist* (one who cuts and arranges hair professionally) in that it made the occupation seem quaint, feminine, and rather gay. No-o-o! (AKA hairbender) Curiously, "too gay" was said of "window dresser" and "interior decorator," too. So they beefed up and became: the "display stylist" and the "interior designer."

My guess was that the hairdresser was using hanky code to say he was into himself.

hairburner • Spiteful for hairdresser (oops, I mean hairstylist).

half-and-half • A bisexual; to split time orally and anally.

I got bored with it being plain, so I decided to go for half-and-half.

Hallowe'en • A celebration of harvest and of unearthly spirits. From the eve of the Christian day of the dead, All Hallows'. Unofficially, a "gay" holiday. (Because it allows all people to show their true selves, in costume—or out of them! Also, because it gives everyone permission to pick up "tricks" and treats.)

hand • The end part of the human arm used for grasping.

hand job • Masturbating oneself or another to ejaculation (and what is considered in the sex-for-hire trade as the simplest, easiest form of exchange).

handball(ing) • To fondle one's own or another's testicles (naked or through clothes); to penetrate one's rear end with the hand (see *fisting*).

When you said you wanted to do a little handballing, I didn't think I was gonna be used as the court!

handmade • Said of a large penis (in that it got that way from lots of handmaking motion: masturbating).

I've tried, but I can't get mine to look quite as handmade as yours.

Handy Andy • A chronic masturbator.

I wonder if Handy Andy is as good around the house as he is with his self.

handbag • What a woman carries with her to keep her necessities; one who is friendly with drag queens. A *favorite handbag* is the most attractive in the bunch.

hanky code • System of covert gay communication where individual males wear various colored hankies, denoting different types of sexual interest, in either the left (active) or right (passive) back pocket. This well-known example of our coded language developed within the leather scene of the early '70s, and was directly related to how gay men previously passed on sensitive information: via one's attire (to show, silently to each other, we existed, as well as to express sexual desire).

happy • Cheerful—and gay.

You're glad, but he's definitely happy.

happy hips • Said of one who walks effeminately.

happy valley • The cleft between the buttocks. To *"ski up and down happy valley"* is to slide one's penis along this crack.

hardcore • Very explicit sexual imagery or activity involving fully aroused male genitalia (see also *softcore*); to have an extreme interest in something.

hardwired • A direct and presumed infallible connection between two or more points; in sexual pleasure terms, when one spot on a man's body directly affects another (ex: a sensitive nipple that if flicked stimulates the inside of his anus).

hardwood floors • A clean-shaven pubic area and anus.

Now that you've got hardwood floors, do you ever have problems with guys slipping inside?

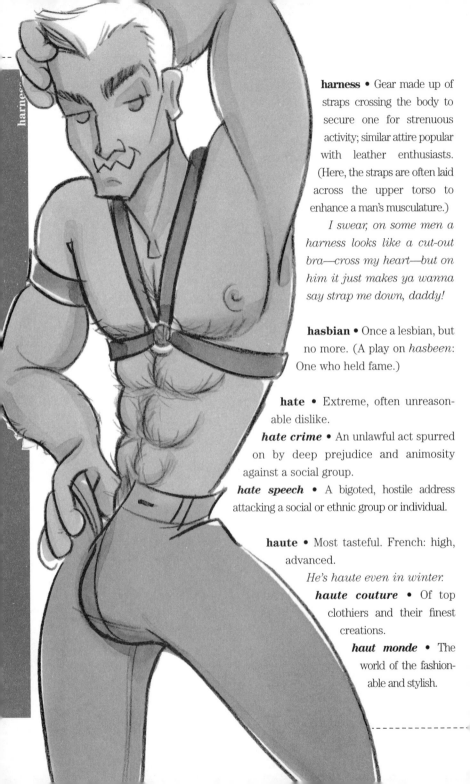

harness • Gear made up of straps crossing the body to secure one for strenuous activity; similar attire popular with leather enthusiasts. (Here, the straps are often laid across the upper torso to enhance a man's musculature.)

I swear, on some men a harness looks like a cut-out bra—cross my heart—but on him it just makes ya wanna say strap me down, daddy!

hasbian • Once a lesbian, but no more. (A play on *hasbeen*: One who held fame.)

hate • Extreme, often unreasonable dislike.

hate crime • An unlawful act spurred on by deep prejudice and animosity against a social group.

hate speech • A bigoted, hostile address attacking a social or ethnic group or individual.

haute • Most tasteful. French: high, advanced.

He's haute even in winter.

haute couture • Of top clothiers and their finest creations.

haut monde • The world of the fashionable and stylish.

he • Of a man.

he-blow • A gay male of the Jewish persuasion (derivative of Hebrew).

he-man • A very masculine man.

he-rags • Of very masculine clothes: construction boots, plaid shirts, etc.

he-she • One who straddles both sexes: a transsexual, a masculine female, or a feminine male.

he-whore • A male prostitute or pronouncedly promiscuous gay man. (AKA Jack's ass)

head • To move forward (leading with your head); the men's room; fellatio; the penis's tip.
I'm gonna head to the head for some head on my head.

head play • A top who taunts and tantalizes a bottom's mind before he goes to work on his body.

healthy • In good overall physical condition or of a sound frame of mind; shorthand for one's HIV status as "negative" or "positive without problems."

heathen • One following a cause that is sacrilegious.

heaven • Used, *gaily*, for when something (or someone) is wonderful (*the show was heaven*). (AKA heavenly)

heavens • Said when one is taken aback.
Heavens, you're bigger than I imagined but no more than I dreamed about.

hedonist • One who looks for or is a slave to pleasure. Greek: *hedone*, pleasure.

"heels over head" • A bottom in love.
I haven't seen him this heels over head since he dated that tumbler from Cirque de Soleil.

height/weight proportionate (HWP) • Noting that one's height is in balance with his weight (ex: someone who is six feet tall would weigh around 180 pounds). Such information is usually noted online, to determine if, whether asked or offered, one is in good enough shape to continue pursuing.

helicoptering • The practice of rotating one's penis in the face of another.

helium heels • Term for a passive gay man or one so sexual he cannot control his desires (as is evident when his feet automatically float upward, taking him instantly into receivership. It happens. Trust me.). (See *"light in the loafers"*)

I hope that helium heels has the sense to take his shoes off—I just had the ceiling painted!

her • Of a woman, or of a gay man (spoken by one who senses in the man a contrived, possibly gay, condition or circumstance). (See *pronoun game, the*)

hereditary • Coming genetically (or learned) from parent to offspring. Latin: *hereditas*, inheritance.

heretic • One with troublesome opinions countering those of Christianity. Greek: *haireisthai*, to choose.

heritage • Something passed down from preceding generations. French: *heriter*, inherit.

hermaphrodite • Old medical term for one who has both male

and female sex organs.

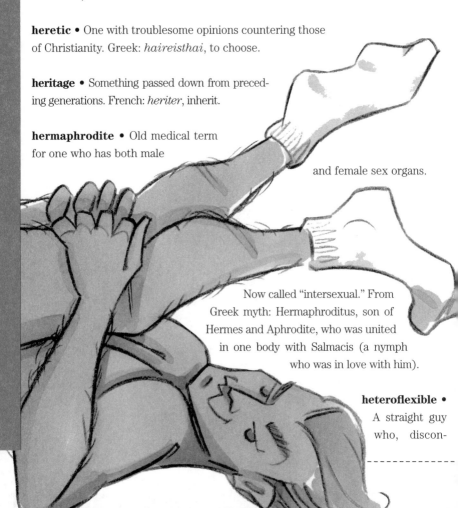

Now called "intersexual." From Greek myth: Hermaphroditus, son of Hermes and Aphrodite, who was united in one body with Salmacis (a nymph who was in love with him).

heteroflexible • A straight guy who, disconcertingly and often on frequent occasion, enjoys the sexual company of other men.

He's says he's a heteroflexible, but it took forever to get his legs into the right position.

heterosexual • From the Greek: *heteros*, meaning "other" and to whom, of the opposite sex, one is attracted. (We say "hetero" as a slightingly shorter version, while the diminutive "het" is meant to be even more demeaning.)

heteronormative • Where being straight is considered the correct state of a society's actions and behaviors.

heterophobia • The unfounded and irrational fear of straight people.

Because of my extreme case of heterophobia, my doctor advises me never to shop in Wal-Mart or dine in Hooters.

heterosexism • Giving dominance to heterosexuality over "minority" sexualities which are deemed inferior.

heterosexual privilege • Favoritism shown to straight people but not those of other sexualities (exs: spousal benefits, visitation rights).

heterosexuality • Characteristic of being straight.

"hide the candy" • Dragspeak for concealing the genitals (candy).

It's impossible to completely hide the candy, when it's the size of a Tootsie Roll big enough to satisfy King Kong.

hideaway • A place deliberately concealed to keep its profile low.

A hideaway is one thing, but do our bars have to be so hidden away that no one can find them?

high heels • One of the three most common active-passive sexual positions (see *reverse missionary*, *doggy style*), where the bottom faces the top, with his legs wrapped around the guy's waist or over his shoulders.

I can't walk in high heels, but who said I was goin' anywhere?

high-risk • That which is greatly subject to danger; of sexual activity and its increased or decreased (low-risk) likelihood of transferring disease, mainly HIV. *At-risk*: Said of those persons often most vulnerable or susceptible to harm.

Sometimes, just being gay is a high-risk behavior.

hijacker • One who plays with himself (or tries to do so with another) on an airplane.

I figured Mr. Friendly Skies was a member of the Mile High Club, but not a hijacker, too.

himbo • A male *bimbo*: an easy woman (casual Italian for "baby," from *bambino*).

I predict that himbo will be doin' the limbo under that Caribbean dude.

him-her • An effeminate man. (AKA himmer; *he-she*).

You'll never catch a him-her in a Hummer, unless it's in the backseat.

"hint of mint" • To show slight gay tendencies.

That hint of mint you say he has is enough to flavor Andes, Certs, Tic Tacs, and Altoids combined.

hinters, the • A place well beyond cosmopolitan culture. German: *hinter*, behind.

hissy • Of disdainful and unfavorable opinion (from *hiss*: a snaky sound of disapproval). (See *meow*)

hissy fit • A tantrum of one who has not gotten their way.

hit-and-run(ner) • Fast, often assaultive action; one who comes—and goes.

The only proof he had of the hit-and-run was the scrape on his rear bumper.

HIV (Human Immuno-deficiency Virus) • A pathogen isolated in the early 1980s that causes (allows for) AIDS. It does this by entering one's system through bodily fluids (semen, blood) and by attacking T-cells, thus hampering the effectiveness of the immune system to fight off illness.

hogtie • A form of bondage, where the feet and/or legs of a man are tied (as would be those of a "pig").

hoi polloi • The masses; Greek for "the many."

What designer Stan Doffish hated most about in-store events was being in contact with the hoi polloi.

hoist • Apparatus to raise a heavy object (used in leathersex scenes). (See *sling*)

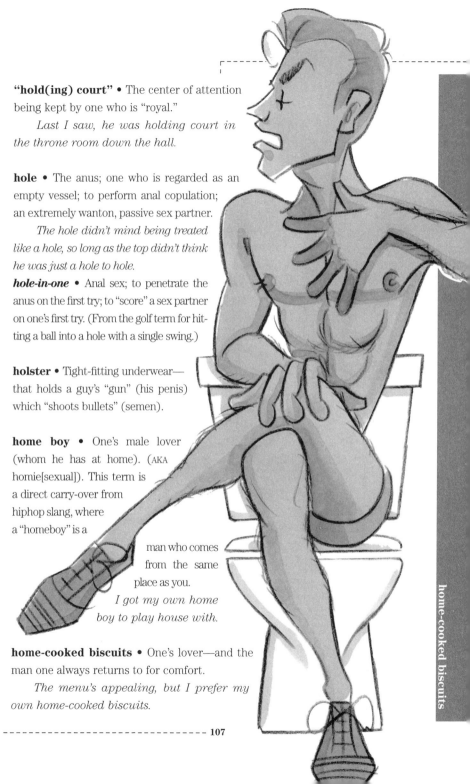

"hold(ing) court" • The center of attention being kept by one who is "royal."

Last I saw, he was holding court in the throne room down the hall.

hole • The anus; one who is regarded as an empty vessel; to perform anal copulation; an extremely wanton, passive sex partner.

The hole didn't mind being treated like a hole, so long as the top didn't think he was just a hole to hole.

hole-in-one • Anal sex; to penetrate the anus on the first try; to "score" a sex partner on one's first try. (From the golf term for hitting a ball into a hole with a single swing.)

holster • Tight-fitting underwear—that holds a guy's "gun" (his penis) which "shoots bullets" (semen).

home boy • One's male lover (whom he has at home). (AKA homie[sexual]). This term is a direct carry-over from hiphop slang, where a "homeboy" is a man who comes from the same place as you.

I got my own home boy to play house with.

home-cooked biscuits • One's lover—and the man one always returns to for comfort.

The menu's appealing, but I prefer my own home-cooked biscuits.

homo- • Greek for "the same"; derogatory shortening of "homo-sexual" (see also *'mo*).

homocentric • Condition where one person's—or all the world's—standards stem from a queer point of view.

Well, it certainly feels homocentric in Barney's Co-op.

homoerotic • Causing and/or attracting homosexual desire.

"The only thing more homoerotic than A&F is the WWE," said he, heading to his water polo game.

homo hit • When something becomes popular among gays.

It's only interesting when one of Madonna's songs does not become a homo hit.

homo-in-training (HIT) • A gay person new to "the life"; one showing the "signs" and/or about ready to come out. (AKA *princess*)

You can tell when some guy is a HIT in high school by the way he carries his books and crosses his legs.

homomasculinity • States of manliness that are heightened when filtered through our eyes, as when we focus our attention on athletic and military archetypes. (The notorious illustrations of Tom of Finland are examples. They are supermen who are also super gay.)

It was as if God had placed an exclamation point on his already tangible (and highly touchable) homomasculinity.

homophile • A fifties term, thought to be nicer than homosexual, that never caught on. (*Phile* means "one who loves." Hence, he was simply "one who loves the same.")

homophobe • One with irrational fear or hatred of gays.

homophobia • The widespread yet unexplainable fear of all aspects of homosexuality. Coined in the seventies by George Weinberg, author of *Society and the Healthy Homosexual*, who, through the term, sought to convey that being gay was not the problem—the problem is with those who are afraid of us.

(internalized) homophobia • Gays who hate being gay or despise another part of the community, such as very effeminate queers; of "heterosexuals" who fear the homosexual feelings they harbor inside.

(religious) homophobia • A particular anti-gay condition that uses the teachings of God as evidence that gays are unnatural. As such, we threaten the security of their just (and heterosexual) society.

homosexism • Ranking gayness superior to heterosexuality.

homosexual • A nonscientific (but scientific-sounding) term to classify those who are attracted to members of the same sex. Coined in the 1860s by Karl Maria Kertbeny, as an alternative to the inflammatory "pederast." Interestingly, Kertbeny felt that homosexuals were more masculine than heterosexual males. But his idea of it was overridden by others' notions that it was a psychological disorder. Today, the word is considered far too clinical-sounding and is infrequently used in casual gay or straight conversation.

homosexual panic • Defense "excuse" used to explain how certain people act out of fear of being perceived as gay.

homosexuality • Conditions of gayness, often framed as being incorrect because they oppose the normal values and dominance of heterosexuals.

(situational/institutional) homosexuality • Sexual intercourse that occurs between men only when women are not available. This happens in prison and in the military, and may be more about showing off one's power and control than it is about desire.

homosociality • An environment where men congregate and, thus, create underlying conditions for homosexuality. These places include barracks, boarding schools, fraternity houses, locker rooms, monasteries, reformatories (and the men's underwear department at Macy's).

"homo we go, les-bi-an our way, me for you and you for me, that's homosexuality" • Childhood chant said mockingly, but innocently(?), of such circumstances.

"honey in the hips" • Said of one whose mid-section moves with appealing fluidity and who is an exceptional copulating partner.

hormone therapy • Regimen where hormones (substances affecting physiological changes) are taken to help develop in a person of one sex the secondary physical characteristics of the opposite sex: estrogens for male-to-female transsexuals; and androgens for female-to-male transsexuals.). *Moning*: When one is in the process of hormone therapy.

horny • Sexually interested or aroused (as shown by having an erect penis, which resembles a *horn*). To have "the horns" or "the fever" (inspired by the classic song written and recorded by Peggy Lee and covered by Madonna) means when one is extremely desirous of sex. To "de-horn" is to have sex after a long period of nonactivity. *Horned out*: To have had too much sex.
"pull in your horns" • Said to one whose attraction to another is too evident (as by an erection).

You might stick the wrong person if you don't pull in your horns.

host • One who opens up and serves guests in his home; a party-thrower; from online exchanges: for one whose place can accommodate a sex partner (see *traveler*).

All his visitors thought he was the host with the most on the ball, and besides, his boyfriend was gone for the weekend, too!

hot-doggin' • To copulate the anus (the buns). A *hot dog*: the penis. A *horn-dog*: a man of extreme horniness.

house • A structure as a dwelling, or place of gathering for one or more persons; a group of individuals under one banner (name).

The House of Cards boys were dealt a severe blow when they lost to the drag queens of the House of Pan-Cake Makeup.
house mother • A nonblood-related maternal figure in charge of a household or group. (See *mother*)
houseboy • One who serves the needs of a home's owners.

Wanted: live-in houseboy, between the ages of 18 and 25, passively disposed and frequently able to handle hard jobs at all hours.

hubby • Affectionately, short for one's husband.

humor, gay • Banter that is characteristically caustic. (No, such a classification does not exist. But many words seem to describe what is funnily fey: acerbic, arch, astringent, bitter, clever, droll, dry, piquant, sarcastic, satiric, and snide among them. Or is it nothing to laugh about?)

humpy • Said of a man who is quite arousing (frankly, *errr*, fuckable), and of anal sex ("to hump," described as like *humping*: moving over a protuberance—and in this instance, the buttocks).

I'm not ready to get over humpy.

Hundred-and-Seventy-Fiver • A reference to the German Penal Code of 1871, which, in Paragraph 175, made homosexuality illegal. During the Nazi era, gay men were arrested under this ruling and sent to concentration camps, but they were not executed. Instead, they served hard labor and, oftentimes, were used for medical testing purposes.

hung • To hang down; to have a large (hanging) penis; and of the query: "how is one hung?" (see the following). (Note: Saying "well hung" is restating what may seem obvious.)

In my stockinged feet I knelt, as he, the hung one, stood by the chimney with care.

"hung like a horse (bull, or hamster)" • Phrase meaning one who is like a "horse" is noticeably large; a "bull" has large testicles; and a "hamster" should keep his skivvies on.

husband • The male spouse; a gay partner (often the one in a relationship thought to be the more masculine/active, balancing his "wife," the more feminine/passive mate). Old Norse: *husbondi*, master of the house. *Husbear and woof*: Bearspeak for the active and the passive partner.

He may look like the husband, but he's really more like the wife.

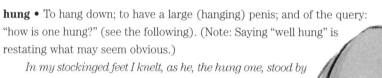

hustler • One who acts in a quick, clandestine manner; a man who takes money from another in exchange for sex. Since "hustle" also means a fast and not fair interaction, when sex is involved you can count on it being speedy and nonreciprocal. Curiously, too, a great many hustlers are straight guys in it for the money. Even so, consider how far one can go just for cash: Supposedly, one's heterosexuality remains intact if he is fellated, but a tad less so if he fellates; he can retain his manhood as the active partner in anal sex—*so long as he closes his eyes*—but he'll have a *very* hard time keeping things "straight" as the passive sexual partner; and might as well confess his queerness if he kisses. (AKA *call boy*, *cocktail*, crack salesman, *gay for pay*, prick peddler, *rent boy*, *swishblader*)

identity • The way by which one, or a group, is known through individual or collective aspects of personality and behavior. Latin: *idem*, the same.

identity crisis • Great unease with one's own or other's expectations of being a certain way.

So long as we are not sure who we are, we will always suffer an identity crisis.

illicit • Not lawful (and often sex-related).

The professor found it necessary to remind his students that not so long ago their sexual acts were considered illicit, leaving them all vulnerable to arrest.

immoral • Not proper, just, or virtuous. Latin: *im*, not.

It would be immoral—if we didn't redo the living room!

immune system • Components (tissue, cells, organs) that weaken or destroy harmful agents, but not beneficial ones, that enter the body.

in-and-out • Reference to heterosexual intercourse, as an act done with a laissez-faire attitude; Britspeak for any sex involving *in*-teraction.

inclination • Tending to move in a way seen as veering from the regular course.

His inclination? To always lie down in bed on his stomach, with his socked feet up in the air and cheeks high.

inclusive • To take all within. Latin: *includere*, to enclose.

Does inclusive mean I have to let just anybody in to my fondue fête?

in crowd • A fashionable, self-contained group.

Can we still be the in crowd when we're all out?

in search of (ISO) • Cyberspeak for a man looking for a specific type.

ISO: hairy, hung, top.

indecent • Running afoul of the public good.

indiscriminate • Not being selective or restrained; wanton.

Even Abel Mounting thought his friend Will Ing was too indiscriminate—buying another red sweater, when he easily owned a dozen.

individuality • The sum total of one's personality differentiating him from others.

The only individuality I'm interested in seeing is each Ajaxx63 model in my bedroom one at a time.

indulge(nt) • To give in, with few limits, to one's desires.

Would it be less indulgent if I did it outside church property?

inequality • When one person or group does not enjoy the same positive circumstances as another.

Sure, I feel inequality—every time you use your Banana employee discount and I don't get something new.

infect • To bring harm.
infectious • Able to bring harmful agents into the body.

inferior • Of a lower level, lesser worth.
inferiority complex • Feelings of one's unworthiness, especially when compared with others.

I think the best way out of an inferiority complex is to buy superior linens.

infidel • One who is without true religion. Latin: *infidelis*, not faithful.

Infidel? No, not since he left for Havana.

innuendo • Circuitous and belittling implication. Latin: by hinting.

A fast innuendo and out—it's what we're all about.

inspector of manholes • A diligent anal copulator (playing on "manhole" to mean "anus").

Once the inspector of manholes finishes his job, things'll open up.

instinct(ive) • Action taken innately in response to an external motivation. Latin: *instinctus*, impulse.

Afterward, his instinct was clearly showing, if not a little worn by the afternoon's activity.

integrate • Gathering together all parts to make a whole. Latin: *integer*, complete.
Sure I want to integrate—with him before the night is over!

intergenerational relationship • An intimate coupling (ex: daddy-boy, mentor-protégé) where one male is older than the other partner, usually by a generation (approximately fifteen to twenty years).

interior designer • One who understands the need for *ambience* (the mood created within a specific realm) and calls it "occasional" when just "table" will do.

intermediate sex, the • Turn-of-the-twentieth-century term for gay people—who appeared to occupy the "space in between" the two extremes of male and female.
No, intermediate sex is not what you have between boyfriends, sweet pea.

Internet, the gay • Cyberspace is very attractive to gay men. But why? Because on it we can be as expressive as our imaginations (and libidos) allow? Or is its relative anonymity comfortingly reminiscent of a time when gay interests were always passed on in some secret manner? Who can say? In any case, the Internet's gay popularity has spawned its own language, but one so vast that even in their almost always abbreviated forms some terms were impossible to include. Still, a few predominant ones are scattered among *Gay-2-Zee*'s entries. Here are a few more—in no particular order— which predate the medium but are in even greater usage because of it: GAM (for "gay Asian male"); GBM (for "gay black male"); GHM (for "gay Hispanic male"); GJM (for "gay Jewish male); and GWM (for "gay white male")

intersexual • That which happens between the sexes; one who has characteristics of both sexes (or is moving from one to the other, as in "transsexual").

You can usually find him at the inter-sexual of his and hers.

"in the life" • Phrase to mean being a (hopefully well-adjusted) part of the gay community.

intolerant • Not accepting of persons with beliefs different from one's own.

invert • Freudian term for a gay person, whose sexual desire turns inward to himself, a man, rather than outward, to a woman. Latin: *vertere*, to turn. Also, "inversion" was an old term for homosexuality.

invisible • Not seen, noticed, or considered.

His family might not notice he's trying to be invisible for them again, but I do.

jack (off) • To give a sudden, continual thrust or pull; to masturbate ("off" meaning "to climax"). From e-*jac*-ulate, which comes from the Latin: *jacere*, to throw. (AKA jerk off) (Note: A "jack-off" can also be one thought of as a low, stupid, or throwaway type. But you knew that.)

jacking • In the process of masturbating. (AKA jerking)

jackoff club/party • Establishment or gathering where males masturbate individually or each other (and where typically no other sex act is involved). (See *circle jerk*)

j/o • Popular abbreviation for "jacking off."

Jacques Pennier • Gayspeak for the store JC Penney, of a peculiar form of wordplay that "queerifies" institutional names. Other examples: Whitey Castel's (for White Castle), Targée (for Target), Homo Depot (for Home Depot), and Needless Markup (for Neiman Marcus).

Let's see if I can find a top to match my bottom at Jacques Penniers.

jaded • Cynical, world-weary, and numbed by the constancy of pleasure. Middle English: *iade*, carthorse, nag.

That ol' queen's green cuz he's hungover—and jaded.

jam • A heterosexual male (abbreviated from "just a man").

I hear that brand of jam spreads easily like melted butter.

jawbreaker • A penis so big you could break your "jaw" with it. (Naw, never happens. Sincerely.)

jock • An athlete or a man characterized by athleticism.

jocker • In prisonspeak, the active male who dominates a passive male. (See definition of "jockstrap")

jockey • An active gay male (taken from the athlete who rides on the back of an animal).

jocks-n-socks • Gay favorite outfit (of a jockstrap and sport socks) that sparingly conveys the essence of all-American manliness. (AKA jox-n-sox)

jockstrap • Male undergarment, perhaps the most homoerotic of any apparel item, that protects the genitals without hindering mobility. This is important! A "jock" originally meant a man's penis. Therefore, a "jockstrap" literally translates into "support for the genitals." Even the trademarked name, *Jockey*, of the underwear maker, means "of a 'jock'" when that still meant a guy's privates. The reason why this is

mentioned: The "jock" many of us worship turns out to be named for his you-know-what. As if most didn't know he was one already. Poetic justice, indeed. (AKA lockerroom tux)

jock-type • One who appears remarkably athletic but is, in real life, probably not a professional athlete.

jolly • Cheerful—and gay.

jousting • Sexual interplay between two men with erect penises (from the medieval game where a coupla guys thrust at each other with *lances*: long wooden weapons with metal heads!).

Judgment Day • The time when God judges one's moral worth for entry into heaven (and when, it has been said, all gay men will regret their entire lives).

Yes, Judgment Day would soon be upon him—and Rod Longfellow worried if he had what it takes to win the annual "Wet Briefs" contest.

K

Kansas • With all due respect to those born and raised there, a "state" we escape from or any place felt dull and behind the times. Derived from the iconic "gay" film *The Wizard of Oz*, in which a sepia-toned Kansas seems downright bland when compared to colorful Oz.

It didn't take a house falling on him to convince Hamilton that he and Burke were no longer in Kansas.

Kaposi's sarcoma • A rare skin cancer that surfaces as purplish lesions and is connected to immune deficiency, therefore is often a major sign that "full-blown"AIDS is present. (AKA KS)

Karma Miranda • A gay hippie-type or one into spirituality. A play on the name of an "old school" gay icon, Brazilian entertainer Carmen Miranda.

Karma Miranda is traveling on a higher plane, but will use my runway when he's ready to land.

kept boy • One whose lifestyle needs are taken care of by a usually more mature and financially solvent male in return for sex. (See *gold digger*)

key code • And a supremely easy one to unlock at that: keys hanging on the left side of the body (leg) mean one is active, keys on the right mean one is passive.

His use of key code only confirmed him as a top pick.

k-hole • A hallucinogenic state one enters when overusing the drug Special K(etamine). Beyond individual instances when one (in past and present gay generations) would seek solace from unfriendly forces in a bottle of booze or "bennies," being queer does not mean you are automatically prone to substance abuse. However, perhaps because of our newfound visibility in the last dozen years, the questionable habits of a few (not all) must share in the spotlight. (See *tweak*)

kidney trouble • Said of one who likes to have sexual adventures in restrooms.

It only takes a second to wizz—unless you're experiencing kidney trouble; then it can take hours.

ki-ki (kai-kai) • A lesbian with the ability to appear both butch and femme; a bisexual; a drag queen or transgendered person sexually attracted to same. (AKA incest)

kink(y) • A peculiarity; exhibiting or attractive to the strange or perverted (especially sexual tastes).

Oddly, queers aren't all kinky.

Kinsey Six, a • A totally gay male. From the scale developed by renowned sexologist Alfred Kinsey for measuring sexual orientation. A person who was a "zero" was considered totally heterosexual, and from one to five was shown to have increasing interest in members of the same sex, you could say bisexual, until reaching the highest point of the range: six. (Note: Kinsey was a four—*your author would be a seven!*—and the numbers were determined by calculating responses to a series of interview questions.)

kitchen cleaner • One who performs anilingus.

I wonder if he'd let me use his kitchen cleaner to work on mine, which are overdue for a good going-over?

kitsch • Something created (like art) that is crude, but often sentimental. (German) (See *camp*)

kneel at the altar • To perform anilingus or fellatio (before a vaunted place). (AKA "worship at the altar," "receive holy communion")

knob polisher • One who specializes in fellating (a "knob-job"); to "shine your knob" is to masturbate.

The knob polisher had a secret to success: using lots of his own spit.

kosher dill pickle • A circumsised penis (from the Hebrew *kosher*: fit to eat). (AKA "cut out to be a gentleman")

His diet allows him one kosher dill pickle a night.

kowtow chow • Fellatio (or, in some cases, anilingus). Taken from the Chinese *kowtow*: to kneel before an authority figure as a sign of respect.

I'd do the kowtow chow for him even if he wasn't my boss.

kumquat • A blob of semen (and play on the name of a small, orangelike fruit). (AKA pearl drop, sugar lump)

Your sheets look like the kumquat harvest came in; whatdja do, bring over all the guys from your gym?

KY • The lubricant originally used by doctors to ease insertion in procedures, as it still is today, medical or, *uhmm*, otherwise.

KY cowboy • An active male. (Note: Supposedly not even the maker, Johnson & Johnson, knows what the "K" or "Y" stands for. If you know, write me!)

label • A descriptive branding, classification, epithet.

My philosophy is: If you're tired of the old label, Mary, go out and buy something new!

lacy • That which is fine and delicate; an effeminate homosexual.

He couldn't be any more lacy if he were draped in a doily.

ladder • An older gentleman into younger ones. Taken from *lad*: a young male.

The handsome young swain knew that the only way to the top of his company was by climbing the old ladder successfully.

laddie/lassie • Code words for identifying children of gay parents to one another in public (school).

lady • Said of one who is particularly genteel. *Ladies*: a group of gay men (*Now, ladies, keep your pants on 'til all the guys get here.*); *Ladyboy*: an extremely effeminate young male or transsexual (a term originating in Southeast Asia's red-light districts). *Lady Godiva*: a queer in the nude who should probably keep his clothes on. *Ladylike*: dainty and indicative of what a gentle and properly behaved woman would possess or how she would behave.

lamb • A young, passive male (often paired with a *wolf*).

lamb to the slaughter • New meat thrown to the predatory gay scene.

lambda • The eleventh letter of the Greek alphabet, "L," and a symbol used by the gay community since the early seventies. Theories as to why it was chosen: 1) "L" stands for liberation; 2) it is an "energy" term in physics and may have been selected to show our collective "power"; 3) the letter, as originally written, implies "balance"; 4) Ancient Spartans felt it meant "unity"; 5) to the Romans it meant: "the light of knowledge shed into the darkness of ignorance"; and 6) Ancient Greek warriors placed it on their shields and paired off with younger men when going into battle (thinking they would fight more fiercely with their lovers, *yup*, alongside).

latent • Here and possible, but not yet clearly present. Latin: *latere*, to lie hidden.
Personally, I think it's better that he's latent than never.

launching pad • A bed (because it's where rockets are shot off).
By the looks of your launching pad, it musta been one of NASA's biggest!

lavender • A color which is a mix of "baby blue for boys" and "pink for girls"—
hence, of the entire gay lifestyle.
lavender convention • A gathering of gay men.
Every time they do a gift show it's like a lavender convention has hit town.
lavender lad • Term used during the '50s McCarthy era for gays working in the
government whose presence was felt to be risky to our national security (because
being secretly immoral left them vulnerable to blackmail).
lavender law • Legal issues (and subsequent rulings) directly involving and affecting the gay community.
"dash of lavender" • To have gayness about.
*You can always find a dash of lavender where people from red and blue
states lightly cross paths.*

layer cake • An active partner's buttocks (cake) atop the passive partner's while
they are in the reverse missionary position. (See *reverse missionary*) (A *three-
layer cake* is when a trio of men are on top of each other.)
*The two of them together was definitely a vanilla layer cake—that was
ready for a generous coating of icing, maybe chocolate cream.*

"lay of the land" • A gay guy who is ready, willing, and able to have sex any place
and at any time.
*Most members had become so familiar with the lay of the land that some
could make out in total darkness—and often did.*

leather • The tanned and hairless hide of animals; the scene of persons preoccupied with the wearing of such garments, along
with the associated sexual and sensate scene. While
it may not be your thing, leather is an
inescapable and important part of the
gay community for compellingly

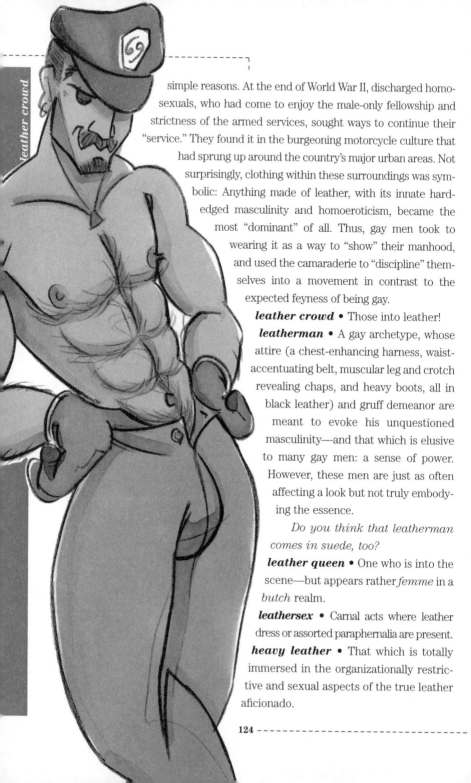

simple reasons. At the end of World War II, discharged homosexuals, who had come to enjoy the male-only fellowship and
strictness of the armed services, sought ways to continue their
"service." They found it in the burgeoning motorcycle culture that
had sprung up around the country's major urban areas. Not
surprisingly, clothing within these surroundings was symbolic: Anything made of leather, with its innate hard-
edged masculinity and homoeroticism, became the
most "dominant" of all. Thus, gay men took to
wearing it as a way to "show" their manhood,
and used the camaraderie to "discipline" themselves into a movement in contrast to the
expected feyness of being gay.

leather crowd • Those into leather!

leatherman • A gay archetype, whose
attire (a chest-enhancing harness, waist-
accentuating belt, muscular leg and crotch
revealing chaps, and heavy boots, all in
black leather) and gruff demeanor are
meant to evoke his unquestioned
masculinity—and that which is elusive
to many gay men: a sense of power.
However, these men are just as often
affecting a look but not truly embodying the essence.

*Do you think that leatherman
comes in suede, too?*

leather queen • One who is into the
scene—but appears rather *femme* in a
butch realm.

leathersex • Carnal acts where leather
dress or assorted paraphernalia are present.

heavy leather • That which is totally
immersed in the organizationally restric-
tive and sexual aspects of the true leather
aficionado.

left • The opposite of "right"; of the political or intellectual *left*: advocates of liberal, not conservative, policy and change.

Just because we're to the left doesn't mean we can't be right.

lesbian • The most used, recognizable, and noninflammatory term for a female sexually attracted to her own sex. Taken from Lesbos, a Greek island where Sappho, a poet of ancient times, wrote lyrically of love between women. (AKA lesbyterian, lezzy, lesbo)

lesbigay • Once popular abbreviation for the community, but now inadequate in its exclusion.

lesbo lad • A straight male who seeks the company of gay women (the heterosexual male version of a "fag hag"). (AKA *Dutch boy*, lesbro)

lesploitation • The use of same-sex female imagery to entice heterosexual men, who often find such instances attractive, at the same time far less threatening, erotically and otherwise, than notions of same-sex male encounters.

LGBTQ • Popular all-inclusive abbreviation for the community ("lesbian, gay, bisexual, transgendered, questioning"), notable for its name placement.

lipstick lesbian • A gay female who affects certain characteristics traditionally expected of women in feminine appearance and actions. While not exactly the opposite, a *Chapstick lesbian* is one who's more into sports than looking pretty.

LUG • Acronym for "lesbian until graduation," of a woman who has those familiar gay relationships in college but ends them after.

power lesbian • A queer female in an authoritative position.

"let one's hair down" • To admit to being gay. Originally, a woman who let her hair down was going from being disciplined in public to being (and becoming) more of herself when her tresses were unpinned in private.

lewd • Overly taken up with sex and desire. Middle English: *leued*, vulgar.

With one button on his 501s strategically unfastened, he was sure to get his message out lewd and clear.

libel • An untrue proclamation that hurts one's standing. Latin: *libellus*, dim.

That fairy's libel to say something queer.

liberal • Generous; not bound by tradition; without bigotry; broad-minded; one who subscribes to such opinions. Latin: *liber*, free.

You can be too liberal—giving of yourself so freely like that.

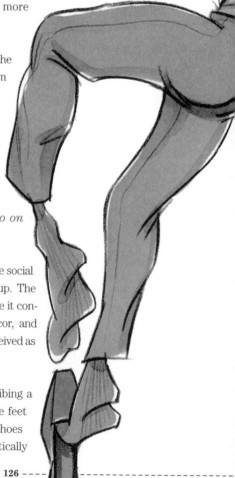

libidinous • Having or showing lustful wishes. Latin: *libido*, desire.

What he does in bed is none of your libidinous, unless you care to join in.

licentious • Not having proper control of one's sexual desires. Latin: *licentia*, freedom.

lickety-split • To perform anilingus. (Also, an older term meaning "to do something with haste.")

If you get Mr. Ice Cream Scoops to come by, I'll be there lickety-split.

life partner • One with whom another has a committed relationship in all aspects of existence; more sexual than just saying "partner."

life preserver • An item thrown in the water intended to keep a person from drowning; a condom. (AKA life jacket)

Do you use a life preserver or just dive right in?

lifesaver • One who is sweet and passive (from the "candy with the hole in the middle").

One more lifesaver, and I can go on to another roll!

lifestyle • A way of being that mirrors the social values and behavior of a person or group. The word often conjures superficiality, because it concerns mainly consumption in dress, decor, and diversion. As such, the gay lifestyle is perceived as the most self-indulgent of all.

"light in the loafers" • Phrase describing a gay male, mainly bottom-inclined, whose feet are expected to smoothly rise out of his shoes and over his head, so that he automatically assumes the passive position for easy penetration. Also heard: "light on his feet," which can also mean one is nimble, but more often means a guy who flies about the room like a "fairy."

This one's so light in the loafers he could top the Rockefeller Center Christmas tree—if he were a top!

Lily Law • Gay for the police (from *lily-white*: that which is colored pure and chaste). (AKA Betty Badge) *Dickless Tracy*: a female officer; and *Whistler's mother*: the head of a police unit.

lily-livered • Said of one who is weak, a coward. A healthy blood-red liver turns lily-white when it is malfunctioning.

limp wrist • Said of an especially effeminate gay male. (AKA *bent wrist*, broke wrist). Whether a "limp wrist" is really a sign of gayness is an unending argument. Plenty of straight men have hands that dangle from their arms like dying tulips. But it is interesting that what appears to be a lack of rigidity becomes a sign of our deviancy.

There's not enough Niagara spray starch in the world to keep that limp wrist straight.

linguist • One who speaks in many languages—or a specialist in oral activity.

He was quite the linguist, until the big throat doctor awed him into silence.

lisper • One who mispronounces words with a "th" sound instead of an "s" or "z." Essentially, a *thithy* (as a sissy has often been mockingly called). Similar to a limp wrist, a lisp has become symbolic of being gay, but it is in no way a true indication. Nevertheless, what is most insensitive is in unfairly attributing the defective angle to both conditions, and then connecting them, making both seem even worse.

load • An amount of material; semen and the acts of ejaculation and anal intercourse. To "lighten your load" is one man proposing to bring another to climax. (See *unload*)

Since I'm here to get you to dump your load, why don't you call me Mack?

locker room • A place where athletes change in and out of uniform, and clean up (a palpably homoerotic environment).

loiterer • One who idles with mischief in mind.
I'm no loiterer, I've got serious business to attend to.

lollipop stop • A roadside rest area (where men go to have sex).
Knowing it was the last lollipop stop for forty miles, he loaded himself up with as many suckers as he could get his mouth on.

long-term relationship (LTR) • Rather clinical-sounding term, used often on the Internet, to state whether one is already involved, is interested in being hitched, or is not interested in any fleeting (quickie) encounter.

longtime companion • One who stays with another for a notable length of time; a gay partner (and too often used by periodicals, in obits, wary of words like "lover" to describe the passing of one's partner).

long-winded • Said of a blowjob that takes a protracted amount of time to reach climax.
The trouble with him is that he's long-winded but short on substance.

lord of the flies • A prodigious and thoroughbred fellator (and title of the William Golding novel about plane-wrecked boys, and a name for Satan in the Bible!).
You better get you some now, before the lord of the flies shows up and unzips 'em all.

lover • One with whom another feels deep emotional and sexual feelings (considered non-gender-specific, often too much so).

"love makes a family" • Phrase that suggests that blood ties are not necessary (or sufficient) to form a group that is supportive, caring, and loving.

"love that dare not speak its name, the" • A euphemism for homosexual love—ummentionable in polite society at the turn of the twentieth century—coined by Lord Alfred Douglas, the intimate of Oscar Wilde.

lube • Short for *lubricant*: a viscous fluid that enables freer movement. The three gayest ones are: petroleum jelly; vegetable shortening, and KY. (Note: All three of these became popular during the seventies long before brands were manufactured specifically for our market's needs. Further indications of their historic aspects: Being that they are both oil-based products, petroleum jelly and vegetable shortening can break down the composition of rubbers. Hence, they were/are ultimately lubes used for "unsafe" practices.) Latin: *lubricus*, slippery.

lip-lubed • Said of saliva having been used as a lubricant.

"lubed up" • One who is ready to go, literally and figuratively.

Any more lubed up and he'll be a faster ride than an Indy 500 pace car.

Lucky Pierre • The guy invited by a couple for a threesome (therefore likely to receive the most attention); the middle man in threeway sex, and likely being penetrated while he is penetrating (AKA the "sandwich filling").

No, you don't have to be named Pierre to be the lucky one.

lure • Means to coax (with seduction).

Daddy, if ya wanna hook that one you're gonna need a bigger lure.

luscious • Abundantly attractive to the senses.

"The butterscotch pudding was luscious!" cooed Lutz Tousay, as his dessert spoon tinkled, loudly, in the now-empty bowl.

macaroni and cheese • An unclean, uncut penis.

He really cooks, but I'm not hungry for another mouthful of his macaroni and cheese.

macho • Spanish for aggressively masculine.

machismo • A strong sense of masculine aggression, dominance.

macho man • One who plays up his masculinity, to the point of not being taken seriously.

macho slut • A sexually active man who, by his aggressive manner, is perceived as a top, but is more than likely to be a bottom.

mad(ness) • Gayspeak for when one is "crazy" for something, or something that is absolutely absurd.

I'm mad for Franz Ferdinand—and I'm forty—isn't that just madness?!

Madame Curie • A gay doctor (and the name of the female chemist who discovered radium).

Your Madame Curie is hot enough to give me a temperature.

Madge • A fusty-sounding woman's name; a fusty gay man (and one of Madonna's many nicknames).

mainstream • The dominant (main) course (stream) of a society's attitudes and behavior.

Gay men are like salmon: born to swim against the mainstream.

majority • The larger part (more than half); the political group with the most authority. Latin: *maior*, greater.

male • Virile; characteristic of a man.

male chauvinist • One who believes without reservations in the dominance of his sex (and sexuality).

male rape • The sexual violation of one man by another. (This type of interaction is almost always about the perpetrator's way to show power, and not about passion).

You can't male rape the willing, and he was ready and able to prove it.

male tail • A guy's backside.

male-dom • The realm of all (straight) men.

male-identified (-oriented) • Recent term for same-sex attraction, but also for anything which is more appropriate for a man. (See *guy thing*)

maleness • Indications of one's masculinity.

M-T-F • Abbreviation for a "male-to-female" transsexual.

mama's boy • One who is distinguished by a deep tie to his mother (and is often shy and affectedly mannered).

man • A male adult.

-man • Compound ending for a professional or social role regarded as male heterosexist and heterocentric (ex: businessman).

He seems more like a boy in blue than a policeman.

man-boy • A decidedly adult-aged male (forties?) with the demeanor, often the look, of one much younger (twenties?), and usually sexually passive.

mangina • Where to copulate with a gay man (oh-so-playfully combining "man" with "vagina").

manhole • The round opening to an internal system of works for one to enter; a guy's anus. (See *inspector of manholes*)

He was going to enter every manhole in the neighborhood until he found one with an opening that was just right.

manly • The correct qualities for a man. (See *unmanly*)

But Monty can't even act manly, Clift.

"man or mouse?" • Question that assumes that as a "man" one is courageous (as he should be), or as a "mouse" is cowardly (as he should not be).

Son, are you man or mouse?

man's man • A servant to a man; an upstanding example of traditional masculinity; a homosexual.

Hudson's a man's man, just like Rock was.

manscaping • The often exacting grooming, shaving, and/or trimming of hair on a man's body (but usually not of a "hairstyle"). Taken from the word *landscaping*: the contouring and arranging of grounds.

manservant • One who tends to another man's needs.

mansex • Men-only erotic interplay expected to be without any soft or romantic aspects.

manual labor • The "job" of male masturbation.

Down at the docks, it was easy to find guys interested in a little manual labor.

manwich • A male sex threesome.

I still had me a banana split after finishing an over-stuffed manwich.

mannerism • An idiosyncrasy of behavior.

The man's mannerisms were what bothered most men.

Mardi Gras • French for Fat Tuesday, climax of the Carnival season, a time of great merriment and abandon before Lent (and, given all its sexuality and costumery, thought a very fun and very gay time). (See *Hallowe'en*)

marginalize • To move to the outer edges (margins) of a larger group and away from its nurturing core.

If they continue to marginalize us, we'll fall right off the map.

Margo Polo • Gay for an Italian man (a play on the name of the Venetian explorer Marco Polo). (AKA a Roman candle, which also works for his penis)

I definitely saw fireworks when Margo Polo pulled out his Roman candle!

maricon • Spanish for gay man. *Mariposa*: Spanish for "butterfly" and "gay."

marriage • A man and woman's legal union as husband and wife; any coupling of similar intimacy—but without the privileges.

front marriage • A union of convenience between a gay

132

man and a lesbian that affords them both all the privileges and benefits of a traditional one.

Any front marriage sets us back a thousand years.

married • Already wed; of being in a very close relationship; code for being straight (or expected to be).
   But he's married!

Mary • Woman's name used to address any gay man (also called a "hairy Mary"), or to indicate that his behavior is gay (*If you didn't act like such a Mary, no one would think you were!*). There is little precise reason why Mary—instead of *Nancy, Madge, Blanche*—became so identifiably gay. It could be because she is so common, especially in classic children's rhymes ("Mary, Mary, quite contrary" and "Mary had a little lamb") or because she rhymes with "fairy." Hmmm. However, there is one most curious connection, which leads us to that holiest of women, the mother of Christ, who conceived without sex. Much as we were, long ago, thought to be lacking.

"Mary, don't ask" • Phrase for when a situation has no explanation suited to a queer's sensibility.
   Why did he serve domestic and not imported? Mary, don't ask—you know how we can be.

masculine • Relating to or suggesting what is traditionally characteristic of a man.
   The only thing masculine about him is in his wearing pants, but it's evidence that falls quickly by the wayside under closer inspection.

masochism • Ritualized erotic conduct in which pleasure comes from the controlled infliction of pain or emotional abuse upon oneself—named for Leopold von Sacher-Masoch, an 1800s Austrian novelist. (See *sadism*)

masquerade • A false covering. In times past, to "masquerade" as a woman, for a man, was to take on a fraudulent identity, and was an unlawful offense for which many gay men were arrested.

massage • A therapeutic rubbing of the body.
   How 'bout I give the back of your throat a massage?

legitimate massage • A body rub given by a licensed professional masseur (as so many can be administered by those without the proper credentials).

masseur • The strong-handed and sure-footed man who rubs your body oh-so well.

master • One in total control of another; in BDS&M activities, the active, dominant partner over a "slave."

masturbate • To play with the genitals (to orgasm). Latin: *masturbare*, to disturb with the hand.

mate • One with whom another is close; of a matched pair; to breed. (Though one can refer to a woman as a mate, it's hardly thought of as the most feminine way to do so.)

mate-swapping • An activity where one man's partner is exchanged with another's for sexual purposes. (See *swinger*)

matinee • A sexual encounter taking place during the middle of the day (as a show would be during those same hours). (AKA nooner)

  In two hours' time I can manage a matinee, but it's always a tight squeeze.

Mattachine Society • A forerunner gay organization founded in 1950, in Los Angeles, by Harry Hay, which sought to change the public's view of gays as deviants to one of an oppressed minority. Their influence peaked in the 1960s, and by the seventies they were seen as too docile. Eventually disbanded in 1987. "Mattachine" comes from an Italian theater character: a jester who spoke the truth to his rulers.

mature • Said of a (gay) man who is expected to be experienced, knowledgeable, and—in a community that cherishes youth—older, but referred to as such in a more palatable way.

maul • Attack by an animal. Bearspeak for having sex with a hairy guy (a "bear").

mauve • A grayish violet; a color, like lavender, which has been associated with being queer for a long time (most notably during the "gay" 1890s, the time of Oscar Wilde, which was also called the "mauve decade").

mayonnaise • A play on semen as the creamy condiment that goes with the meat

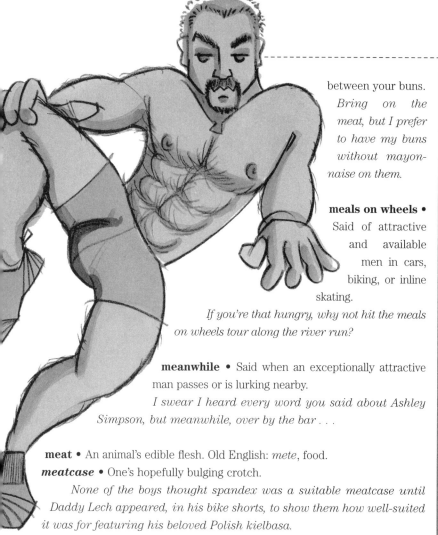

between your buns.
Bring on the meat, but I prefer to have my buns without mayonnaise on them.

meals on wheels • Said of attractive and available men in cars, biking, or inline skating.
If you're that hungry, why not hit the meals on wheels tour along the river run?

meanwhile • Said when an exceptionally attractive man passes or is lurking nearby.
I swear I heard every word you said about Ashley Simpson, but meanwhile, over by the bar . . .

meat • An animal's edible flesh. Old English: *mete*, food.
meatcase • One's hopefully bulging crotch.
None of the boys thought spandex was a suitable meatcase until Daddy Lech appeared, in his bike shorts, to show them how well-suited it was for featuring his beloved Polish kielbasa.

meat market • Any sizable gathering of gay men, but particularly one with a lusty attitude and look.
I wonder if there's any salami left in the meat market at this hour?

meat rack • Anywhere men congregate—to the side, on a rise—frankly offering themselves for sex.
The only cuts I got from the meat rack last week were from the bramble thorns.

fresh meat • When a new potential partner enters a bar, or the "scene" in general.
If ya can, I'd take a closer look at that fresh meat out under the daylight, cuz it's looking a little past the sell-by date in here.

prime meat • A man who is physically and/or emotionally a cut above others.

meek • Passive and easily put upon. Old Norse: *mjukr*, soft.

I don't know about inheriting the whole world, but I'd give that meek guy a piece of me to keep for a while.

ménage (à trois) • French for a "household for three," also used to mean a sexual threesome ("under one roof"). (Note: Threeways often involve women. But at least two persons must be of the same sex. So, there is at least bisexuality if not total homosexuality present.)

M4M (Men for Men) • Cyberspeak acknowledging that the contents or intentions (of the site) are for those with a same-sex attraction.

men's • Possession of a man.

men's liberation • The '70s movement which advocated a man's freedom from his traditional roles of breadwinner and warrior (and, consequently, allowed him to be somewhat gayer if he chose).

men's magazine • Periodical intended for the educational and pleasurable pursuits of heterosexual men, including "girlie," "sporty," and yes, even "fashion" publications.

men's room • Place where guys go to relieve themselves (and where others have gone to act as relief facilitators).

mentor-protégé • A mentor is a learned and responsible counselor (from Mentor, who, in Greek myth, taught Telemachus); a protégé is one whose care and career are guided by a person of counsel and influence. Latin: *protegere*, to protect. (See *intergenerational relationship*)

men-ziz • Dragspeak for plural of "man."

So many men-ziz, so little of me!

"meow" • The sound a cat makes—and an acknowledgment that someone has said or done something "cattily." (AKA "Milk?"; see *hissy*)

Mercury • Roman myth. Messenger of the gods, and himself one of commerce, travel, thievery (noted to be "fleet of foot").

Delivering flowers to an attractive client in that skimpy uniform, you could always tell when Mercury was rising to the occasion.

merry • Full of gay spirits. Old English: *mirge*, pleasant.

merry-go-round • Of sex between those already familiar to or friendly with one another. (One man sleeps with another, who sleeps with another, and so on, until eventually, the match-ups come full circle.)

I've been on this merry-go-round long enough to have encircled my fingers around every pole at least twice—if not more.

messenger boy • One who transports goods back and forth among businesses.

The messenger boy had two boxed items he was hoping the customer would accept: one big and the other better than average-sized.

Metropolitan Community Church (MCC) • A gay religious institution begun in the autumn of 1968 by Pentecostal Reverend Troy Perry, who was defrocked twice for being homosexual, and, after a failed suicide attempt, came to believe God really loved him. The twelve members in his first congregation grew to today's 40,000-plus.

metrosexual • A straight guy who appears to have absconded with the look, style, and mannerisms associated with gay men (or, as we like to call him: a "closet case"). Though it's a relatively new phenom, some have tried shortening the term to "metro" because the addition of "sexual" is thought too queerly erotic. (AKA "just gay enough") (See *gay vague*)

Every gay man knows that the problem with a metrosexual is that he changes course just when you see him pullin' into your station.

midnight cowboy • Hustler or gay man on the prowl late into the evening.

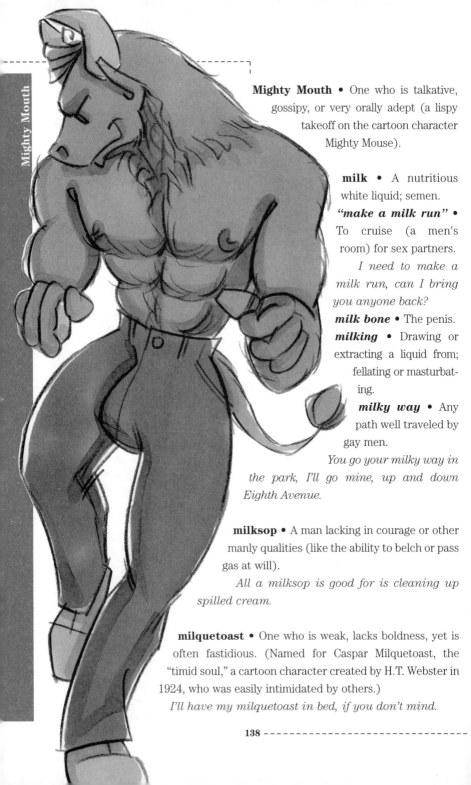

Mighty Mouth • One who is talkative, gossipy, or very orally adept (a lispy takeoff on the cartoon character Mighty Mouse).

milk • A nutritious white liquid; semen.

"make a milk run" • To cruise (a men's room) for sex partners.

I need to make a milk run, can I bring you anyone back?

milk bone • The penis.

milking • Drawing or extracting a liquid from; fellating or masturbating.

milky way • Any path well traveled by gay men.

You go your milky way in the park, I'll go mine, up and down Eighth Avenue.

milksop • A man lacking in courage or other manly qualities (like the ability to belch or pass gas at will).

All a milksop is good for is cleaning up spilled cream.

milquetoast • One who is weak, lacks boldness, yet is often fastidious. (Named for Caspar Milquetoast, the "timid soul," a cartoon character created by H.T. Webster in 1924, who was easily intimidated by others.)

I'll have my milquetoast in bed, if you don't mind.

mince • To speak or walk in an obviously prim, halting, indecisive manner. Latin: *minutia*, smallness.

Too bad he's not a knife, he could mince all the veggies for our chopped salad.

-minded • Compound ending meaning "to have a particular feeling."

closed-minded • Not willing to open one's self to the conditions of others. (ant: open-minded)

narrow-minded • Only able to see things within a limited range. (ant: broad-minded)

small-minded • Not able to see the whole picture. (ant: big-minded)

So what if he's small-minded, as long as he's large where it counts!

minority • The smaller of two groups, with possibly less authority relative to the other (from *minor*: of lesser importance).

I don't mind being in the minority, if he's of a sizable majority.

minotaur • In Greek myth, a creature half-man, half-bull, to whom young men (and young women) were given in sacrifice in his labryinth.

It better be something good at the door, thought the minotaur, to disturb his watching The View.

minty • Gay; having gayness about one's self. Of *mint*: a pleasantly aromatic scent or taste.

I'm not brazenly gay, I'm minty fresh!

misconception • An incorrect impression. From *mis*: wrong; *conception*: thought.

The only misconception about him is that he's a natural blond.

miscreant • One thought of as low or evil. Middle English: *miscreaunt*, heretic.

If I'm a miscreant, than you are surely a Miss de Meanor!

misfit • A person who, by not being able to fit in, is felt to be troublingly different.

I may be a misfit, but no one has complained that I wasn't tight enough!

miss(y) • A (young) unmarried woman; one given her particular attitudes.

Missy misses his man.

Miss Thing/Thang • A drag queen or any person, gay or straight, who has attitude to spare. The original usage of this term started with African-American females, and was carried over by their gay sons, who understood its sassy nuance. Interestingly, a great deal of gay language is attributable this way, in that all minorities experience similar problems with the white heterosexual hierarchy.

missionary position • Term for the "man-on-top" sexual position. (Coined in the nineteenth century by Christian missionaries who believed that this was the right and natural way for people to be during intercourse.) (See *reverse missionary*) *Missionary work*: Trying to convert a heterosexual male to homosexuality.

Mister Man • Emphatic dragspeak for a male who thinks a great deal of himself, one of considerable masculinity, or one in obvious authority (policeman).
Someone should tell Mister Man that a bit of his sister is showing.

Mister Sister • A drag queen.
Tell me, is that a hairy woman or a Mister Sister?

mixed • Jumbled together; any situation where a crowd can consist of all kinds: gays and straights, blacks and whites, men and women.

'mo • Short for "homosexual," used mainly for gay men by straight men.

moaner • One who makes orgasmic sounds during sexual intercourse (and even louder during climax).
I heard moaner was back in town doing his usual unspeakable things.

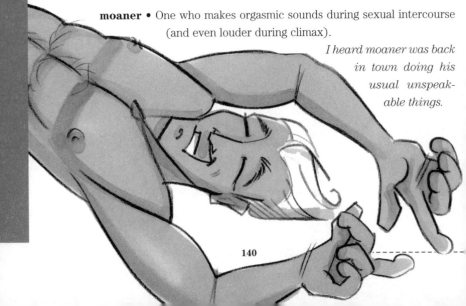

model • A gay hustler, but one who, like an escort, offers his services under a different and legitimate guise. In this case, to "pose" for a client—in private.

molest(er) • To expose to unwelcome or inappropriate sexual behavior; one who acts in such a manner. Latin: *molestus*, troublesome.
Molester—isn't he the professor you slept with in high school?

molly • An effeminate man. (Also, a prostitute, a gangster's "moll," and the definitely gay "Miss Molly." Good golly!)
mollycoddle • A man who is overindulged and kept from harm, usually by his mother. From *molly* and *coddle*: to pamper.

money shot, the • The moment of orgasmic ejaculation, as shown on (pornographic) film, alluding to the fact that this is the scene guys pay to watch.
He thought the money shot of Farley Cummings was worth about half what the DVD cost.

monogamous • Of a relationship kept intimate between just two people; to be sexually faithful to the other in a two-person coupling.
Of course I'm monogamous; I'm just sleeping with one guy while he's away.

Moody Judy • A gay man given to emotional swings. (Yes, again the association goes back to our connection with Judy Garland, well known for her variable temper.)

morals • Standards of right and wrong as they especially apply to sexual behavior. Latin: *moralis*, custom.

morning dew • Gay men still on the prowl after a late night out.
All the morning dew about was due to spontaneously erupt.

morphadite • Lost language variant of "hermaphrodite," meaning to have innate bisexual tendencies, as per Sigmund Freud. (AKA moffie, mophy)

mortal sin • A transgression so vile that it takes sanctity from one's soul, leaving it damned unless forgiven before death.
What better way for me to cleanse myself of a mortal sin than at the baths?

motel time • During a bar's closing, when the urgency to find a partner becomes most evident. (AKA crush hour)

I am happy to say that there will be no room at my inn when motel time is announced.

mother • One who bears and tends to a child, or children; one who acts in a maternal fashion; an older gay male expected to be wise, caring, and gentle (AKA mother superior). **mothered** • Looked out for with maternal excess.

It's because she mothered him too much when he was a boy.

motor mouth • One who fellates with the continued intensity of a machine.

Turn motor mouth on and he'll run all night until you're finished.

mouse • A small, timid animal; a timid, cowardly, and passive male. **mousy** • Resembling a mouse's behavior or looks.

If he acted any more mousy, Jake was sure his date, Heath, was gonna order some Gouda.

movie extras • Those "normal" everyday people used as background filler in the film of one's gay life.

This is where Farrell breaks through the crowd of movie extras to whisk Colin off in his limo.

Mrs. (missus) • A married woman (but originally an abbreviation for "mistress," a woman in authority); one man's effeminate male partner.

muff diver • One who performs cunnilingus (oral stimulation of the female genital area), used often by gay men for lesbians and the occasional hetero male. (AKA knishkebobber, bumper sticker)

muffin • A very attractive young man (with, no doubt, a hot pair of them ready for nibblin' on). (See *stud muffin*)

I get my day started devouring a muffin, preferably low-fat.

multiple partners • Clinical accounting for the many persons one encounters by being sexually active.

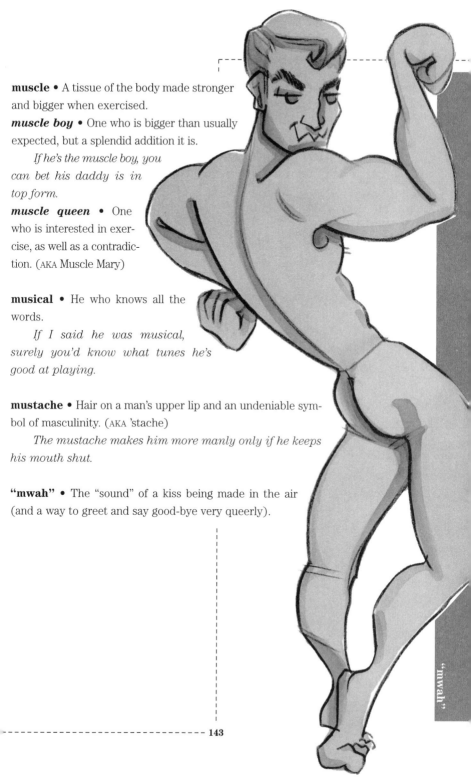

muscle • A tissue of the body made stronger and bigger when exercised.

muscle boy • One who is bigger than usually expected, but a splendid addition it is.

If he's the muscle boy, you can bet his daddy is in top form.

muscle queen • One who is interested in exercise, as well as a contradiction. (AKA Muscle Mary)

musical • He who knows all the words.

If I said he was musical, surely you'd know what tunes he's good at playing.

mustache • Hair on a man's upper lip and an undeniable symbol of masculinity. (AKA 'stache)

The mustache makes him more manly only if he keeps his mouth shut.

"mwah" • The "sound" of a kiss being made in the air (and a way to greet and say good-bye very queerly).

"mwah"

namby-pamby • One who is bland, weak (from a satirization on the name of 1700s poet Ambrose Philips).

nameless • Anonymous (of the many sexual encounters of the sexually active).
They weren't nameless, I just didn't think it necessary to ask.

Nancy • Popular woman's name, like Mary, for an effeminate man or homosexual. Sometimes Nance and Nancy boy.

Narcissus • Greek myth. A man so taken by his own beautiful reflection in a pool of water that he was turned into a flower. (AKA Narcissy) A *narcissist* is one so in love with himself that he is unaware of others, and *narcissism* is a fixation on one's body, and a characteristically male and highly homoerotic trait.

nasty • Something vile (also, rough sex, but that which is compelling in its rawness). Old French: *nastre*, bad.

"nature or nurture?" • A paradoxical question that considers whether one's (sexual) orientation stems from innate or learned causes.

neatnik • One who is preoccupied with tidiness (from Yiddish and Russian: -*nik*, suffix, "belonging to").
Nathan, why can't you be a neatnik like your friend Matthew?

nefarious • Of severe wickedness. Latin: *nefarius*, criminal.

negative • As in "not," and AIDS-speak for one whose condition does not show the presence of HIV. (AKA "neg")

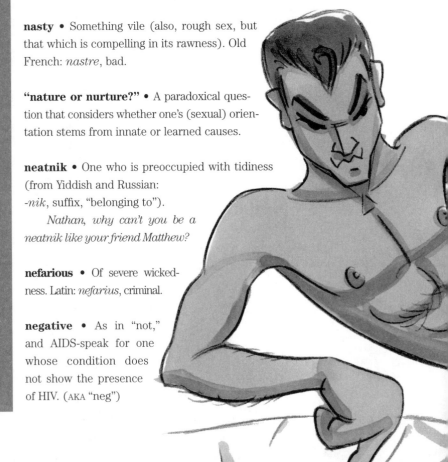

nelly • Well-known description for any gay male (but usually one acting especially effeminate), or just behavior felt to be girlish. Like many "names" for gay men that come from women, "nelly" is a nickname for Eleanor, Ellen, and Helen.

nellyectomy • A fabled "operation" wherein a masculine-behaved gay (or even straight) man instantly loses his macho affects and becomes instantly gayer.

I thought the guy was so butch until he walked through the doorway and opened his mouth to speak—and poof!—it was like the dude had undergone a nellyectomy before my very eyes!

neocon • A "new conservative" person, who blends progressive with traditional values; an out gay male who espouses rightist (even closeted) behavior. (AKA homocon)

He says he's a neocon, but that old dog sure was doin' a bunch of tricks last week, and none of 'em were new.

nephew • A passive young male sought by or in the company of an older gay male "auntie" or "uncle." (Note that in all instances where gay is insinuated to be feminine, one is never referred to as a "niece.")

nervous type, the • One whose jittery, unsure behavior equates him with gayness. (AKA nervous nelly)

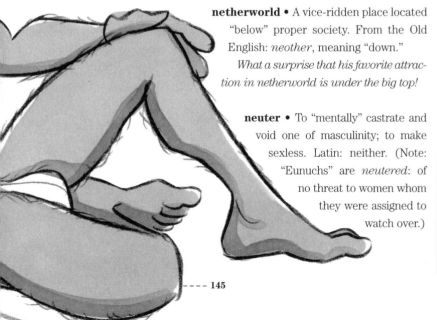

netherworld • A vice-ridden place located "below" proper society. From the Old English: *neother*, meaning "down."

What a surprise that his favorite attraction in netherworld is under the big top!

neuter • To "mentally" castrate and void one of masculinity; to make sexless. Latin: neither. (Note: "Eunuchs" are *neutered*: of no threat to women whom they were assigned to watch over.)

new • Recent.

newbie • A gay man just into the scene (shortened from "newborn").

newcummer • A gay man having his first experiences with same-sex play.

That newcummer made such a splash last night that I'm still drying off!

new guard • The current leather scene, not restricted to the original all-male set-up (which has been viewed as sexist and homophobic). (See *old guard*)

nightlighter • One who sleeps with another man's partner. From *nightlight*: a device used to comfort one in the dark.

No guy need fear when that nightlighter is on, but their boyfriends should.

ninny • A silly-acting, foolish person. Italian: *ninno*, baby.

nipple play • Erotic stimulation of a man's teats. (Yes, they can be quite sensitive.)

no • A refusal—and surprisingly, as something we hear too often, something we often use to deny others.

"no cologne" (because it makes you smell like a sissy?)

"no drag queens" (because they are *too* gay?)

"no white sneakers" (because they make you look like a wuss?)

"no women" (because they remind us of being men?)

"no strings attached" (NSA) • Cyberspeak designation for a sexual encounter predetermined to have no likelihood of relationship entanglements.

non-biological • Not related by blood.

nonconformist • Not following accepted beliefs, customs, practices.

Would I be a nonconformist—if I wore Hanes instead of a designer tee?

non-dairy creamer • A gay man, especially one who is active.

He found his favorite non-dairy creamer—and an all-night diner—in the same place in Boystown.

non-op • Short for *non-operative*: A transsexual who has *not* undergone gender reassignment surgery, but who considers himself or herself to be of the opposite sex.

normal • A typical condition. Latin: *norma*, a carpenter's square; *normalis*, according to the square.

In a normal situation he would be straight.

nuance • A subtle gradation in level. Old French: *nuer*, to shade.

The only nuance about him is the lighter tone of L'Oréal he's using.

number • One countable in a series; a casual sexual partner (with whom one engages quickly so as to go on to others); one regarded as a readily available commodity.

He lost count after his last number.

numbers game, the • To have sex combining all the numerical positions: *69, 99,* and *39.*

obscene • Repellent to those decently behaved; that which disgusts morally.
What we do is obscene—and I'd love to see more.

obvious • Not difficult to understand; lacking subtlety.
If the guy were any more obvious, he'd be sneezing confetti, farting air freshener, and have landing lights on the sway of his back.

odd • Queer.
oddball • One whose peculiar behavior is not expected or ordinary.

old guard • Of the leather scene as it was originally intended: a masculine-expressive endeavor for men only. (See *new guard*)
That old guard can use some Right Guard.

oncer • A guy who sleeps with someone a single time, or is afraid of commitment.
He may be a oncer, but I got him twice that evening.

one • Singular.
one-night stand • A sexual encounter with someone not expected to be seen again; a person you sleep with only once. (See *oncer*)
He can manage another one-night stand as long as he's lying down.
one of the boys • A gay man among many.
one of them/those • An outsider dismissively noting the presence of someone gay.
one-on-one • A sexual encounter taking place between just two men.

"on fire" • In flames; a total "flamer." (See also *en fuego*)

"on tour" • Said of those who are slumming in the gay scene.
He said he was just on tour, but asked to be taken where he could see the scenes from behind.

open • Unrestricted; honest; a relationship that allows for sex with others together or individually.

"open for lunch" • An unzipped fly.
He's always open for lunch; too bad what he offers is so unappetizing.

"openly gay" • Said of a gay person who, seemingly, has no reservations about his sexuality being known to the public. (See *out*)

operatic • Overly dramatic (and, like "musical" and "theatrical," a euphemism for being gay, because, *hey*, don't we all love opera?!). *Opera queen*: one who does.
It ain't over 'til that horny opera queen gets rammed by a Viking.

oppress • To treat wrongfully. Latin: *opprimere*, to press against. The "oppressed" are those kept beneath the oppressors.
Honestly, how possible is it to oppress someone who's always on his knees?

oral • Of the mouth; sex involving the mouth (fellatio). (See *French*)
His favorite toothbrush wasn't around, so he decided to go out and find some new oral stimulation.

orientation • A clear show of thought and direction. From *orient*: to position to measure. Latin: "where the sun rises."
If there was any question as to his orientation, all you had to do was look at how queerly he moved.

Oscar • Registered name for the statuette given annually by the Academy of Motion Picture Arts and Sciences. This name is included only because certain interests are considered gay. And indeed, we do seem preoccupied with the entertainment industry and these awards in particular.

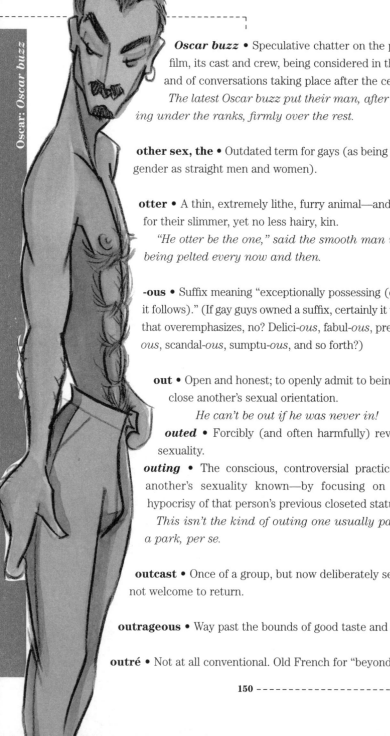

Oscar buzz • Speculative chatter on the potential of a film, its cast and crew, being considered in the festivities; and of conversations taking place after the ceremony.

The latest Oscar buzz put their man, after years working under the ranks, firmly over the rest.

other sex, the • Outdated term for gays (as being not the same gender as straight men and women).

otter • A thin, extremely lithe, furry animal—and "bearspeak" for their slimmer, yet no less hairy, kin.

"He otter be the one," said the smooth man who fancied being pelted every now and then.

-ous • Suffix meaning "exceptionally possessing (of that which it follows)." (If gay guys owned a suffix, certainly it would be one that overemphasizes, no? Delici-*ous*, fabul-*ous*, preci-*ous*, lusci-*ous*, scandal-*ous*, sumptu-*ous*, and so forth?)

out • Open and honest; to openly admit to being gay; to disclose another's sexual orientation.

He can't be out if he was never in!

outed • Forcibly (and often harmfully) revealed homosexuality.

outing • The conscious, controversial practice of making another's sexuality known—by focusing on the hurtful hypocrisy of that person's previous closeted status.

This isn't the kind of outing one usually partakes of in a park, per se.

outcast • Once of a group, but now deliberately sent away and not welcome to return.

outrageous • Way past the bounds of good taste and reason.

outré • Not at all conventional. Old French for "beyond."

outsider • One not belonging to or removed from a well-formed group and its circumstances. (AKA loner)

over • Gayspeak for when something (or someone) is past its moment of main interest.
His latest CD? O-ver!

overs and unders • Said of a gay crowd mixed with active (overs) and passive (unders) men.

oversexed • Exceeding usual sexual interest or engagement.

overt • Not at all secret. Old French: *ovrir*, to open. (See *covert*)
Hunter took Tab's smooch as an overt gesture of his feelings.

Oz (The Emerald City) • A colorful, exciting, and "gay" place where dreams are expected to come true (although, if one were of a simpler mind, you could have fulfilled the same wishes right at home). From the film *The Wizard of Oz*. (AKA New York, San Francisco)

P

package • A bundle; the impression given of a man's genitals through clothing (AKA box). (See *basket*) A *surprise package* is a penis that turns out to be much bigger than expected.

packaged goods • One who is well-dressed and good-looking.

At holiday time, Bergdorf's has some splendidly wrapped packaged goods in their men's store, ready to take as gifts for your eggnog party host.

packing • Stuffing; making the crotch (genitals) appear larger (AKA prop the prick, pushing box); questioning a man's penis size (*Whatcha packing there, dude, about eight?*); a lesbian wearing a strap-on dildo (to appear to have a penis).

If you're feeling tight, I'm sure you can handle the one packing lightly over there.

padding • Filling something to make it appear present (as when a drag queen stuffs a bra, or a garment worn by a transgendered person to affect the look of their desired sex).

pagan • One without religion, or of different religious beliefs. Latin: *paganus*, country dweller.

paint remover • One who assaults especially effeminate types (who are expected to wear makeup [paint]).

He got hold of some paint remover that stripped him the hard way.

palimony • Money given in support by an unmarried couple's chief provider to the lover/companion after separation. The unwed-divorced version of *alimony*. Latin: *alimonia*, sustenance.

Lee gave Scott palimony, but they were hardly buddies since the split.

palsy-walsy • In or giving the appearance of a relationship troubling to the viewer. (A double intensive of *pal:* a friend.)

You get palsy-walsy with one of 'em and they always try to get too close.

Pan • From Roman myth. The very playful god of fields and forests, who had the upper torso and head of a man with a goat's legs, horn, tail, ears, and beard. (See *goatee*)

pansy • A colorful, frilly flower thought to resemble a face (from the French: *penser*, to think); a gay man, especially one thought colorful and frilly of manner.
bouquet of pansies • A group of gay men.

Rather redundant that he was carrying a bouquet of pansies while on his way to be part of one, n'est-ce pas?

pansy patch • The gay area in a park. (AKA piccolo park)

The specimens in the pansy patch had gotten very seedy lately.
pansy without a stem • A lesbian.
pickled pansy • Drunk and gay.

pantywaist • A man considered fey and ineffectual, taken from the notion that he is no bigger around than the band on a woman's intimate apparel and, therefore, would be of little consequence or imposition.

No pantywaist is worth gettin' your drawers all up in a knot.

papi • Spanish for father, gayspeak for daddy.

paraphilia • Peculiar, transgressive, or possibly harmful sexual interests that are deemed obsessive and run counter to normal practices of intimacy. (See *kink*)

Paraphilia on purpose, or did he just brush your behind accidentally?

parent • One who begets, raises, and/or protects a child. Latin: *parere*, to give birth.
legal parent • One into whose care a child is lawfully given.
Parents, Families and Friends of Lesbians and Gays (PFLAG) • A national organization, started by Jeanne Manford in 1972, charged with dispelling notions of homophobia and heterosexism within families and between the mainstream and the gay community.

second-parent adoption • Process for a non-biological person to become a legal guardian along with a partner's biological status.

pariah • One who is unwanted. (From the Paraiyan, a large caste of southern Indians who often became domestics and were regarded by Europeans as emblematic of all the lower Hindu classes.)

If pariah Carey dressed better, maybe he'd have more dates.

partner • One brought together with another in common interest; used as a non-inflammatory term to denote one as another's lover. *Sex partner*: One with whom another engages in erotic interplay but not romantic intimacy.

party • A celebration of merriment and abandon.

party boy • One who is prone to use artifical substances to enhance his experiences, sexual or otherwise.

That party boy would go to the opening of anything—even if it was a book.

party favor • The "gift" of mood-enhancing drugs that an individual (freely) receives at a get-together.

Do me a party favor, and let me snort some of yours.

party-and-play (PNP) • Cyberspeak for sex (play) involving or allowing the use of drugs (party). (AKA plug-and-party)

splash party • A sex party where the main activity is group masturbation (to orgasm).

pass(ing) • To occur without notice or conflict; to go around publicly as a heterosexual while feeling it is necessary to keep one's homosexuality hidden; for a transgendered person, to be accepted as their intended opposite sex without pause after medical procedures have taken place. Latin: *passus*, step.

passive • To take in or bear without resistance; to be a sexual submissive: The "bottom." Latin: *passivus*.

He's so passive, I bet there isn't a single guy he doesn't give the right of way.

past • A period in one's former life kept hidden or thought of with regret.

Judging by the harsh looks, that dude's past just became his present tense.

pastel • A pale color; a light shade; shades of gayness.

All that hard work toiling in the sun, and he's still pastel.

patriarchy • Classic social system where, by right, men (fathers) control all institutions and women (and gay men) are given secondary status. Latin: *pater*, father. It should be made clear that within the queer community, gay men often perpetuate this type of authoritative organization.

peacock • A vain, "dandy" male (who, like the bird, shows off his plumage to attract attention).

When all was said and done at the end, a peacock always had his tail to work.
peacock palace • A men's clothing store with a large gay clientele.

pearl • A drop of semen.
pearl diver • One who fellates ("goes down" in search of "pearls").

The most skilled pearl diver doesn't come up until he's got what he went down for.
pearl necklace • Semen shot on a partner's neck or chest.

Personally, I think a pearl necklace is the only kind of jewelry that looks good on a man.

pederast • A man who has sexual relationships with a boy; a "sodomite." Greek: *paiderastes*: *paidos*, (boy) child; *erastes*, lover.

pedophile • An adult who desires (and often acts on having) sex with children. Greek: *paidos*, (boy) child; *philos*, beloved. Every

pedophile

time this word is read or spoken, too many think, unfairly, that a gay man is involved—even though girls are far more often violated by straight men. Is this because a transgression against a boy, at the hands of a man, is considered the more vile act, therefore, the one that leaves the most indelible and troubling impression?

peevish • Discontent, ill-mannered, contrary. (AKA petulant)
Wilson was still being peevish, weeks after Luke and he disagreed on the new davenport.

penile • Of the sex organ of the male, the penis (which is not a muscle, but spongy tissue that swells with blood from stimulation). *Phallic:* Relating to the phallus (the penis)—and informing of every other thought in a gay man's mind (or, for that matter, every straight man's).
As gay men continue to grow, do their penile thoughts increase, too?

perfectionist • One who takes offense if things are done poorly or do not meet extreme standards.
I'm not a perfectionist, I just want everything to be right for the cotillion.

perineum • The area between the scrotum and anus. (See *t'ain't*)

persecute(d) • Subject to painful conditions (because of race, gender, beliefs, sexual orientation). Latin: *persequi*, to pursue.
Yes, I feel persecuted—when I'm expected to wear something flattering every time I go out.

persnickety • Caring too much about small details; snobbily difficult. (AKA finicky)

persona non grata • One whose presence, after some untoward action or condition has become known, is undesirable. Latin for "person not acceptable."
If I was persona non grata for not knowing it was a Gwen Stephani remix, you should leave town for not knowing which Olsen twin is which.

pervert • To direct away from what is right; one who engages in acts not considered normal. *Perverted:* Something or someone thought incorrect.
perversion • A (sexually) deviant act. (The previous both stem from the Latin: *per-*

vertere, to overthrow, *per*: through; *vertere*, to turn.)

pestilence • An often deadly and widespread disease; an insidious influence.

I tell ya what a pestilence is—that cheap cologne you're wearing.

Peter Pan • James Barrie's fictional characterization of a young lad who refused to grow up and spent his time in Never-Never Land with other "lost boys," and a tiny fairy; one who is older but acts and dresses (usually quite inappropriately) like someone much younger.

It appeared as though Peter Pan was being played by someone's daddy, instead of by a boy, but he was surprisingly agile when it came to fly across the stage and still quite youthful-looking in his green tights.

phase • A short-lived occurrence. Greek: *phasis*, appearance.

By the look of the things, he's entering his phase-out period.

pheromone • A chemical made by one of a species, able to affect the mating behavior in another. Greek: *pherein*, to carry; *mone*, short for "hormone."

I hear they're making a big stink about gay men and straight women responding to the same male pheromone.

phone sex • Erotic telephone talk leading to climax. (See *cybersex*)

piano bar • Liquor-selling establishment where the main attraction is the playing of standards by a pianist and singing by various invited performers and patrons.

Porter wondered if there was anything more off-key, yet comforting, than the guys belting out show tunes at Cole's, the piano bar down the block.

picky • Extremely finicky.

You weren't so picky with your selections in that backroom.

piers, the • A platform extending from the shore out over water—frequently used for gay gatherings.

I'm headed to the piers, ya wanna go down with me?

pig • An untidy animal; one who is gluttonous; one who has an insatiable sexual appetite. *Pork*: To fornicate, usually with a porky (as in able to be had, not heavy) pig.
pig boy/bottom • One who wallows in his wanton passivity. Oink! (AKA piglet)
pig sex • As "raunchy" and often as "raw" as it gets. A *pig pile*: an orgy.
"not my pig; not my farm" • Said when the lascivious ways of a friend are not another's responsibility to correct. Akin to "not my (slutty gay) brother's keeper."
"stuck like a pig" • To be anally copulated (without any doubt about it!).

"ping" • The sound a gaming machine makes when registering a hit; the internal/external noise a gay man makes when recognizing another, usually in a setting not thought conducive to queers. (See *gaydar*)

"Ping" went the strings of my heart when I finally saw another friendly face in the crowd at Friday's.

pink • A pale red color; to be politically left-leaning; of girlishness. If "pink is for girls" and we are, agree or disagree, said to be like them, we are also stuck with anything color-related, including wearing it, to be gaily connected, hence:
pink dollar • Of spendable "gay" money, which we are supposed to have in greater supply because we have fewer traditional expenditures.
pink panther • A militant-minded gay man (derivative of the '60s activist group the Black Panthers).

He wanted to be a pink panther, not to fight but to wear the catsuit.
pink pants • A gay man (whose lower half is clad in queerness).
pink posse • A gay clique; a group of powerful gay men; fey men who surround another.

The only thing a pink posse is good for is doing a chorus line.
pink power • The influence of the gay community over or in conjunction with that of mainstream society. (AKA purple power)

Why is it that the more

we exert our pink power, the redder the state they recede into?

pink triangle • An emblem used during the Nazi era to mark someone as homosexual, that has since been inverted (with the point down instead of up) and made into a symbol (since the '70s, more so with the advent of AIDS) of the gay community in acknowledgment of its struggle for acceptance and pride.

pipe • A very important piece of equipment in a plumber's box. (AKA plumbing)
pipe cleaner • One who shines the plumber's pipe and checks it for leaks.
pipe fitter • One who takes the plumber's pipe out back to where there's the best connection for it.
pipe fixture • A condom.
pipe laying • Taking the plumber's pipe around back and dropping it in place—hoping it'll fit nice and tight.

pissy • Stingingly indignant, arrogant. *Piss elegant*: One whose lofty airs are a sham.
He just got stung by the pissy one's decorating bill, but never minded being pissed on every once in a while.

pitcher • One who throws the ball (to a "catcher") in baseball. In sexual terms: the active male, especially in anal copulation. (AKA *top*)
Everything around the pitcher's mound was seeded and ready to go.

pit job • Sexually gratifying action involving the armpit.

pixie • A whimsical, elfin type. Scandinavian: *pyske*, small fairy.
Poking a pixie with a stick will not hurt him—I swear.
pixie dust • Glitter; and gay sexual desire spread around.
It was like someone had sprinkled pixie dust at the party, and all the guys got that twinkle in their eyes.

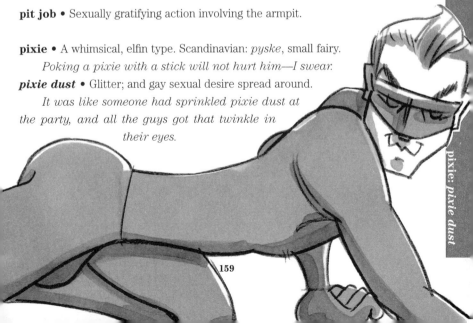

plague • A far-reaching calamity (often thought to be deserved by its victims). Latin: *plaga*, blow, wind.

play • To spend one's time in amusing recreation; sexual activity.

"play checkers" • To jump around a lot in a bar looking for a *pickup*: one to take home for sex.

"play pick up the soap" • An imaginary game, where the one who bends to get the object wins and should expect to receive more than a handful of cleanser as his prize. (See *"drop the soap"*)

You can't really play pick up the soap with a guy who doesn't stand up straight to begin with.

"play squirrel" • To grab some nuts (another's testicles). *Play chipmunk:* To suck on another's testicles.

"play the fruit market" • Said of a (straight) male considering being a hustler.

Winter is the best time to play the fruit market in Fort Lauderdale.

playboy • One who is sexually active, a pleasure-seeker, lives alone in a groovy pad, is unmarried, and loves bunnies(!).

player • An active participant; a sport's team member (see *coach*).

"playing chopsticks" • Two guys masturbating each other. (Taken from the familiar piano tune performed as a duet.)

"play(ing) on the side" • To sleep with someone other than your "significant other" (with or without a partner's knowledge).

playroom • A space used for (sexual) recreation. (AKA playspace)

"plays with dolls" • Said of a young male whose leisure interests may be cause for concern.

He plays with dolls just so that he can get his hands on a little couture.

playtime • The period set aside for having fun.

playtoy • An object used for fun; a passive male aggressively handled by an active partner. (AKA *boy toy*, *fuck toy*)

plow • To furrow a fertile field; recently popular gayspeak for anal sex (with an expectation it will be done deeply and thoroughly).
plow boy • The young farmhand who either works the fields or tends to the landowner's equipment while it does some intense plowing
  The farmer was planning to sow his seeds as soon as the plow boy arrived.

"pluck some feathers" • To have relations with a "quail," "chicken," or "turkey." *Plucky*: said of one who is most attractive, anally.

pocket pool • Playing with (masturbating) one's genitals from inside a pocket.
  He's so good at pocket pool that for a while there I didn't know where my balls had gone.

poised • Free from artifice or shame; composed.
  Isn't it amazing how he can be so poised—in that position!?

polari • A collection of slang that was, arguably, the most authentically gay of any ever used. It developed in Britain, during the '50s and '60s, first as a way to talk among ourselves without being understood by outsiders—and was quite popular with those who worked in the cruise ship and, of course, entertainment industries. Ironically, it fell out of popularity as "gayness" became better known, everywhere. Hence, the necessity of a "secret" language became obsolete. In a way, this can be said of much current gay slang, in that our assimilation has rendered specialized terms too contrived. (See *bona*)

politically correct (PC) • Supportive of sweeping, often excessive, redress of past unfair treatment of others (such as those with a differing sexual orientation).

poly- • More than one. Greek: *polys*, many.
polyamorous • Romantically and sexually attracted to many persons regardless of sexuality or gender. (See *sexuality: pansexual*)
polygamous • Able or wanting to have sex with more than one person at a time.

poof • Britspeak for gay, with the implication that the man is soft and easily vanquished (as in a "poof" of air). (AKA poofter)

"pop it in the toaster" • To have (anal) *morning sex* (that which occurs when all partners have just arisen).

I get up, pop it in the toaster, and by the time we're finished so's my brewin' coffee.

popinjay • One who is chatty and self-interested. Old French: *papegai*, a parrot.

Only minutes after the popinjay popped onstage, the audience was as ready to pop him in his upturned nose as the hero was.

poppers • Amyl nitrate sealed in ampules that "pop" when opened, owing to the release of vapors built up inside. (AKA Rice Krispies, 'cuz they "snap, crackle, and pop")

poppycock • Meaningless talk. Middle Dutch: *pappekak*, to defecate.

Boys, stop this poppycock and get on with your poetry reading.

popsicle • A sweet treat on a stick, that melts onto your hand no matter how fast you lick it (re: an erect penis that leaks precum on one's hand). (AKA Creamsicle)

porn star name • The (obviously) made up "public" name—usually of an erotic nature—of an actor in sex films who knows it is unwise to use his real one.

I bet I know the kind of action Neal Downing gets into!

positive • The state of having HIV. (AKA poz)
poz-4-poz • Cyberspeak for one with HIV seeking the company of another for sex and/or companionship.
poz-friendly • One who is knowing and accepting of another's condition (and quite often open to having sexual relations with that person), but not likely "poz" himself.

post-gay • Period after the acknowledgment (and possible acceptance) of gayness—in an individual or group context—and of the questionable conditions in its aftermath. *Pre-gay*: Said of the time, usually in childhood development, before signs of gayness become obvious. Logically, this would also be the child's pre-straight period.

Post-gay, pre-gay? How about present, gay, and accounted for?

post-op • Short for *post-operative*: a transsexual after having sexual reassignment surgery.

post toasties • An attractive delivery man or postman (from the classic breakfast food of the same name).

potato • A white guy.
potato queen • A non-white man who prefers white guys.

powder puff • A cushy pad for applying powder to (a woman's) skin; a male of no consequence. *Powder puffs*: white sneakers; *cocoa puffs*: dirty ones.

"powdered and perfumed" • Gay men dressed and ready to go out.

power • The might or authority of a person or group. Latin: *potere*, to be able.

prance • To strut or springily move about.
   Dashing Rudolph couldn't help but prance when he heard Mr. Claus, the dance director, was making him first string over that vixen, Donner.

precious • Dainty, artificial, or too refined; a title for a dainty someone. Latin: *pretium*, price.
   His delicate kerchief was as precious as he was.

preen • To gloat or care excessively over one's appearance. Old French: *proindre*, to anoint with oil.
   Why preen if you're so fond of steam?

preference • Liking for one more than another. Latin: *praeferre*, *pre*, before; *ferre*, to carry.
   If I really had a preference—do you think I'd choose this color scheme?

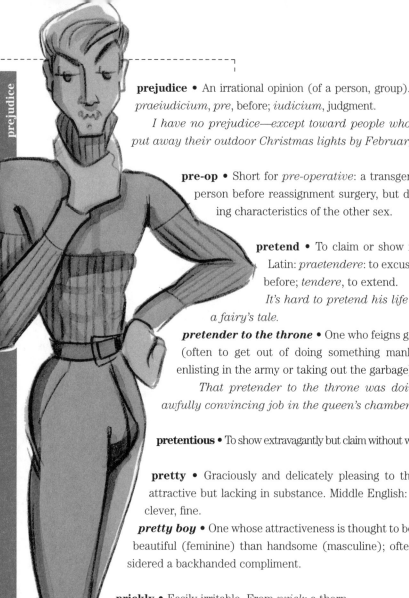

prejudice • An irrational opinion (of a person, group). Latin: *praeiudicium*, *pre*, before; *iudicium*, judgment.

I have no prejudice—except toward people who don't put away their outdoor Christmas lights by February!

pre-op • Short for *pre-operative*: a transgendered person before reassignment surgery, but displaying characteristics of the other sex.

pretend • To claim or show falsely. Latin: *praetendere*: to excuse; *pre*, before; *tendere*, to extend.

It's hard to pretend his life is not a fairy's tale.

pretender to the throne • One who feigns gayness (often to get out of doing something manly, like enlisting in the army or taking out the garbage).

That pretender to the throne was doing an awfully convincing job in the queen's chambers.

pretentious • To show extravagantly but claim without warrant.

pretty • Graciously and delicately pleasing to the eye; attractive but lacking in substance. Middle English: *prety*, clever, fine.

pretty boy • One whose attractiveness is thought to be more beautiful (feminine) than handsome (masculine); often considered a backhanded compliment.

prickly • Easily irritable. From *prick*: a thorn.

I hate it when he gets prickly in public, but in bed it's another story.

pricknic • An orgy. (AKA oyster stew)

There were too many half-empty baskets at yesterday's pricknic to make it a really big success.

pricktures • Images of men with erect penises. (*Prick*: penis)
It gets way too hard for me to look at pricktures all day long.

pride • Awareness of one's own value (hopefully demonstrated more than once a year).
He still had his pride, and, thankfully, his 2Xist on.

prig • One who behaves with conceited and overly proper manners and speech.
The prig was a twig or was it the witch was a switch?

prim • Exacting and respectable to the point of affectation. Old French: *prin*, delicate.

Prince Albert (PA) • Notorious piercing of the penis head (through the slit) favored by phallic narcissists (and devil-may-care toothchippers), and named for the royal mate (of Queen Victoria) said to have had one himself.
His Prince Albert has been in a lot of cans.

princess • A king or queen's daughter; one having the manner and sway associated with such status; the "feminine" of prince and, *ahem*, a soon-to-be queen. (See *homo-in-training*)
princess with a pink wand • A straight woman out with a gay man (who may be working for her, so she is not as friendly as a "fag hag" would be).

Princeton rub • Non-penetrative sexual act, where one's penis is rubbed between the other's thighs (or both abdomens), often fully clothed. Named for the university where it is said to have become popular. (AKA college fuck, college style)
The Harvard man pressed on with his studies after enjoying a Princeton rub.

prissy • Unnecessarily decorous. Likely a blend of "prim" and "sissy."

privacy • The state of being sheltered from the presence of unbidden intrusion.
He thought they were safe in the privacy of his apartment . . .

private • Kept close to the individual. Latin: *privatus*, not in public life.
. . . but doing it in private was no guarantee . . .

procreate • To conceive offspring. Latin: *procreare: pro*, forward; *creare*, to create.

procreate

. . . unless he did it to procreate, which of course he and his boyfriend were not . . .

profane • Showing little care for what is sacred. Latin: *profanare*, to desecrate.

. . . and that made it all the more profane an act.

profile • An outline of notable detail (on the Internet: a listing of mainly physical statistics and relationship interests); the way one's body, especially the back-side, looks from the side. Latin: *profilare*, to draw a line forward.

He said he was getting his profile into shape—and he succeeded.

promiscuous • Having numerous sexual interactions with a variety of partners. Latin: *promiscuus*, possessed equally.

They were too promiscuous . . .

prone • Having a tendency; facing down-ward. Latin: *pronus*, leaning forward.

. . . and the longer he stayed the more prone he would be to do it again . . .

pronoun game, the • The locution by which a gay man refers to another in female rather than male terms ("she" instead of "he"). Often, this is done in jest ("She's" such a big ol' mess, isnt he?) and for both gay and straight persons. But it can be used protectively, as when one is in the company of hostile, anti-gay-seeming forces. (*Uhmm,* "she" was busy tonight having drinks with "his," *err,* "her" girlfriends.) However, the need for this kind of subterfuge is happening less and less. At the same time, a lot of us refrain from the practice because it calls to mind the time when everyone thought we were nothing but a bunch of "girls." (This is far more a gay male than a gay female habit.)

proper • Conventionally fitting and exacting of societal rule.
  . . . and that just wasn't proper.

prophylactic • Defending against disease; a condom. Greek: *prophulassein*, to take precautions against.

protection • To keep from harm; a condom. Latin: *pro*, before; *tegere*, to cover. (AKA raincoat)

protein • Semen (which is made up largely of it).
  Why go out for a protein drink when you've got your own portable dispenser?

protest • An involved group or individual announcing and enacting formal disapproval and challenge. Latin: *protestari: pro*, before; *testari*, to testify.

proud • Experiencing (deserved) self-respect.
  He was out—and proud—and had never felt better.

provoke • To push to anger. Latin: *provocare*, to challenge.
  Sister, we provoke just by existing.
provocative • Leaning toward provocation or sexual arousal.

prude • One worried about looking proper. (The "feminine" of "proud.")

prurient • Having an unbalanced attraction to lascivious matters. Latin: *prurire*, to yearn, itch.

puff • A quick expelling of air; a light baked good; a soft pad; one of no significance; a gay man. (French: *pouf: bouffer*, to blow out, also *bouffant*)

"pull the covers" • To accidentally or intentionally expose another's homosexuality.
  I could hardly pull the covers on one whose bed has lain bare for so long.

"pull(ing) the train" • Said of one (or the lead) male anally copulated by a slew of others (who sometimes link up behind one another).
  That caboose's hitch could pull the train from New York to LA!

pump-and-dump • Starkly graphic term for anal copulation to quick climax (*pump*: hard, repeated action against; and *dump*: to leave stuff behind).

punishment • A penis so large one is not able to accommodate it comfortably.

The punishment seemed excessive, but he was willing to do the hard time now, feeling it would get easier soon enough.

punk • A badly behaved young man (derived, some say, from the Chinese for "rotting wood"). A "punk" also meant "prostitute (female or male); a criminal's apprentice; and, if incarcerated, an older inmate's passive sexual partner."

pup(py) • A young dog; one who is playful and inexperienced—and often troublingly full of himself.

I believe he's out walking his puppy, Stud, and his pussy, Willow.

puritan • Strictly moral. Latin: *purus*, pure.

pussy • One who is weak, unmanly. From "pussycat" (see following), and, to some degree, that most intimate of female body parts.
pussy boy • A very passive young male (who is basically treated like a woman, sexually). (See *boy pussy*)
pussycat • One who is "soft," an easy mark.
pussyfooter • One who behaves timidly or with undue extra caution (as in moving about with the noiseless steps of a cat). (See *tenderfoot*)
pussy-whipped • Said of an easily controlled man.

pweenis • A tiny penis, a wee weenie.

Sadly, there can never be much between us—if all you have is a pweenis.

Q • Short for "queer," but in and of itself identifiable as such.

quail • A just-visiting young gay male approached by an older male. Named for the migratory bird, which is edible like a domestic "chicken."

Spring was here, and he was ready for some quail, having had enough locally grown chicken.

quaint • Darlingly old-fashioned; strange. Middle English: *quiente*, clever, expert.

My, isn't he a quaint ol' thing?

queen • A female monarch; one who acts with high-mindedness; a gay man (often with extreme attitude and a feeling of sovereignty over others). Though it is often assumed that the use of "queen" was a natural match for our estimable presence, a "quean," from which the word emerged many years ago, meant an unpleasant wanton woman. "Queen" is also widely used to mark one's interests and actions as satiric and excessive. The latter quality would seem to dissuade some from its use. It speaks of uncontrolled behavior. But oddly enough, heterosexuals are now frequently using the label, so one can no longer say this is done just from gay interests. Still, many supreme examples throng the pages of *Gay-2-Zee*, and on the following page are more.

queen bee • The most self-important (or successful) queer in a group; a woman in the company of a gay man. (See *fag hag*)

queen bitch • The meanest Mary of them all. (AKA evil queen)

queen for a day • Said of a straight guy involved, temporarily, in some sort of "fabulous" activity. Evocative of the camp classic fifties TV game show, where ordinary housewives were briefly treated to a life befitting a queen (with lavish gifts, like washing machines, vacuum cleaners, and blenders!).

For just bein' queen for a day, he was awfully good at handling my royal carriage.

Queen Mary • A plus-sized pansy.

queen of clubs • He who loves the nightlife.

queen of denial • A gay man who will not accept his lot in life.

queen of hearts • A Casanova queer.

He was a jack of but one kind of trade, yet still the queen of hearts.

queen of scotch • A sissy who loves the sauce.

queen of spades • A gay man of color (and not considered a very PC thing to say).

queen without a country • A gay man who thinks he's "all that," but isn't; a gay guy who finds himself where the nightlife (or general gay scene) is limited.

I was in Branson for a week one night, and felt like a queen without a country.

queeny • Behaving with extreme effeminacy (but usually not 'tude).

queer • Not expected; odd; one who is strange; all gay people.

queer bait • Said of an attractive (straight, young, slight) man who could tempt someone gay, but may not be able to fend off such unwanted advances.

"Queer Eye" effect, the • From the "reality" series *Queer Eye for the Straight Guy*, in which five gay men set about making over "straight guys" using their "gay sensibilities." The "effect" is on how such interplay is viewed. Previously, one's sexuality in such highly visual fields was only suggested. Also, heterosexual men, who never believed they could need or get advice from the gay perspective, have now become more willing to accept it openly.

Queer Nation • Political activist group, formed in 1990, which was, among other things, instrumental in reestablishing the meaning of "queer" to the point that peculiarity could be read as strength and diversity. ("We're here. We're queer. Get used to it!")

quel • Gayspeak French for "what (a)" and often used negatively: *Quel rat!*

questioning • One who is in the process of identifying sexually and is asking, internally and externally, for guidance and confirmation. (What the "Q" represents in GLBTQ.)
   After all that questioning, I hope he comes out with the answer everyone else already knows.

Quilt, The AIDS Memorial • Conceived in 1985 (and made official in 1987 as the Names Project) by San Francisco gay-rights activist Cleve Jones, the quilt is a commemoration of those lost to AIDS, as represented by panels made by loved ones in memoriam. The inspiration for the quilt came while Jones was organizing a yearly candlelight march for slain city supervisor Harvey Milk. Jones learned how many San Franciscans had died of AIDS up to that point, and asked for each name to be written on a card. Affixed to the walls of the city's federal building, it was said to look like a quilt, and thus the idea was born.

quippish • Fast with witty, off-the-cuff remarks. Latin: *quippe*, indeed, ironic.
   He was wild about Oscar's quippish way.

quivers, the • To shake rapidly and involuntarily, as when frightened, nervous (or how an arrow string vibrates); how a passive partner's anus supposedly behaves in anxious anticipation of sex. (AKA pussy quivers)
   Was that an earthquake or did that bottom boy just have the quivers?

R

radaring • When a person, in the presence of one whose sexuality is ambiguous (transgendered), tries to detect specific gender indications by scoping broadly. (Related to the character Radar O'Reilly, in *M*A*S*H*, the soldier who was never sure how to address female officers.)

radical • Far from the usual; one who wants extreme changes made to the current system. Latin: *radix*, root.
> *Wouldn't it be wonderfully radical—if we all didn't shave our chests?*

raid • An unexpected forced entry by law enforcement into a place thought to house and abet unlawful goings-on.
> *I hear Lily Law is planning a raid on Stonewall tonight.*

rainbow • The natural bow of light arcing in the sky after a storm (post-calamity), promising happier times—and why we, and other groups, have embraced its prismatic look and meaning as an emblem.
rainbow family/tribe/village, the • A supportive group of usually non-blood-related persons (of different colors, ethnicities, and sexualities) having chosen or happy to be in the same place together.
rainbow flag, the • Internationally known symbol for the GLBTQ community, chosen to show our diversity, designed for the 1978 Gay Pride Parade in San Francisco by Gilbert Baker. The flag's original version had eight and not the usual six colors: red (life), orange (healing), yellow (the sun), green (nature), blue (art), and purple (spirit). Unfortunately, manufacturers could not make the hot pink (sexuality), and the indigo (harmony) was dropped to keep the flag symmetrical. (We are nothing if not consistently neat.)
rainbow rod • A long penis that arcs downward (often ending in one's golden pot).

rake • A man with little morality (who, when he was identified as such in the 1600s, was said to engage in sex with both women and men while retaining his masculinity. You go, girl!). (AKA cad, roué, scoundrel)

rally 'round the flagpole • To show one's allegiance by gathering around a symbol; when two (or more) men show their "patriotism" by fellating another man's "pole."

random • Without regular or edited structure.
> *I consider the men I encounter as surprises, not random.*

raunch(y) • (Of sex that is) obscenely vulgar, dirty.
His raunch is definitely on the border of going too far.

raw • Natural, not refined; naked; unbridled sex; unprotected sex.
raw jaws • One who is new to fellatio, or one who has performed it to exhaustion.

reach-around • To masturbate one's passive partner from behind—mainly during anal copulation.

reach-under • To go at a guy, sexually, from underneath a partition (as in a men's room).

read • To comprehend the meaning of (by nonwritten means); to speak your mind about another. A *reading*: the lengthy exposé of another's faults.
"read your beads" • Dragspeak to mean "chastising by speaking of the many nasty realities of another." This term is taken from the notion that all gay men wear imaginary beads—like those that sniping society dames would wear.

real • Honest; when one has affected the look of someone else to the point of convincing others.
real man • One whose looks, actions, thoughts, and behavior leave no question that he is the true embodiment of the traditional masculine ideal.
real time • To be physically present for sexual activity, rather than on the phone or Internet.
realness • Measure of how successfully one can be a "type" that is not who you really are.

His high-minded attempt at real-ness came tumbling down when he leaned over in his miniskirt.

rear admiral • A commissioned naval officer; a gay man (usually the active partner).

rear admiral

The rear admiral felt it his duty to be present whenever an exceptional recruit was coming through, even if it meant being there during the physical and, sometimes, a necessary rectal exam.

receiver • Opposite of "giver"; the passive "bottom" sexual partner.

reciprocal • Returning an equal action. In other words: doing unto another (blow) as he has done unto you (be blown).

recruit • To actively try to enroll (a new member, involuntarily, into a group to strengthen it). French: *recruter*, to grow again. (AKA draft)
recruiting center • Any place where gay and straight men intersect in vulnerable ways: restrooms, locker rooms, necktie counters, and florist shops around Valentine's Day.

rectal exam • Anal sex (playing on the medical procedure, where one's rectum is thoroughly checked out by a professional).

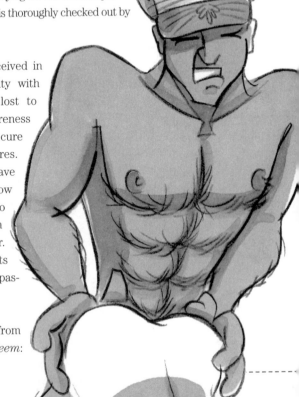

red ribbon, the • Conceived in 1991 to indicate solidarity with and concern for those lost to AIDS, and to create awareness of the ongoing quest for a cure and preventative measures. The ribbon was said to have been inspired by the yellow ones used at the time to show support of American troops in the first Gulf War. Red was selected for its associations with blood, passion, and anger.

redemption • Saving from transgression (from *redeem*:

to cash in; Latin: *redimere*: *re*, again; *emere*, to buy).

The only redemption he was interested in was getting enough frequent-flyer miles for a trip to Mykonos.

red-light district • The city area where prostitution and other naughty things are expected to occur. From when a red light placed in a window meant dirty stuff was happening inside (which itself comes from the biblical story of Rahab, a prostitute who aided the spies of Joshua by marking her house with a scarlet rope).

I don't mind the bars all being in the red-light district, but it's never been my color.

regular guy • One who poses no threat of being different, and whose actions can be predicted to take a traditional course.

He was surprised that one so queer could be such a regular guy.

reign • A gay man's influence over others.

After hearing the guffaws for the new queen's remarks, he sensed his reign as the group's wittiest bitch was nearly over.

relaced • One who tries being straight, but happily returns to being queer.

He's relaced, but so tightly I could barely squeeze in during our reunion.

release • To let go; to climax, ejaculate (also said if one "climaxes" at the end of body work services).

I don't feel like leaving unless I get a release at the end.

rent boy • A male prostitute—for whom payment allows for his "temporary occupation." (AKA pay for play)

repartee • Talk marked by witty interplay. French: *repartir*, to retort.

I will repartee him to ribbons when he gets home.

repent • To feel reproachful for having (or not having) done something after taking a second look. Old French: *repentir*, to be sorry.

He would repent—after noticing most of the men who wore Hollister were half his age.

repent

repertoire • All those with whom one has had intimate relations; all that one is willing (or not willing) to do sexually. From the French, for the full complement of works that an actor, player, or ensemble is ready to perform or has performed in the past with much success.

I hear his repertoire is short but sweet, so you can still make your train.

repress • To keep down, exclude by force.

Don't repress—that's what maids are for.

Republican • One favoring a conservative government created for, not by, individuals. Latin: *res publica*, thing of the people.

When I said, "Screw him, if he's a stuffed shirt, rep tie–wearin' Republican," I didn't think he'd actually do him from behind the guy's desk!

repulsive • To cause disgusted avoidance. Latin: *repellere*, to drive back.

Repulsive to me—is wearing synthetic anything!

resignify • To take a symbol and give it a different meaning or restore its original definition. (AKA reclaim)

resistance • The ability of an organism to fight off illness.

respect • A show of appreciative, deserved regard. Latin: *respicere*, to look back at.

I'll show you what gets respect—if I may drop my shorts.

responsible • Showing good judgment, sound thinking, and answerable to one's own behavior. Latin: *respondere*, to reply.

I was responsible: I asked his name before undoing his jeans.

rest area • A roadside place for drivers to stop, relax, and relieve themselves.
It seems silly to call it a rest area if all the men are gettin' busy.

retail therapy • Shopping as a way to be happy (from TV's *Will & Grace*).
A little retail therapy at Brooks Brothers will suit you just fine.

reverse discrimination • Action against a group that was previously the beneficiary of privilege.

reverse missionary • A gay sex "twist" on the standard "straight" missionary position, where the passive male partner is lying facedown with his active partner on top. (See *bottom: "bottom's up"*)

reversion • Going back to a former state (as when one was straight, then gay, then straight again).
I had a reversion myself—when I paid off my Nordstrom's card and was able to shop there again!

rice • A starchy food staple (in Asia); an Asian gay male. (Note: Often "rice"—as in "white as"—is used to indicate Caucasian men. But so is "potato" and more!)
rice and potatoes • Asian men and white men together, socially or sexually.
Some dark meat would go great with those rice and potatoes.
rice pudding • The semen of an Asian man.
rice queen • A white boy greatly attracted to Asian men; *potato queen*: a non-white (usually Asian) male attracted to white boys.
sticky rice • Asian men who like each other.
You know a touch of Wesson helps separate sticky rice.

Right, the • Classification for the politically conservative; those who believe they are proper and take the high(er) road; the opposite of "left" (an unnatural condition).
Can a guy remain on the Right with a left hand up his rear?
right wing • A group on the conservative "side" (from political assemblages during the French Revolution which seated conservatives to the right of the center, opposite liberals on the left).
righteous • Thought to be without fault (and excusable for violent acts); something felt to be excellent. Old English: *rihtwis*, right plus wise.

right(s) • One's privilege(s), birthright(s), even without documentation or precedence, which usually must be legislated.

    constitutional rights • Those which are written into the highest authority of our nation.

    gay rights • Those which should be, but which we must struggle for.

    human rights • Those belonging to all, without restriction to country, class, race, sex, or orientation.

    states' rights • Those which are lawful only within a state's borders.

rim(ming) • The edge; engaged in activity along the edge; oral stimulation of and around the anus. (See *lickety-split*)

    rimadonna • One who enjoys anilingus (a play on "prima donna").

    rimmer • One who performs anilingus.

role play • To behave with the characteristics of another; in sex, for one to take on the persona of another whose traits are sexually stimulating. Examples of "gay" role play: daddy-boy, coach-player, ranger-camper, executive–delivery boy, schoolmaster-schoolboy.

"roll out the red carpet" • Something done for an occasion that warrants great fanfare; to use one's tongue (red carpet) to perform anilingus with great zeal.

    After I roll out the red carpet in back, I'd

like to cover his whole front with it, too, from the top of his head to his toes.

roommate • One with whom another shares a household (and though it is expected that such pairings are platonic, suspicions arise given the close quarters). (AKA roomie)
Technically, I don't think you can call him a roommate after doing that.

rosebud • An undeveloped rose; the anus (which resembles one) especially of an inexperienced gay man.
pick-a-rosebud • To be the first to *prick* the anus of a male virgin.

rough • Characterized by coarseness.
rough sex • Intercourse which is raucous and may cause physical harm. (Woo-hoo!)
rough trade • A very aggressive, even cruel and physically abusive partner. Taken from the era when many gay men paid for sex with straight men—"trade"—who were disengaged performance-wise and nonreciprocal to the point of violent deflection.

royal jelly • What a "queen" bee makes.

rubber • Misleading yet popular name for a condom. (Correct in that they are elastic, but not in the material used.)

rubdown • An energetic massaging of the body meant to stimulate/relax the muscles (often a prelude to sex). (Note: This category of "massage" does not require legally certified practitioners.)
"rub-and-tug" • To masturbate (*tug*) one who is receiving a massage (*rub*).

rumor(ed) • Unverified, frequently disturbing information spread by word of mouth.
For Immediate Release: Stylist-to-the-stars and rumored homosexual Harry Teasing was laid to rest during a lavish service that featured his request for white orchids, white-tuxedoed ushers, and cages full of white doves freed into a white cloud-strewn sky.

rumpy-pumpy • Cutesy term for gay anal (rump) intercourse (pump).

runway • Owing to our close fashion ties, anywhere that gay men traipse (especially past others, like in a bar or down a street in a "gayborhood"). (AKA catwalk)

Russian roulette • A deadly game of chance (named for its country of origin), where a gun's cylinder is loaded with one bullet, then spun (like a roulette wheel) and given to a player to pull the trigger at his own head and at his own peril; used to describe any recklessly endangering activity (ex: "bare" sexual intercourse between gay men).

Is it still playing Russian roulette in an orgy full of Romanian men?

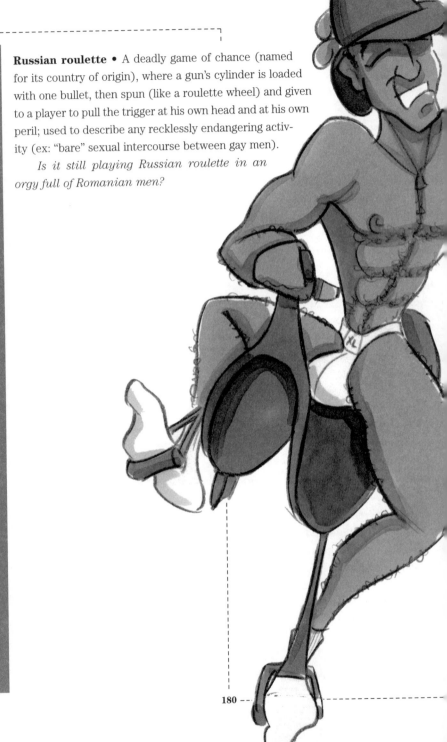

saddle • A seat a rider uses on an animal; the butt.

in the saddle • To anal-copulate; in BDS&M encounters, descriptive of one who is in a sling.

saddle up • To prepare for sex (usually with a condom); to have anal intercourse. *Pardner, I need you to saddle up first before we go for a ride.*

sidesaddle • Said of a gay man having sexual intercourse with a woman. Taken from the way in which a proper lady rides a horse.

sadism • Ritualized erotic conduct in which pleasure comes from the controlled infliction of pain or emotional abuse upon another. Named for the Marquis de Sade, a French writer whose works were preoccupied with sexual violence.

sadomasochism (S&M) • The well-known combination of sadistic and masochistic behaviors for sexual pleasure (usually engaged in with predetermined limits). Are all gays *mean queens* (those who are into sadomasochism; sometimes *sadie-masies*)? Hardly. But there is a compelling excuse for what attraction there may be. Aside from the onetime "disorder" connection, BDS&M play has a lot to do with power. This is something many gay men felt (and still feel) they don't have—outside a private dungeon playroom.

safe • Protected from harm; not into kinky, harmful, or unprotected sex. Latin: *salvus*, healthy.

safe, sane, and consensual • A way to say one is only interested in protected, normal, and mutually agreed upon acts of sex.

safe sex • Erotic interactions where partners take preventative measures (minimally by wearing a condom or maximally by avoiding anal and/or oral contact) against the spread of infectious illnesses, especially HIV.

safe word/gesture • In BDS&M sex, a predetermined word, or physical sign (if speaking is not possible!), used to call an immediate end to the proceedings.

safest sex • Masturbation (in that the threat of passing infection from potentially disease-transmitting fluids is minimized).

SAGE (Services and Action for Gay, Lesbian, Bisexual, and Transgender Elders) • Organization founded in 1977, and charged with making sure the maturing gay community respects and integrates with its older generations.

salt and pepper • White and black men together.

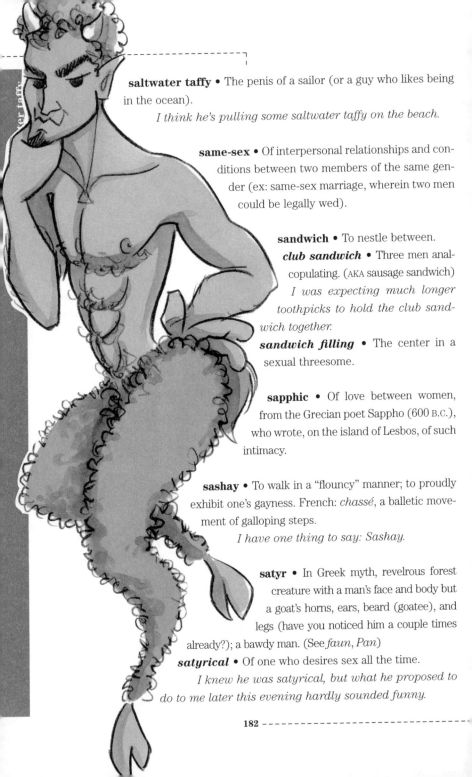

saltwater taffy • The penis of a sailor (or a guy who likes being in the ocean).

I think he's pulling some saltwater taffy on the beach.

same-sex • Of interpersonal relationships and conditions between two members of the same gender (ex: same-sex marriage, wherein two men could be legally wed).

sandwich • To nestle between.

club sandwich • Three men anal-copulating. (AKA sausage sandwich)

I was expecting much longer toothpicks to hold the club sandwich together.

sandwich filling • The center in a sexual threesome.

sapphic • Of love between women, from the Grecian poet Sappho (600 B.C.), who wrote, on the island of Lesbos, of such intimacy.

sashay • To walk in a "flouncy" manner; to proudly exhibit one's gayness. French: *chassé*, a balletic movement of galloping steps.

I have one thing to say: Sashay.

satyr • In Greek myth, revelrous forest creature with a man's face and body but a goat's horns, ears, beard (goatee), and legs (have you noticed him a couple times already?); a bawdy man. (See *faun, Pan*)

satyrical • Of one who desires sex all the time.

I knew he was satyrical, but what he proposed to do to me later this evening hardly sounded funny.

"Save the drama for your momma" • Dragspeak for not having any time for unneccessary histrionics.

"scared straight" • Behavior modification technique where the evils of homosexuality are used to frighten a person (back) into heterosexuality.

scaredy-cat • One who is timid, or made easily afraid (attributed to our friend Dorothy Parker, c. 1930).

scat • Excrement. Why does this word appear in many of my gay language references? Is it because it and we are so disgusting?! Or that it's part of extremely humiliating BDS&M play? But if we're supposed to be so fastidious, it makes little sense. If you can figure it out, let me know!

scene, the • A realm of activity. Greek: *skene*, stage. Typically, the "gay" scene encompasses nightclubs, fashion events, sex clubs, baths, saunas, gyms, cocktail parties, bars, liberal political events, and bake sales. *Non-scene*: not part of the scene, usually said of a person who hasn't any interest in such places or activities anyway.
scenery • Backdrop; one to whom another is attracted, but hard to approach.
    The scenery at the boys' school was great, but it was wiser to watch from afar.
scenic • Quite attractive (re: worth a sightseeing trip).
    The short walk around his front and back was every bit as scenic as the long route we took through Yosemite.

screamer • An extremely flamboyant gay man (given to loud outbursts and such).
screaming fairy • Double intensive for an obvious gay male (who behaves in such an excessively fey manner that he may be the gayest man you'll ever meet).

screen • One who acts as concealment for another. Middle Dutch: *scherm*, shield. (AKA *beard*)
    Truthfully, I'd say no matter how well dressed, a skinny drag queen makes for a pretty flimsy screen.

scrumptious • Delicious and delectable.
    Those cinnamon-dusted truffles are absolutely scrrrumptious!
scrumpy • One who looks good enough to eat. (AKA scrumpable)

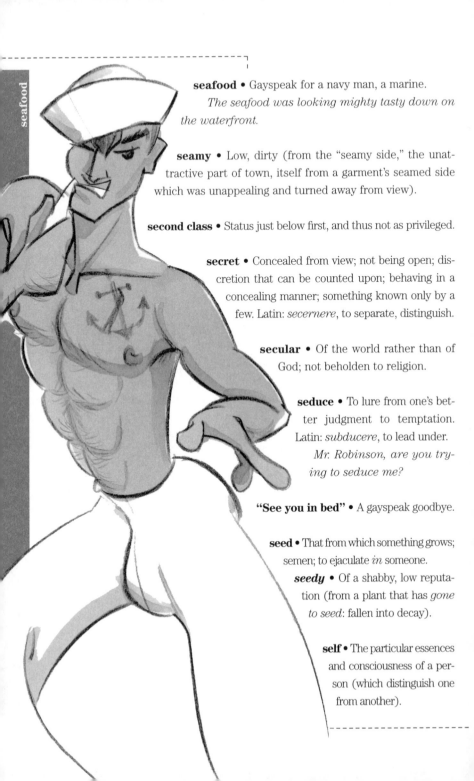

seafood • Gayspeak for a navy man, a marine.
The seafood was looking mighty tasty down on the waterfront.

seamy • Low, dirty (from the "seamy side," the unattractive part of town, itself from a garment's seamed side which was unappealing and turned away from view).

second class • Status just below first, and thus not as privileged.

secret • Concealed from view; not being open; discretion that can be counted upon; behaving in a concealing manner; something known only by a few. Latin: *secernere*, to separate, distinguish.

secular • Of the world rather than of God; not beholden to religion.

seduce • To lure from one's better judgment to temptation. Latin: *subducere*, to lead under.
Mr. Robinson, are you trying to seduce me?

"See you in bed" • A gayspeak goodbye.

seed • That from which something grows; semen; to ejaculate *in* someone.
seedy • Of a shabby, low reputation (from a plant that has *gone to seed*: fallen into decay).

self • The particular essences and consciousness of a person (which distinguish one from another).

self-loathing • An extreme dislike of who one is.

self-love • To be in full support, often excessive, of who one is.

I hear he's got plenty to self-love.

self-pity • Sorrow for one's perceived condition of having been wronged.

semiotics • The study of interpreting nonverbalized signs, considered part of how a group communicates.

What would your semiotics say about his erect penis?

señoreater • One who likes Latino types. (AKA *bean queen*)

sensitive • Quick to feel and see (what others are feeling, seeing); easily offended; touchy. Latin: *sensatus*: sensate.

sentimental • Easily moved by a feeling that is not logical reason; overly emotional. Latin: *sentire*, to feel.

sero- • From *serum*: prefix describing blood separated into its fluid and solid parts.

sero-convert • When blood (serum) tests go from having no condition to testing with it (going from HIV-negative to positive).

sero-discordant • When blood (serum) does not match; a couple where one partner is HIV-positive and the other negative.

serosort • To separate those with HIV from those without it.

serve • To behave submissively, in indebtedness or obedience to another. Latin: *servus*, slave.

serviceable • Ready to be given pleasure (hopefully, worthy of such attention).

service-oriented • When one is inclined to pleasure another. (This guy is always the passive type. An active partner so disposed is specifically called a "service-oriented top.")

service-oriented disability • When a man in the military, a place of extreme "homosociality," finds himself having sex with other men.

For a soldier with a service-oriented disability, he doesn't show many signs of suffering.

service station • A passive male who fulfills all the sexual needs and desires of an active male, without expecting any "service" in return.

Using that service station makes me feel like a Lamborghini.

session • A meeting; a BDS&M sexual encounter (because most are quite well-organized). Latin: *sedere*, to sit.

sex • That by which an organism is determined—male, female, intersex—based on their reproductive organs and functions; all forms of erotic behavior.

sex crime • An unlawful or forced sexual activity.

> *Remember, until recently it was essentially a sex crime just to be gay.*

sex offender • One who perpetrates and is convicted of a sexual crime.

sex pig • One of voracious carnal appetite (often a bottom, who, like the animal, can be sloppy and gets stuck a lot). (See *pig*)

sex-change • When a person of one sex approximates the biological/physical characteristics of the opposite sex (often called *sex-reassignment surgery*: which *restores* one to the condition felt to be originally intended).

sexual • Of sex, sexuality, the sexes, and erotic desires or activities.

sexual abuse • To force oneself lasciviously upon another.

> *The therapist explained to Billy, the kid, that even though he had enjoyed it, what Mr. James did was still sexual abuse.*

sexual harassment • Abusive behavior enacted by an authority figure against a subordinate as a way to coerce sex from that person.

sexual identity • Where one sees himself, erotically: straight, gay, bisexual, transsexual.

sexual objectification • The treatment of a person (by others or oneself) as nothing more than a means to erotic gratification.

sexual orientation • The sex to which one is naturally attracted. (See *orientation*)
His sexual orientation is just where I hoped it would be: low to the floor.

sexual preference • The sex that one "prefers" (which is our problem with the term: it implies that homosexuality is not innate, and, as such, is considered the wrong choice to make).

sexuality • Concern or interest in carnal activity (and of its range and orientation). The following are all sexualities:

ambisexual • One interested in all sexes.

asexual • One seeming to have no interest in sex.

hypersexual • One overly interested in sex.

monosexual • One who behaves exclusively within his sexuality (and considers any overlap incorrect).

pansexual • One with no or very few sexual limitations. (See *poly-: polyamorous*)

psychosexual • Of the mental processes involved in sexuality.

sexualize • To give something an erotic edge (often where none is warranted).
He vowed not to sexualize everything, as he adjusted his cock ring, pulled on his jockstrap—shifting his penis to maximize its size—and went hunting in his closet for the tight and faded jeans with the holes under both ass cheeks.

sexually transmitted disease (STD) • Any malady passed on through sexual contact. (Formerly, venereal disease. From the Latin: *venereus: venus*, love.) It's only to be thorough that I've listed the following, and not because I think we are promiscuous (see also *AIDS, HIV*):

chlamydia • Causes sterility.

(genital) herpes • A virus causing genital sores.

gonorrhea • Treatable affliction of the genitals and urinary tract. (AKA the clap)

hepatitis A, B, and C • Viruses causing inflammation of the liver. A and B are curable, C is not.

syphilis • Oldest known STD, effectively treatable with penicillin. If left unattended, it can be fatal.

shade • To cast a darkening over; a variance in intensity; one's haughtiness, scorn, or the ability to remark to another with nuanced insult.

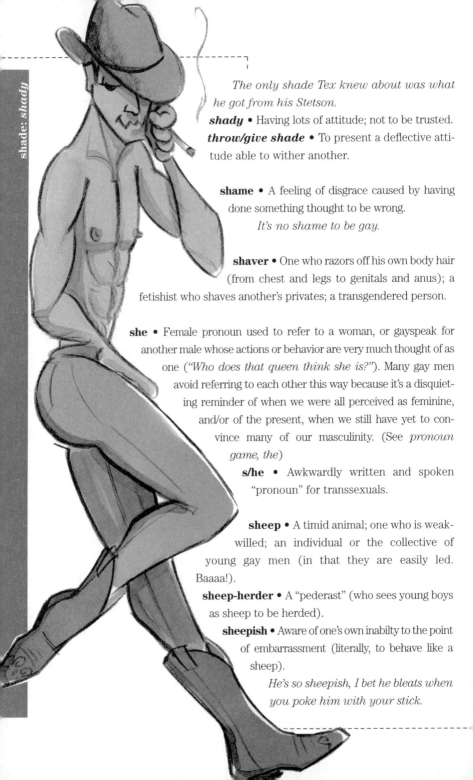

The only shade Tex knew about was what he got from his Stetson.

shady • Having lots of attitude; not to be trusted.

throw/give shade • To present a deflective attitude able to wither another.

shame • A feeling of disgrace caused by having done something thought to be wrong.

It's no shame to be gay.

shaver • One who razors off his own body hair (from chest and legs to genitals and anus); a fetishist who shaves another's privates; a transgendered person.

she • Female pronoun used to refer to a woman, or gayspeak for another male whose actions or behavior are very much thought of as one (*"Who does that queen think she is?"*). Many gay men avoid referring to each other this way because it's a disquieting reminder of when we were all perceived as feminine, and/or of the present, when we still have yet to convince many of our masculinity. (See *pronoun game, the*)

s/he • Awkwardly written and spoken "pronoun" for transsexuals.

sheep • A timid animal; one who is weak-willed; an individual or the collective of young gay men (in that they are easily led. Baaaa!).

sheep-herder • A "pederast" (who sees young boys as sheep to be herded).

sheepish • Aware of one's own inabilty to the point of embarrassment (literally, to behave like a sheep).

He's so sheepish, I bet he bleats when you poke him with your stick.

she-male • Widely used to refer to a male-to-female transsexual (derived from "female").

she-man • An effeminate gay or a butch lesbian (derived from "he-man").

"shop by phone" • To hire an escort (hustler).

shop door • The fly opening in a man's pants or underwear. (AKA barn door)

short circuit • A very small penis.

shortcake • Quick anal sex.
With my schedule, I'm lucky to get one piece of shortcake a week.

showbiz • The gay life, in that it is constant play-acting and razzle-dazzle.

showstopper • An extra-large penis (that gets everyone's focused attention).
When he pulled out the showstopper, everyone in the crowd just came together in their seats.

shrimping • Sucking on another's toe (which gives the appearance of a small, curling crustacean); a *shrimper*: a toe-sucker. ("Shrimping" is also the very difficult act of fellating someone at the same time as anal-copulating him. For this to work, it helps if the top is very flexible and both are very well endowed.)

shun • To intentionally stay away from one who has done something bad. Old English: *scunian*, to abhor.
shunary • A book that has all the dirty stuff censored out.

shy • Lacking boldness; to draw back in fear.
He's so shy, that sweet little boy who caught my eye.

sick • Defective, unwholesome.
You people are sick.

sidewalk sale • Available gay men gathered after a bar's closing hours.
The pickin's at the sidewalk sale were better since their summer restocking.

sign(al) • That which intimates the existence of; a specific way of communication.

significant other (SO) • Term frequently used by gays (and unmarried straights) for a person with whom another shares a long-term, intimate commitment ("significant" in that he is "more than just"; "other" to mean "one of two").

silly • Exhibiting little wisdom, sense, responsibility and too much giddiness; a ninny.

sin • A religious or moral transgression, especially when undertaken intentionally. *Sinful*: known for wickedness.

single • The state of a person being solo, without a partner, unmarried, unaccompanied (after a certain time, considered a troubling, desperate state).
   I wonder why he's still single.
single-sex • Functioning within one sex; same-sex. Reader, would you consider that in this day and age, any single-sex activity is going to be thought of as "gay," even when it's not at all, like the guys' bowling league or a fishing tourney?

sir • Respectful address for an elder male, or one taking the active vs. the passive sexual role. From the English: *sire*, one who fathers.
   Whatever you say, sir!

sissy • Meaning to be "like a sister"; a cowardly, effeminate man (and of all gay men, in that we are a sort of sorority?) (AKA sis).
sissy bar • A gay watering hole.

sister • A female sibling; one who is regarded in an affectionate, sisterly way. Also used by gay men: for one of whom another is fond; of all gay men collectively; and of one who acts with extreme femininity.
   Check out the sister—is he too queer or what?!
sister act • Sex between a gay man and a straight woman (implying that it is an *act*: not genuinely involved); two drag queens or effeminate guys together.
sister boy • One who shows womanly tendencies; in Japanese, *sista-boi*.

"sitting on a gold mine" • Said of "well-rounded" men who do not allow themselves to be anally penetrated (often unapproachable heterosexual males). From the phrase meaning the potential for riches is very close at hand but is going untapped.

He was sitting on a gold mine worth more than Fort Knox.

sixty-nine (69) • Mutual fellatio represented as an ideograph of numbers resembling two curling bodies in opposition. *68*: of oral sex when only one is fellated.

sixty-six (66) • Anal copulation represented as an ideograph of numbers resembling one body directly behind another. (AKA ninety-nine)

size queen • One who desires men with large penises. (AKA whaler)

skeet shooting • Ejaculating through the air and onto another man's face (and/or into his mouth). (See *facial*)

For safety reasons, I'm leaving my old target behind, undisturbed, while I started up skeet shooting to keep from getting out of practice.

skinny • Thin often to the extreme of unhealthiness; a weakling. If one has to think about gayness in terms of body type, what's the first one that comes to mind? Skinny? This is not to say we don't come in all shapes and sizes. We do. But the implications of being skinny as weak may imply that any man who is is without power—certainly against more aggressive (manlier) forces. Further, doesn't mainstream culture always ask its men "to put meat on their bones" as an act of patriotism (so they're better prepared for defense)?

skippy • One who *skips*: leaps lightly about.

slanderous • Falsely speaking or reporting something that causes harm to another's standing. Latin: *scandalum*, cause of offense.

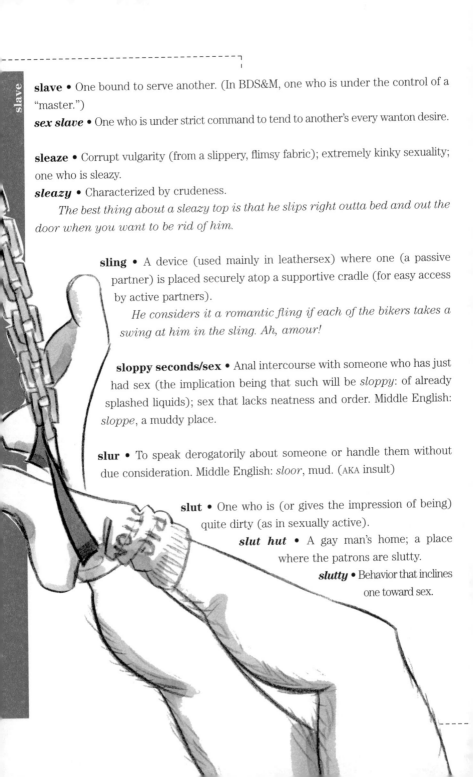

slave • One bound to serve another. (In BDS&M, one who is under the control of a "master.")

sex slave • One who is under strict command to tend to another's every wanton desire.

sleaze • Corrupt vulgarity (from a slippery, flimsy fabric); extremely kinky sexuality; one who is sleazy.

sleazy • Characterized by crudeness.

The best thing about a sleazy top is that he slips right outta bed and out the door when you want to be rid of him.

sling • A device (used mainly in leathersex) where one (a passive partner) is placed securely atop a supportive cradle (for easy access by active partners).

He considers it a romantic fling if each of the bikers takes a swing at him in the sling. Ah, amour!

sloppy seconds/sex • Anal intercourse with someone who has just had sex (the implication being that such will be *sloppy*: of already splashed liquids); sex that lacks neatness and order. Middle English: *sloppe*, a muddy place.

slur • To speak derogatorily about someone or handle them without due consideration. Middle English: *sloor*, mud. (AKA insult)

slut • One who is (or gives the impression of being) quite dirty (as in sexually active).

slut hut • A gay man's home; a place where the patrons are slutty.

slutty • Behavior that inclines one toward sex.

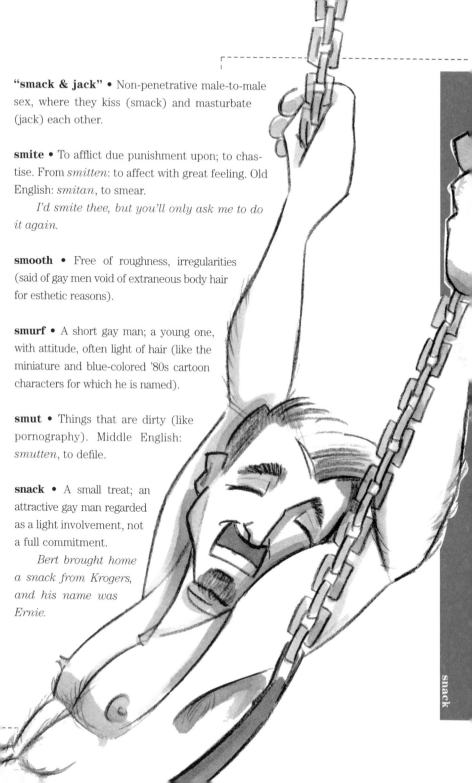

"smack & jack" • Non-penetrative male-to-male sex, where they kiss (smack) and masturbate (jack) each other.

smite • To afflict due punishment upon; to chastise. From *smitten*: to affect with great feeling. Old English: *smitan*, to smear.

I'd smite thee, but you'll only ask me to do it again.

smooth • Free of roughness, irregularities (said of gay men void of extraneous body hair for esthetic reasons).

smurf • A short gay man; a young one, with attitude, often light of hair (like the miniature and blue-colored '80s cartoon characters for which he is named).

smut • Things that are dirty (like pornography). Middle English: *smutten*, to defile.

snack • A small treat; an attractive gay man regarded as a light involvement, not a full commitment.

Bert brought home a snack from Krogers, and his name was Ernie.

snack bar • A gay establishment offering more than drinks to please its customers.
It was your usual popular gay dive, until they opened up the backroom and it became every cream puff's favorite snack bar, too!

snackpack • A jockstrap, brief underwear, or bikini-cut swimsuit.

snake • A long, slithering reptile; a penis.

"charm a snake" • To give one an erection.

snake charmer • One who fellates exceptionally well.
My understanding is that the snake charmer has his own alluring python.

snake pit • Any place where gathered gays might be somewhat hostile to outsiders (straights) entering, like a sex club.

snake venom • Semen.

snap • The quick snapping of one's fingers in emphatic response to the moment; to quickly become aware; a classic "drag" gesture used when one is feeling contemptuous, or just to punctuate the proceedings (AKA a royal command); to tense up one's sphincter during anal sex. *His snap almost crackled and popped my you-know-what!* Middle Dutch: *snappen*, to seize.

sneak queen • One who is regularly unfaithful in his relationship(s).

snippy • Acid-tongued.

snit • An agitated, annoyed state; one who is in such a state.

snivel • To complain weepingly.

snow • White persons, or that which is white; semen; cocaine.

snow flurries • Short-term white involvement in any non-white community (sexually, socially, and politically).
Summer or not, any time Gay Pride rolls around, you can expect snow flurries.

snow queen • A non-white man who is attracted mainly to white men (or fond of cocaine, in which case one would "shovel snow").

snow storm • An immense amount of ejaculate.

snowballing • The sex act of passing ejaculated semen from mouth to mouth.

snowbanks • A white guy's buttocks or those set off by the much tanner skin on the rest of his body.

I wouldn't mind digging my way into those snowbanks on a cold night.

snowblindness • Caused when someone dyes his hair blond.

snowflakes • Gay white men.

snowplow • Said of anally copulating a white male.

"so gay" • Said, insultingly, when something (or someone) is perceived as being unacceptably queer.

social • Among people.

social disease • A sexually transmitted malady; a communal thought or action that brings potential harm.

I'll tell ya what a social disease is: letting regular ticket holders fill out the VIP section.

social pressure • Force brought on by one's community to be a certain way not always natural to the individual.

social worker • One who loves to greet those newest to the scene (by offering his bed); said of white men who date non-whites (this use is old and very un-PC).

Sodom • Any place thought to be full of vice and immorality (New York City, San Francisco, New Orleans, Las Vegas); from the ancient city so depraved it was destroyed, along with Gomorrah, by God. *Little Sodom*: a gay enclave. (See following)

You might think it Sodom by the Sea, but I still left my heart there.

sodomy • Various sexual acts (from anal sex to bestiality) considered outside the norm (of procreative intercourse) and, thus, what's considered gay sex behavior (and derived from Sodom, see preceding). For all who have never feared for the consequences of their actions in bed, you should remember that it wasn't until 2003 that individual states' sodomy laws were judged unconstitutional—in the settling of the landmark Supreme Court case *Lawrence vs. Texas*. Only thereafter were such acts undertaken privately by consenting adults considered their own business. Just prior to the ruling, it was still an offense, punishable by imprisonment, to have sex with a person of the same sex (and for a woman to fellate a man) in nearly one-third of America's states. It was only during the latter half of the twentieth century that states had even begun to exorcise these laws of their own accord. A final thought: Three of the high court's judges remained dissenters, as were most social conservatives, feeling that to allow such actions, even by those consenting, *naturally* opens the way for "sleeping with animals" and "incest."

sodomite • One who commits an act of sodomy, which was mainly thought of as anal copulation, and why all gay men were called sodomites for a long time—which is how many still refer to us. (See *bugger*)

soft • Tender; weak.
softcore • Sexual material considered to be of a tempered explicit nature (*soft*: subdued; *core*: essence). (See *hardcore*)
softspoken • With a gentle manner.

soirée • Gayspeak French for an evening social affair.
   Sister, you'll be sorry if you miss my soirée on Saturday.

solo • An act by a single performer; in gay porn, one man occupying himself with various acts of self-pleasure. Latin: *solus*, alone.

son • One's male child or someone watched over by a parental figure; the passive partner of a "daddy" (see *boy*).

sophisticate • One who is worldly and fine, not simple or naïve; to adulterate. Greek: *sophos*, clever, wise.

sordid • Morally foul. Latin: *sordere*, to be dirty.
   That the orgy was a sordid affair with a variety of nasty men was a given.

southern belle • A gay guy from south of the Mason-Dixon line.

south of the border • An exotic place to visit; said of gay men contemplating being with a woman, indirectly, and her genitalia, directly.
   He gets around, but never travels south of the border.

Speedo • Well-known swimsuit manufacturer and maker of brief styles seemingly favored only by and indicative of a certain classification of men—others being aghast at the mere mention.

He was quick to peg the guy in the Speedo.

sperm donor • One who donates his semen for purposes of artificially induced procreation; one who loves to "get off."

He's the kind of sperm donor who will give until you hurt.

spineless • Without courage (as a *spine* is necessary for support of the body).

spiritual • Relating to God and the soul.

I prayed that no one else would be wearing the same Marc Jacobs shirt as I; is that spiritual enough?

spit roast • Sex act where one "middle" man is penetrated both anally and orally by two others (and, presumably, can be spun around like an animal on the fire).

splendiferous • Brilliantly grand. Latin: *splendere*, to shine.

Newman thought the glitter-dipped invitations were splendiferous—and couldn't wait to tell The Paper Cut Above the Rest card shop owner Paul how he felt.

sport • Physical activity governed by rules and engaged in competitively; term of endearment from (usually) an older to a younger male (who might be rambunctious but pleasing company). The notion that there is such a thing as a "gay" sport is far-fetched, though we surely engage in some more than others. Certainly some sound queer, like badminton, shuttlecock, croquet, figure skating, and wrestling.

spouse • One's partner in marriage; one's partner without the legality of same (as with gay couples). Latin: *spondere*, to pledge.

"spray tonsils" • To ejaculate into someone's mouth.

spread-eagle • Passive sexual position, where a face-up or face-down partner's legs and arms are outstretched, sometimes tied, leaving him vulnerable and powerless against aggressive acts. In BDS&M sex, this is a favored stance of those who choose the controlled, submissive, and punishable role. In law enforcement, this is a position where a suspect's arms and legs are placed widely apart to enable frisking for concealed weapons. (Oh, officer!) (Note that all are taken from the noble bird when in full flight.)

"squat to pee" • Said of one who is extremely effeminate (in that the position is how a woman urinates).

squeal(er) • To be tight, anally; one who cries loudly (in pain or pleasure); too weak-willed to keep a confidence.

squeamish • Quick to feel illness, or shock, or to turn from disgust.

squirrelly • Behaving sneakily and eccentrically (like the small animal).
Everyone cover your nuts, squirrelly is here.

stag • An adult male deer; a man without the accompaniment of a woman; men-only gatherings.
stag-hag • A straight male who likes the company of gay men, or the reverse. (See *fag stag*)

stand and model (S&M) bar • An establishment where preening patrons assume unapproachable, mannequinlike stances about the room. Thus, not a congenial place to meet a potential intimate—but a great place to get the scoop on recently dumped film and TV stars. (AKA bowl of wax fruit, garden of touch-me-nots) Alternatively, an S&M bar is favored by sadomasochists.

stats • Abbreviation for one's "statistical" information: age, weight, height—often used in Internet profiles.

status • One's current health in relation to HIV (positive or negative); one's standing in comparison to others.

special status • Particular conditions not given to everyone.

Of course I deserve special status—I'm her publicist, for goodness' sake!

status symbol • A possession believed able to convey (and increase) one's social or economic prestige.

steak house • An establishment where pieces of meat are the speciality; a sex club.

The steak house had a scare last week when someone thought they were offering fish, but it turned out the seafood was a bunch of sailors on leave.

stealth • Getting by unnoticed; of a transsexual successfully living as the desired sex without question.

steam room • A usually sex-segregated place, where nude or toweled men congregate amid the hot vapors of forced water (and will engage in erotic play if the opportunity avails itself).

Nasal passages aren't the only paths opened in the steam room.

stereotype • An often over-simplified but consistent conception; one seen as embodying an accepted image. Greek: *stereo*, solid; *type*, printing. (See *cliché*)

stigma(tize) • A sign of disgrace; to label as reproachful. Latin: a tattoo indicating slave or criminal status.

stonewall • To block out; name of the Greenwich Village bar where, in the early morning hours of June 28, 1969, a riot broke out between gay patrons—most of them drag queens and effeminate queers—and overly harassing police, sent there in a raid specifically intended to help then-mayor John Lindsay clean up the city's unruly and unwanted elements. We as a community "fought back" for the first time at Stonewall, and that is why the vast majority of pride festivities are held during the latter part of June. But the timing is everything for another reason, too: Many of the multitudes that had gathered there that night in 1969 were grieving the loss of Judy Garland, the old school gay icon who had passed away days before.

straight (STR8) • Without deviation; rigid; a heterosexual.

straight and narrow • Behavior restricted to that which is of very little or no deviation from the norm.

straight-acting • Giving the outward look and attitude of a heterosexual male to attract and deceive (thinking in both cases that this is the more suitable or attractive way to appear).

strait-laced • Extremely tight, moral (from women's bodices, bound to impede movement).

He's strait-laced during the day, but loosens up enough to get tied at night.

"strike a pose" • To stand in a manner that is most flattering for the viewer.

When it came time to strike a pose, he had us beat with his au naturel homage to Lady Liberty.

stripper, male • A guy who takes his clothes off (to music), working in a passively objectifying and "female-oriented" occupation (other examples: flight attendant, nurse, secretary). (See *go-go boy*)

stud • A male animal kept expressly for breeding purposes; an exceptionally sexual male (can be of a gay male, but considered more heterosexual—owing to his procreative skills).
stud muffin • Like a stud, but maybe younger, maybe smaller, definitely sweeter—and more likely gayer.
studly • Having very masculine qualities.

studious • Given to intense study and being alone, rather than cavorting.

stylish • Of current fashion(s).
stylist • One who designs or consults on decorating, dress, or beauty.
   Is there a single stylist who isn't?

sub- • Below, beneath, under, secondary.
subculture • Group within a greater group.
sublimate • To alter oneself to conform with what's regular.
submissive • Yielding to the authority of another; a "dominant" partner's passive plaything. *Subspace*: where a submissive male's mind goes while engaged in sex.
subtext • Underlying meaning.
subversive • Undermining the established.

suck • To draw into the mouth; to perform fellatio (see *cocksuck*).
"Suck my dick" • An insulting directive, like "fuck you," so common that many forget its original slight, which is that when one man tells another to do it, he is demanding that the other perform a denigrating and emasculating act.
"You suck" • Meaning that one has done another ill. However, since it is truncated from "you suck dick," it again equates the fellator (hello, us!) with degeneracy.

sugar daddy • An older man who supports a younger man (with something "sweet": money). (See *daddy*)

suggestive • Tending to offer something improper for consideration. Latin: *suggerere*, to pile up.

sumptuous • Suggesting lavish expense. Latin: *sumptus*, expense.

"That shade of sapphire makes the room look sumptuous, don't you agree?" asked Willis, of his partner, Bruce, who was too busy admiring the furniture store's sales help to answer.

sunflower • One who loves to tan, usually younger.

superb • Of rare excellence. Latin: *superbus*, elegant, superior.

"What? Oh yes, you're right, it's superb," said Bruce back to Willis, finally, after deciding the clerk most decidedly was not.

superficial • Just on the surface; shallow.

supine • On one's back; passive.

suppressor • One who forcibly keeps others, felt not acceptable, from moving upward. Latin: *supprimere*, to press under.

I don't mind a suppressor, as long as he uses my tongue.

susceptible • Easily overpowered or influenced. Latin: *suscipere*, to take up from below.

Any man is susceptible, under the right circumstances.

swallow • Ingest. *Swallower*: one who willingly ingests semen (ant: spitter)

swan • A "male-to-female" transsexual (in that "she" will go from an ugly duckling to something beautiful).

swap • To trade.
swap cans • For partners to take turns anally copulating each other's "can": buttocks.
swap loads • For partners to fellate each other to the point of ejaculation and ingestion. (AKA shot for shot)
swap spit • For partners to (sloppily) open-mouth kiss.

sweet cheeks • One with notable, delectable buttocks. (AKA *candy ass*)

swing(er) • Back and forth movement; from the Swinging Sixties, when one would unin-

hibitedly pursue unusual sexual behavior, then go back to a more traditional mode. Though often begun in a heterosexual context, the occurrence of bi- or homosexuality was/is quite prevalent.

"swings both ways" • A bisexual (based on baseball terminology for a batter who can strike at a ball from either the right or left side of home plate). (See *switch hitter*)

swish • To rush back and forth with a rustle (the sound made by gowns as they brush past something); a gay man (who, it is assumed, walks in an exaggeratedly swiveling, "swishy" manner). (See *"walk with a lisp"*)

Did a breeze just disturb the drapes, or did a swish happen by?

hip-swishy • Overt feminine movement of the buttocks.

swishblader • Any gay man; an active gay male; a straight guy who has sex with a gay man (here, "blader" takes on an ominous tone). (See *blade*)

swishy • Effeminate.

switch hitter • A bisexual; one who can top (dominate) or bottom (submit) within a single encounter. From baseball jargon for a right- and left-handed batter.

sword • The penis.

sword swallower • A fellator.

swordfight(ing) • Mutual play between two erect men. (AKA *jousting*, pole vaulting)

sybarite • One dedicated to pleasure and luxury. *Sybaritic*: marked by extravagant fancy. From the ancient city of Sybaris, known for the posh existence of its people.

symptom • Indication of a disorder. Greek: *sumptoma*, a happening.

syrupy • Overly sentimental. (AKA sugary)
   *When you told me I would get stuck on him, I
didn't think you meant he was so syrupy.*

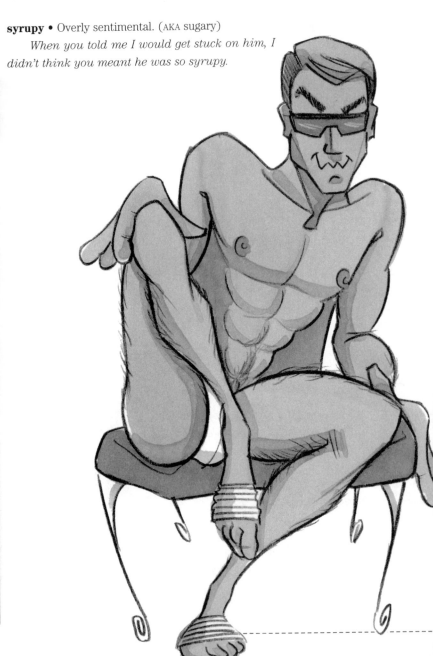

T • Short for "testosterone," used mainly by transsexuals.

taboo • Forbidden by social custom or personal aversion. Tongan: *tabu*, prohibited.
If Owen and Vince kiss, a taboo won't be broken—it'll be obliterated.

tag hag • One who cares only about the manufacturer of something. (AKA label queen)

tag team • Intense sex activity where two (or more) active partners take turns anally copulating with one passive partner. From wrestling, where one competes against the opposition after being designated by a teammate, upon completion of his part in the competition.

tailgator • Gay men (especially active ones) who frequent the beach and resort communities in search of "tail" (bottoms).
I got a tailgator on my ass—and it's exactly where we both want him to be!

t'ain't • The perineum, translated to mean "it ain't one (the scrotum) or t'other (the anus)"; also *taint*: to spoil the sanctity of something. Old French: *ataindre*, to touch upon.
The guy didn't taint me, cuz he never got near my t'ain't.

"take it like a man" • Phrase to mean accepting something with stoicism (as would be the right and expected way for a man to behave under even the most dire circumstances), but usually spoken to one who is exhibiting signs of weakness.

"take the veil" • For one of us to go straight, by marrying (as one who "takes the veil" is actually a nun who weds God), or to remove oneself from the possibility of sex (as one would when entering a convent).

talent • Potential partners (sexual or otherwise).
talent scout • One who is always on the lookout for "talent" (his next boyfriend or just his next sexual encounter).

tansie • A gay man (rhyming with "pansy," and relating him to an expected fondness for tanning at the beach); *tansie's formal*: a brief-cut swimsuit.
A tansie's not my fave flower, but I'd like to see the bloomers off that one.

taste • The ability to tell what is excellent or right.

He's got taste, all right, but I bet it's saltier than you think.

tastemaker • One who decides or affects current styles.

tats • Short for "tattoos" (used often in "profiles").

tattletale • One who talks openly of secret things; a gossip (*tattles*: reveals; *tales*: stories).

taunt • To insult mockingly. Middle French: *tanter*, to provoke.

T-cell • A Thymus-derived cell necessary to fend off viruses in one's immune system.

tea • An afternoon gathering, begun in England, featuring comestibles and beverages elegantly served; gay gatherings held in bars and clubs at the same time (but especially Sundays). A *lo(w)-tea* and *hi(gh)-tea* are quite similar socials that precede one another—"low" before "high"—but end before usual evening business hours. A *tea dance* is a more formalized, involved version of "tea" that features—*badump-bump*—dancing! The existence of gay teas can be traced back to when we began traveling, in obvious numbers, to weekend resort communities like Provincetown and Fire Island (where it is said the very first was held, in 1966, at the Blue Whale). There, teas were the only daytime diversions available—at least that one could speak of openly—and we were quick to make them our own. Bear in mind, though, it was illegal for men to dance with each other until the late seventies. Also, before they were known solely as drinking (and dancing) functions, a "high tea" was when gay guys gathered to smoke marijuana.

    tea room • A public lavatory cruised by gay men. Here we've taken one of life's most base functions and sweetened it by giving it the name of the places where fine ladies go to sip liquid refreshment. Ah, aren't we clever? (AKA teahouse)

    teabagging • Sexual act where one "dips" his scrotum (like a tea bag into a cup) into and out of the mouth of a partner.

teacher's pet • One who is especially favored by one in authority.

team player • One on the same side as yourself; a fellow gay male.

He's not a team player now, but I suspect he can be coached over to our side.

tease • To pester; to provoke desirous thoughts and not give satisfaction; one who teases.

temperamental • Given to extreme mood swings (from *temperament*: one's way of being). Latin: *temperare*, to moderate.

Cross him at your own peril, he's the temperamental kind, ya know.

tendency • General movement in one direction (from *tend*: to care for).

tender • Frail and gently emotive.

tenderfoot • One not hardened to roughness (of one's foot not able to stand much coarseness).

testosterone • Hormone responsible for secondary-stage male characteristics (deepening of voice, height gain, hair growth).

that • To refer to or single out.

"that look" • A specific appearance, as when a guy acts way beyond just wanting to have sex, and/or when he's showing definite aspects of gayness.

"that spot" • A location "inside" a passive partner which, if reached, sends him into euphoria.

Keanu knew he'd hit that spot when Brad banged his noggin on the headboard.

"that way" • Noting that a person is likely moving in a queer direction (and said often about us, demeaningly).

"That's so gay" • Noting when something is especially queer seeming, like a pink flamingo or a floral-print shirt.

theatrical • Of the theater; grandly surreal, affected behavior; and, like "musical," euphemistic for being gay (in that the

"theater"—full of actors, drama, costumes, and show—is a comfortable milieu).
Theater guild: a gathering of gay men. (AKA *drama club*)

third sex, the • Mid-twentieth-century term for being gay (as if we were neither man nor woman). (Note that lesbians have been referred to as the "fourth sex.")

thirty-nine (39) • Of anilingus represented by an ideograph of numbers resembling one person facing another's buttocks.

"thou shalt not . . . " • Arguable beginning to the biblical edict, translated many different ways, which goes more or less like this: "And with a male thou shalt not lie down as with a woman; it is an abomination." This is interpreted by the devout to mean homosexuality is a near-irredeemable transgression.

three • A trio.
three B's, the • The triumverate of gay cruising locales: bars, baths, beaches; and/or what one can expect of a quality encounter: a blowjob, bed, and breakfast.
three gets, the • The trio of actions one hopes will take place with a Mr. Will-Do-for-Now, or when under time constraints: 1) get in—or get home; 2) get off; and 3) get out.
three-dollar bill • As in being "as queer as a . . ." (A *nine-dollar bill* is three times as gay!)
three-letter man • A gay man (or "fag"), referring to the three letters contained in each word.
threeway • Any type of sexual endeavor where three persons are involved (typically, a couple and an invited extra partner, but, of course, it could be just a trio of really close friends).

tight • Kept close; hard of body; of one's anus being exceptionally firm—and, thus, not easy (*butt* preferable) to penetrate.
tight end • A "top" (from football, the one who passes the ball, often to a *wide receiver*).
tight-assed • Prudent, chaste, or uptight (in that nothing can go in or come out).
　　Since when has being with someone tight-assed been a problem for you?
tighty-whities • Body-hugging, brief-cut men's underwear—in a color meant to give the impression of spotless male essence.

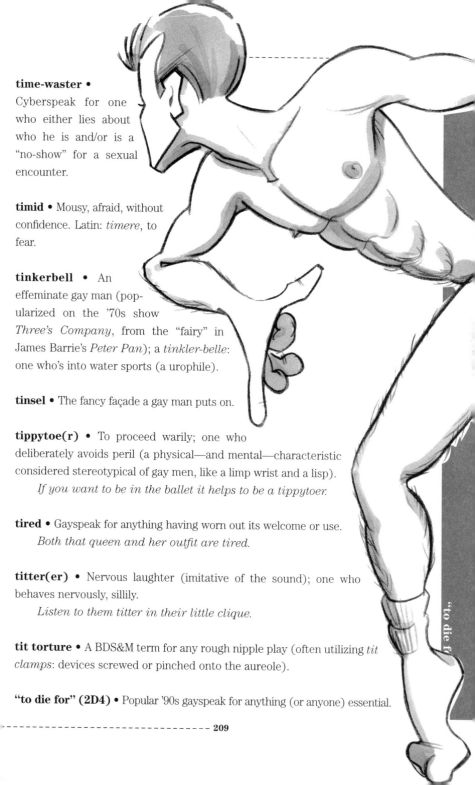

time-waster •
Cyberspeak for one
who either lies about
who he is and/or is a
"no-show" for a sexual
encounter.

timid • Mousy, afraid, without
confidence. Latin: *timere*, to
fear.

tinkerbell • An
effeminate gay man (pop-
ularized on the '70s show
Three's Company, from the "fairy" in
James Barrie's *Peter Pan*); a *tinkler-belle*:
one who's into water sports (a urophile).

tinsel • The fancy façade a gay man puts on.

tippytoe(r) • To proceed warily; one who
deliberately avoids peril (a physical—and mental—characteristic
considered stereotypical of gay men, like a limp wrist and a lisp).
If you want to be in the ballet it helps to be a tippytoer.

tired • Gayspeak for anything having worn out its welcome or use.
Both that queen and her outfit are tired.

titter(er) • Nervous laughter (imitative of the sound); one who
behaves nervously, sillily.
Listen to them titter in their little clique.

tit torture • A BDS&M term for any rough nipple play (often utilizing *tit
clamps*: devices screwed or pinched onto the aureole).

"to die for" (2D4) • Popular '90s gayspeak for anything (or anyone) essential.

token • An indication; a representative of one group alone among others totally of another (who often discriminate against that person).

tolerance • The ability to accept in others practices and beliefs other than your own. Because this word derives from "tolerate," often defined as "enduring with forbearance," its use is problematic in suggesting the new condition is a burden just bearable for others. Those tolerated want to be fully embraced.

"too close for comfort" • Phrase for those feeling threatened (physically and emotionally) by the proximity of another who they feel is a threat or a bad influence.

top • One who prefers the active, aggressive role in sex. A top is more than an anal copulator (or, for that matter, the fellated one). His "role" is also the more masculine (straighter) when paired with a bottom, who, it is assumed, takes on the more feminine (gayer) position. If, in this rather natural pairing, the psychosexual dynamic is not obvious, it should come to mind when a top finds himself in bed with another aggressive partner. There, the power struggle—over who does the penetrating, who sublimates his natural desires, and who is emasculated—takes on telling dimensions. Realize, too, that a top (the highest level?) is not expected to subordinate himself to serve, but is to be served. Which further elevates him above the bottom (the lowest point?).

top drop • An active partner feeling inadequate during or after play.

topping from the bottom • Taking charge of sex from the passive position. (See *bottom: bossy bottom*)

torch singer • One who specializes in singing torch songs (mainly a woman, who, at all costs, will "carry aloft a flame" for a man).

torch song • A tune in which an unrequited love is lamented.

tormentor • One causing another great pain; a bully. Latin: *torquere*, to twist, torture.

toss-a-salad • Term for anilingus as an act in and of itself (sometimes combined with fellatio), but often as a prelude to anal intercourse (in a sense, to mix and make it ready for serving).

total • Complete (used to denote one's unwavering position: a total bottom, a total top).

"to thine own self be true" • Quote from Shakespeare's *Hamlet*, particularly "gay" relevant in that the meaning—honest personal awareness—is any person's most important first step to happiness. The entire passage, spoken by Polonius to his son, Laertes, goes: "This above all: to thine own self be true, and it must follow, as the night the day, thou canst not then be false to any man."

touchy-feely • To be overly sympathetic and sentimental in an often intrusively physical way.

I don't mind those guys bein' touchy-feely, as long as they're not touchin' and feelin' on me.

tourist • One who is visiting a place; a straight person checking out the gay "scene." (See *"on tour"*)

towel boy • In an athletic setting, one (less likely to have participated in the activity) who passes out cloths to just-showered men.

trade • To exchange; random sexual encounters; one available for sex: a male prostitute (but specifically *and* historically, one who is paid to make himself available to be serviced—fellated—by gay men). As an exchange, this seems hardly fair or just, but such were the circumstances of a time when it was also expected that "trade" be straight—*but not always so*—whose usual upright position made him better than the one who was bent. *Do (and did) him for trade* were also quite common expressions at the time, which suggests the imbalance of the interaction. Interestingly, another expression—*Today's trade is tomorrow's competition*—implied that most hustlers were just one day away from coming out (and it was very often true).

trade

trait • A traceable aspect (of one's personality). Latin: *tractus*, a line.
Most boys outgrow that trait. Most.

trans- • Prefix to mean "across, to cross, to change."

tranny • Belittling word for "transsexual."

tranny chaser • One attracted to transsexuals.

trannyfag • One who is a gay female-to-male transsexual. Did you get that?! (AKA transhomosexual)

transacademic • A scholar on the trans community.

transactivist • One who advances the causes of the trans community.

trans community • Transgenderists, transgendered men and women, two-spirit folk, crossdressers, intersexuals, and gender-variant individuals, identified as their own group within the gay community.

transdyke • A lesbian male-to-female transsexual. Get that, too?! (AKA tryke)

transfriendly/transpositive • One who is supportive of the endeavors of the trans community, and/or attracted to those within it.

transgender(ed) • A person of one sex with the characteristics of the other: a masculine woman, a feminine man. A transgendered person is not the same as a transsexual, in that he or she, in their present anatomical condition, is often not interested in seeking a physical alteration, as does a transsexual. Further, the term "transgender" can categorize the entire queer community, in that it implies a fluidity back and forth between real and learned notions of what is masculine and feminine, gay and straight, male and female.

transgenderist • A man who appears (in dress and manner) as a woman for professional or lifestyle reasons, going so far as to make physical alterations with the exception of penis removal. This term is used interchangeably with "drag queen," "crossdresser," and "transvestite," but those are of mainly temporary assimilations, whereas a transgenderist's interests are often not so fleeting.

transsexual • A person of one sex who has undergone surgical procedures to become the opposite sex. (AKA turnabout, Danish pastry [from when these procedures were performed mainly in Denmark])

transvestite • One who "wears" the style (and manners) traditionally associated with that person's opposite sex. (AKA *crossdresser*) Latin: *trans*, cross; *vestire*, to dress. Not only is saying "transvestite" outdated, its origin—in *travesty*: a grotesque imitation, a ridiculous parody—forever cast a shadow over those who do not see their situation as ugly and out of bounds. (See *TV*)

trapper • Bearspeak for a smooth-bodied male who is attracted to hairy men.

travel(er) • Cyberspeak for one who cannot accommodate another in his home, so is compelled to take sex to an intended "host" partner's place, or elsewhere.

For sex, will travel. And so Will did, with his Coach backpack packed.

trend • The direction in which something (a style) currently tends to move. Middle English: *trenden*, to revolve.

trendsetter • One who initiates or popularizes current fashion.

trendwatcher • One who looks for new currencies of style to inform others, or to be self-aware.

trendy • In with the latest fad or fashion. (AKA mod squatters)

Being gay is so-o-o trendy.

très • French for "very" and gayspeak for anything that may be "too much."

trick • An illusory event meant to reach a quick end (from its original definition as "an unlawful act that must be kept covered"); a casual, inconsequential sex partner. (AKA *one-night stand*, floater).

trick out • To have sex outside of a committed relationship.

trick towel • Cloth used for cleaning up after casual/random sex encounters (usually not of the best quality available).

It's a sin to use a Pratesi as a trick towel when you've got Wamsutta!

"turn a trick" • Of sexual interactions done successively, often for money.

"trip to the moon" • To have sex with the main emphasis being on anilingus.

I'll hit Uranus next, after I take a trip to the moon with this guy.

troll • A creature of Scandinavian folklore depicted as a devilish imp who lives in dark places and "patrols" in an endless search; an unattractive (often older) and relentless gay man. *Trolling*: to cruise for sex in a notably wanton manner and with lessened standards of what one will accept in a partner. Middle English: *trollen*, to wander about.

trolley dolly • Britspeak for a gay flight attendant. (AKA cart tart)

trophy boy • One who is a prize (whom another, an older male, proudly shows off as a "win" to others). (AKA prestige piece)

tryst • A specific meeting made in secret between lovers. Old French: *triste*, a waiting place in hunting.

tuck • To pull together and turn in to secure; hiding one's penis in an outfit where it might show.
  Those drag queens really know their tuck.

Turk • A sodomite, from the impression that many Turkish males were/are well acquainted with male anal copulation (but are not necessarily gay). (See *Greek*)
Turkish delight • Of the candy, gay for an anal sex virgin.
Turkish wrestling • A form of the male-to-male body contact sport even more homoerotic than usual.

turkey • A wild bird domesticated for food; a bird served on special occasions; a failure or one who is a flop; a young gay man, but not as youthful or common as a "chicken."
  Thanksgiving wouldn't be the same if I wasn't spending the afternoon basting a turkey.
turkey stuffing • Oh jeez, if you have to ask at this point!

turnover • A pastry where part is filled and covered by another part before baking; a passive gay partner.

turtleneck • The foreskin of an uncircumsised penis.
  I don't mind a turtleneck as long as your head pops out easily.

tutti-frutti • An Italian ice cream blended with chopped nuts and candied fruits;

one who acts effeminately, a tad nuttily, and definitely fruitily.

TV • Gayspeak short for "transvestite." A *console TV*: a large, lounging drag queen (*console*: a stationary cabinet).

tweak(er) • To sharply twist; one who is heavily under the influence of a drug, mainly crystal meth(amphetamine).

twee • Overly darling. Baby talk for "sweet."
If you had your choice to sleep with twee dull Dean and twee dull Dom, whom would you pick?

24-hour girl • Dragspeak for one dressed up in women's clothes all the time (and it can be a real girl!).

twerp • One who is detestably inconsequential. The term has no exact origins, but one far-fetched tale is of gay interest. It theorizes that the name comes from T.W. Earp, a student union president at Oxford in the early 1900s, who inspired loathing in the hearts of rugged rugby players by being "the last, most charming, and wittiest of the decadents."
My theory is that between the four, a twerp would be the first one on his knees before a geek, a dork, and a nerd.

twilighter • A person in the "middle" (from the time in between day and night when all has a "purplish" cast).
He was a twilighter with a sunny disposition and dark passions.

twink(ie) • A young gay male (post-teen, pre-mid-twenties) of slight build, memorable for his "outer packaging," and not his "inner depth." From the golden-colored (blond), phallic-shaped snack cake, invented in the 1930s, of little nutritional value, sweet to the taste—and, lest we forget, cream-filled!
How cute: a twinkie goin' down on a Twinkie.

twinkle toes • One who flits about in sparkling merriment.

twit • One who is annoying and silly (perhaps from "nitwit" or Old English: *aetwitan*, to reproach).

twitter • To speak chirpingly or giggle nervously.

twixter • Britspeak for a bisexual, or a person who gives the impression of being between the sexes: a masculine female or feminine male. (AKA tweener)

two-handed • A penis so large it can accommodate the grasp of a pair of hands. (Bring it on!)

two-spirit • Of transgendered people, mainly from African and Aboriginal tribes, who feel their dual essences of the sexes are beneficial characteristics. (See *berdache*)

type • Influenced by another. Greek: *tupos*, impression.
    He's the jock-type and he's the straight-type and he's the A&F-type, but I'm just me, the gay-type.

U-B-2 (you be too) • Cyberspeak to mean when one person of specific conditions (usually healthy—HIV-negative—and/or drug-free) notes that his sexual interests are restricted to those whose circumstances are exactly the same.

über • Gayspeak German for "extra."
Ober was über hot in bed.

un- • Prefix meaning "not"—and of way too many words often used to describe us, among them: *undesirable*: not wanted; *unnatural*: not right; *unfit*: not suitable; *unhealthy*: not good for you; *unorthodox*: not regular.

uncle • Any parent's brother; a frequent form of address for a close but non-blood-related male; a usually older, watchful gay man, sometimes partnered with or seeking a younger "nephew," and not as effeminate as an "auntie."

uncut • Uncircumsised, of a penis that has not had its original foreskin removed (preferred by many as the natural and more manly state).

undercover man • A gay man who keeps his sexual identity hidden, or one who does his best work "under the covers."

underground, the • Below the earth's surface; something kept hidden; a clandestine operation.

understand(ing) • To comprehend; to know and be sympathetic toward; an agreement between two.

unicorn • Creature of fable, symbolic of singularity (and "gay" in its uniqueness). Latin: having one horn.

unisex • That which can be undertaken or utilized interchangeably by both sexes. The androgyny of such things seems unsuited to straight men (gay, too) who need to make clear their sexuality and sex.

unity • All in harmonious accord. Latin: *unus*, one.

unload • To ejaculate (in recently gay-popular "hard" sex terminology; see *load*). (AKA shoot, blast a load, bust a nut)

unmanly • Not what a male should be (ex: dishonorable, cowardly, feminine). Everything "unmanly" has an effect on gay identity. Any man thought so is *queerly* considered, because it puts us just a step away from being womanly—and who is seen more often straddling or crossing that divide than we?

unusual • Not common; queer.

"Up yours" • Short for "up your ass"— and another way to say "fuck you." Consequently, another way to stick it to those who happen to like taking it up the butt.

Uranian / Urning • No longer used terms for homosexual and homosexuality, derived from the Greek *ouranos*, meaning "heaven"—coined by pioneering gay-rights advocate Karl Heinrich Ulrichs. "Urning" specifically implied that gays were noble, their same-sex attraction from Aphrodite Urania (see *hermaphrodite*), daughter of the god of the skies, Ouranos. *Urano-dioning*: Ulrichs's term for bisexuality. (See *dion*)

urbane • Metropolitan. Latin: *urbanus*, of a city.
We're the urbane of dull America's existence.

ursine • Like a "bear" (but not an active member of that gay subset). Latin: *ursus*, bear. *Ursophile*: one who is slim and hairless, but goes for "bears." (AKA *trapper*)

vaccine • A preparation that encourages antibodies to battle pathogens in the body.

vacuum cleaner • A machine of immense sucking power; one who likes to fellate, and does it extremely well. (AKA a Hoover, from the well-known maker of household cleaning appliances)

valley of decision • The small of the back, right before the buttocks (where one may pause before committing to anal sex).
He lingered along the valley of decision, guessing at what wonderful events were to come.

vanilla • A sweet, basic flavor; a white guy; of "traditional" sexual activity (kissing, masturbation, fellatio, and copulation?!) and not of the unusual, kinky, raunchy, hard-core, raw, or rough kind. The origin of "vanilla" comes from the Latin: *vagina*—yes, Virginia, *that* vagina!—which meant a sheath covering around a stem; you figure it out from there.

vanity • Inflated pride (often over one's appearance); something without use. Latin: *vanus*, empty.
If vanity thy name is woman, then what type of man be vain?

vapors, the • Said of someone who is going to or in an urgent mood to visit the baths.
Did it really sound like a cold, or is he having a case of the vapors again tonight?

Vaseline Towers • Any building where there resides a large population of gay men. (Although "Vaseline" is a once-popular form of lubricant used for naughty activities, any name brand could work just as well in its place.) (AKA stack-o-fags)
Was it a slip-up to go to Vaseline Towers? No, but it will be.

vegetarian • One who eats only plants (and never any "meat"); a gay man who does not fellate; a lesbian (theoretically not a meat-eater). A *vagitarian*, derivative of a "vagina" and "vegetarian," is a cunnilinguist.

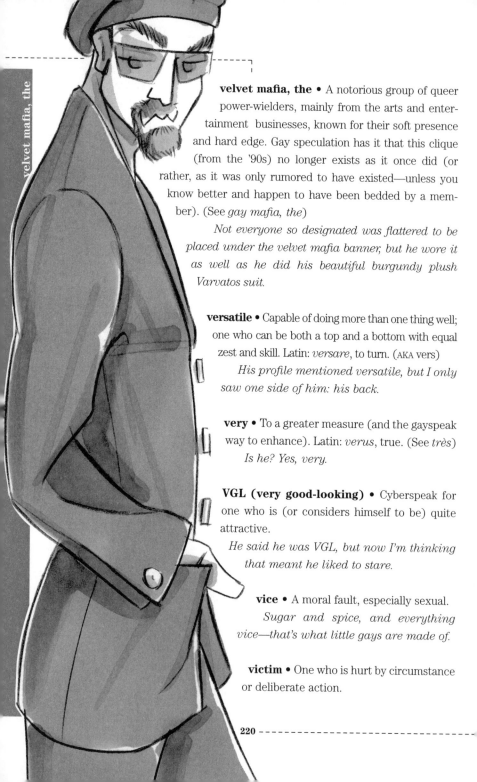

velvet mafia, the • A notorious group of queer power-wielders, mainly from the arts and entertainment businesses, known for their soft presence and hard edge. Gay speculation has it that this clique (from the '90s) no longer exists as it once did (or rather, as it was only rumored to have existed—unless you know better and happen to have been bedded by a member). (See *gay mafia, the*)

Not everyone so designated was flattered to be placed under the velvet mafia banner, but he wore it as well as he did his beautiful burgundy plush Varvatos suit.

versatile • Capable of doing more than one thing well; one who can be both a top and a bottom with equal zest and skill. Latin: *versare*, to turn. (AKA vers)

His profile mentioned versatile, but I only saw one side of him: his back.

very • To a greater measure (and the gayspeak way to enhance). Latin: *verus*, true. (See *très*)

Is he? Yes, very.

VGL (very good-looking) • Cyberspeak for one who is (or considers himself to be) quite attractive.

He said he was VGL, but now I'm thinking that meant he liked to stare.

vice • A moral fault, especially sexual.

Sugar and spice, and everything vice—that's what little gays are made of.

victim • One who is hurt by circumstance or deliberate action.

vile • Without morals, low.

viral load • Measured concentration of virus in the blood.

virgin queen • One who will allow anal sex only after he is in a committed relationship (from *virgin*: one who has not had sexual intercourse, often until marriage).

virile • Of an adult sexual male or of the powerful male spirit. Latin: *vir*, man.
He was too virile to be one of them.
virility • Manliness, strength.
But why do you think one's virility has anything to do with his sexuality?

virulent • Of great contagion. Latin: *virus*, poison.
virus • A noncell entity able to cause illness. Latin: *virus*, poison.

vivacious • Animated and spirited.
He's one of our most vivacious talents.

vogue • What's "in fashion."
voguing • An early-'90s dance, perhaps the only true "gay" one, which integrates quickly done "poses" (taken from the pages of the eponymous high-style magazine).

voyeur • One who watches rather than participates in sex, for pleasure. In this age of safer sex, it's not terribly surprising to find that a voyeur is no longer seen as so sinister as he once was. (See *watch queen*)

vulgar • Crude. Latin: *vulgus*, the common people.

vulnerable • Easily hurt, emotionally and physically. Latin: *vulnerare*, to wound.
Those with the least protection are the most vulnerable.

waffle • To be indirect; a light baked good (flimsy until toasted!); a very effeminate male.

waiter • One who "remains in expectation" in public restrooms, hoping to "serve the needs" of those who enter.

"walk with a lisp" • Said of one who is gay and behaves exaggeratedly so.

He walks with a lisp and runs like a girl.

"walks like Tarzan, talks like Jane" • Gayspeak phrase descriptive of a male whose outward appearance is unquestionably masculine (great body) but who, when he opens his mouth, sounds so feminine as to change completely one's previous impression. (AKA "See Tarzan, hear Jane")

wallflower • One whose timidity and awkwardness make it difficult for him to engage socially. From a "flower" who sits by a wall at a dance waiting for a partner.

The florist, after his success at the floral show, doffed his shirt at the closing dance, and was clearly a wallflower no more.

wank • Britspeak for masturbation.

wannabe • One who wishes to be someone else; a straight person curious about gayness (see *gay vague, metrosexual*). A *wannabe breeder*: someone gay wanting to be straight.

wanton • Excessive, sexual, and without scruples; one given to immorality. Old English: *wan*, without; *towen*, discipline.

"wash and go" • Where one cleans up immediately after sex and leaves hurriedly.

watch queen • A gay sex "voyeur" (AKA peek freak); one who likes to look at himself "in action" in a mirror; the one who keeps a lookout, in any intimate situation liable to be interrupted by unfriendly forces.

water boy • One whose main task it is to liquidly refresh thirsty athletes.

water sports • The sexual act(s) of urinating upon another for pleasure (considered "disciplinary" behavior, where the one peeing is in power and "humiliating" his partner—who still finds gratification in the act).

weakling • Said often of a male who cannot easily perform a typically manly task.
    Even with a hundred pounds of solid muscle added on the outside, he still felt like a 98-pound sand-abraded weakling on the inside.

"wear it out" • Dragspeak phrase imploring another to take something to its extreme.

wearmark • "Worn-out" area which draws the onlooker's attention to specific areas on another's clothes: mainly his crotch and buttocks.

wedgie • Prank where one's underwear is pulled up (wedged) between the buttocks. Of all life's mischievous acts, this is possibly the most hurtful to the young boys who are its targets. In one fell swoop, the young lad's budding masculinity is compromised and his power rent asunder.

weenie • One without effect, insignificant. This term has three possible origins: 1) from *wean*: to take nourishment (therefore, of one who cannot take care of himself); 2) from *wee*: very small; and 3) from a name for a frankfurter (which, via the same connection, makes it/him a "penis," too).

weird(o) • Noticeably strange; different; one who deviates from most.
    Honestly, I think it's a little weird that being gay isn't so queer anymore.

welcome wagon • The one who gets the honor of having a virgin male first.

If he snacks on any more hors d'oeuvres, they're gonna have to wheel that welcome wagon out, and no guy is gonna find that a welcome sight.

well- • Prefix for "outstandingly done." In many ways, gay men are superlative. But are we, as many think, so well-groomed, well-spoken, well-bred? In any case, speaking of outstanding things . . .

well-hung • Endowed with a much longer than average penis. "Hung" means of greater length, too, so to say "well-hung" is technically an overstatement. (Too, we're not all well-hung. But that's one exaggeration most would like to see.)

wet dream • A dream during which ejaculation occurs (a *nocturnal emission*); a man who, seeming to have come to life from one, is so attractive as to cause the onlooker to have a wet dream.

whack • To hit/remove with forceful intent.
whack job • A male-to-female transsexual.
whack off • To masturbate ("whack the weasel").

wham bam • Quickie sex (from the longer sentiment: "Wham, bam, thank you, Sam").

whimper(er) • To weep or protest softly; one given to crying (see *wimp*).

whimsical • Known for its fanciful aspects, and its gayness.

whine(r) • To protest childishly; one who harps.
Boys don't whine.

whipping boy • One who is punished for his master's misdeeds.
The whipping boy was so quick to undo his britches and bend over, his master wondered if it was possible that the youth enjoyed being lashed.

white party • The circuit party where attendees are expected to wear all (or some) items white in color. But it is not expected that they will behave in a manner that befits such pure effects. (In the beginning, these functions were called "white" because it was the color of semen and only masturbation was permitted.) (See *circuit*)

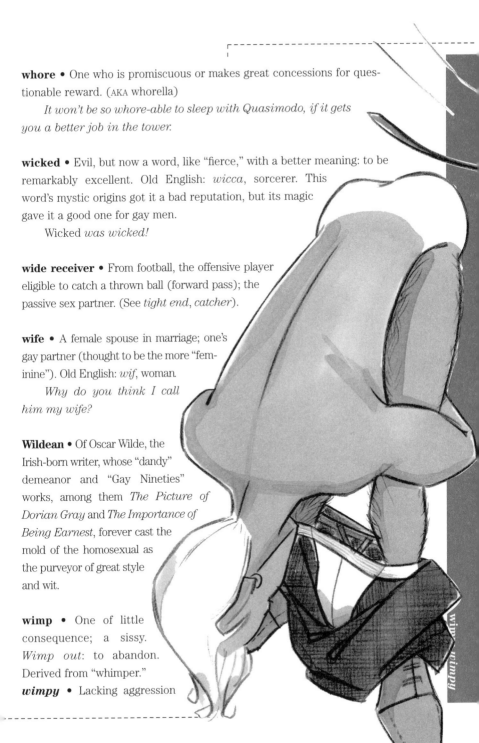

whore • One who is promiscuous or makes great concessions for questionable reward. (AKA whorella)

It won't be so whore-able to sleep with Quasimodo, if it gets you a better job in the tower.

wicked • Evil, but now a word, like "fierce," with a better meaning: to be remarkably excellent. Old English: *wicca*, sorcerer. This word's mystic origins got it a bad reputation, but its magic gave it a good one for gay men.

Wicked *was wicked!*

wide receiver • From football, the offensive player eligible to catch a thrown ball (forward pass); the passive sex partner. (See *tight end, catcher*).

wife • A female spouse in marriage; one's gay partner (thought to be the more "feminine"). Old English: *wif*, woman.

Why do you think I call him my wife?

Wildean • Of Oscar Wilde, the Irish-born writer, whose "dandy" demeanor and "Gay Nineties" works, among them *The Picture of Dorian Gray* and *The Importance of Being Earnest*, forever cast the mold of the homosexual as the purveyor of great style and wit.

wimp • One of little consequence; a sissy. *Wimp out*: to abandon. Derived from "whimper."
wimpy • Lacking aggression

(derived from the above, and popularized by J. Wellington Wimpy, the timid character from *Popeye* cartoons).

wince • To helplessly flinch from pain (or the expectation of it).

wishy-washy • Indecisive; without force of personality (a double intensive of *washy*: that which is diluted).

wispy • One who is frail. From *will-o'-the-wisp*: Will, a lad, who is slight among the *wisp*: the palely lit and thin grassy marshes. (AKA winsome)

witchy • Full of spite. From a *witch*: a nasty-tempered woman (possibly with magical powers).

wit(ty) • One expressive in a keen and fast manner about incompatible things; perceptively funny.
  You fuckin' guys are always so galdarned witty.
witticism • A clever remark (blending "witty" and "sarcasm").
  To wit, they were not the types to waste a whit of witticism on wastrals.

wolf • One with a voracious sex drive (from the animal who relentlessly stalks its prey); a "bear" male who is like an "otter" but more aggressive.

woman • An adult female; a gay man of extreme feminine behavior. Old English: *wifman*, wife of man.
womanly • Suggestive of an adult female. (See *girl: girlish/girly*)
woman's work • Occupations thought to be better done when performed by a female.
  But, son, what possessed you to think you'd be any good at woman's work?

woodworker • One skilled in crafting hardwood; a happy fellator (who works with *wood*: an erect penis).
  The naughty woodworker was busy chiseling away at his trojan, not realizing the irony that this was the closest he had come to handling one in years.

"woof" • The sound a dog makes; bearspeak for a sign (or sound) made noting someone's attractiveness, usually a "bear" himself. (See *"grrrr"*)

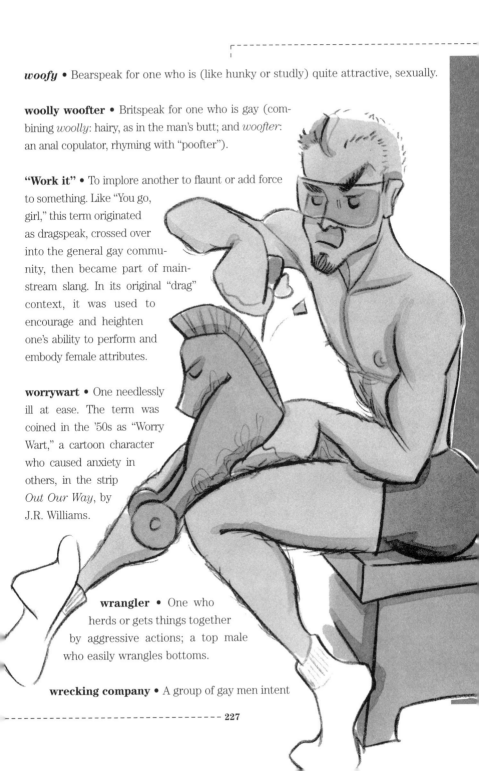

woofy • Bearspeak for one who is (like hunky or studly) quite attractive, sexually.

woolly woofter • Britspeak for one who is gay (combining *woolly*: hairy, as in the man's butt; and *woofter*: an anal copulator, rhyming with "poofter").

"Work it" • To implore another to flaunt or add force to something. Like "You go, girl," this term originated as dragspeak, crossed over into the general gay community, then became part of mainstream slang. In its original "drag" context, it was used to encourage and heighten one's ability to perform and embody female attributes.

worrywart • One needlessly ill at ease. The term was coined in the '50s as "Worry Wart," a cartoon character who caused anxiety in others, in the strip *Out Our Way*, by J.R. Williams.

wrangler • One who herds or gets things together by aggressive actions; a top male who easily wrangles bottoms.

wrecking company • A group of gay men intent

on startling straights (by *wrecking*: messing up the order of things).

They called themselves a wrecking company, but acted like they were in the one for the ballet.

wrestle • To grapple with powerfully (from the Old English: *wreasten*, to twist); a quite (perhaps the most) homoerotic form of male-to-male contact sport.

Coach Strap was encouraged that his jocks were so enthusiastic to learn how to wrestle properly that they practiced on their own time—and without having their official uniforms yet to wear, managing only frayed athletic supporters and holey gym socks.

wrinkle room • A gay bar patronized mainly by elderly men. (AKA crow's nest, wax works)

writers, gay • Since *Gay-2-Zee* is a dictionary of gay words, I thought it would be interesting to include the names of men who made their way by writing—*gaily*. A whole list would be too large to include, so I decided to whittle it down to just a dozen—along with a notable work—whose mention *may* cause a slight stir. (Listing either a Capote, a Coward, or a Cunningham would, or should, hardly be a surprise.) These scribes (composers, poets, too) are all widely considered to have been gay (or at least bisexual). For most, the true nature of their sexuality was never accepted publicly. More often, it was denied. Thus, their lives (and loves) remain "as rumor has it."

Bernstein, Leonard (composer, *West Side Story*)
Copland, Aaron (composer, *Fanfare for the Common Man*)
Eliot, T. S. (poet, *Old Possum's Book of Practical Cats*)
Inge, William (playwright, *Picnic*)
James, Henry (writer, *Washington Square*)
Mann, Thomas (writer, *Death in Venice*)
Maugham, Somerset (writer, *Of Human Bondage*)
Melville, Herman (writer, *Billy Budd*)
Proust, Marcel (writer, *Remembrance of Things Past*)
Waugh, Evelyn (writer, *Brideshead Revisited*)
Whitman, Walt (poet, *Leaves of Grass*)
Wilder, Thornton (writer, *Our Town*)

wry • Of drolly ironic humor. Middle English: *wrien*, to turn.
How wry you all are.

wuss(y) • An unmanly man. From "wimp" combined with "pussy" (both in the soft, "cat" sense, and less of a woman's vulnerable private parts).

X • Short for the sex-enhancing drug Ecstasy; labeled as "explicit" in content.

xobile • Able to search for, transmit, and receive sexual materials over wireless devices (combining "x," for "explicit," with *obile*, short for *mobile*: able to take with).
   Sexually speaking, he was as xobile as his cell.

X-pic • From the Internet, images of persons totally nude and/or in explicit sexual circumstances.

XXX • Sexually explicit materials that show full male erections and graphically depicted male-to-male sexual inter-actions.

yellow • Quite afraid.

yellow-bellied • One who is, in his "guts," a coward.

yestergay • One who was queer, but now settled into a heterosexual life.

"You go, girl!" • Famed dragspeak phrase that means praise for another's actions or empowerment for those yet to be undertaken. This expression originated within the African-American female community—then came to us via the gay sons of these women. But ever since the mainstream took to using it, the impact and importance within our community has dropped off to the point of almost non-use.

None of us could tell if he was saying a hello "yoo-hoo" or a goodbye "you go, girl"; the hand gestures he used for both were identical.

"yoo-hoo" • The gayspeak way to greet or call one's attention.

young(er) • Being of less age than someone or something else (and a focus in the gay community—on one's own and other's youth or youthful aspects—both troubling and promising).

Youth is wasted on the young.

The above is a famous quote from the esteemed playwright George Bernard Shaw, who, it has been said, wasn't gay. In fact, he was supposed to be quite the womanizer. But surely one of his most well-regarded works, *Pygmalion* (which became the basis for the musical *My Fair Lady*), could be read *queerly*. No? Yes? But of the entire contents of *Gay-2-Zee*, that is precisely the point. We all read into things what we want to read. And with that, I take you to "Z" end of the book . . .

Z

zero tolerance • Completely unacceptable.

He had zero tolerance for their toleration bullshit.

zing(er) • A barbed remark that succeeds in making clear its point.

zipper • Closure device found on the fly of men's pants (derived from the sound made when the pull was quickly drawn upward).

zipper club • An establishment where sex is readily available.

Not only was he president of the zipper club, he was a client, too.

zipper dinner • Fellatio. (AKA zipper sex)

zipper morals • Standards of conduct that are easily bent or lowered..

zshoosh • To do oneself or something up right. (Pronounced "juge.")

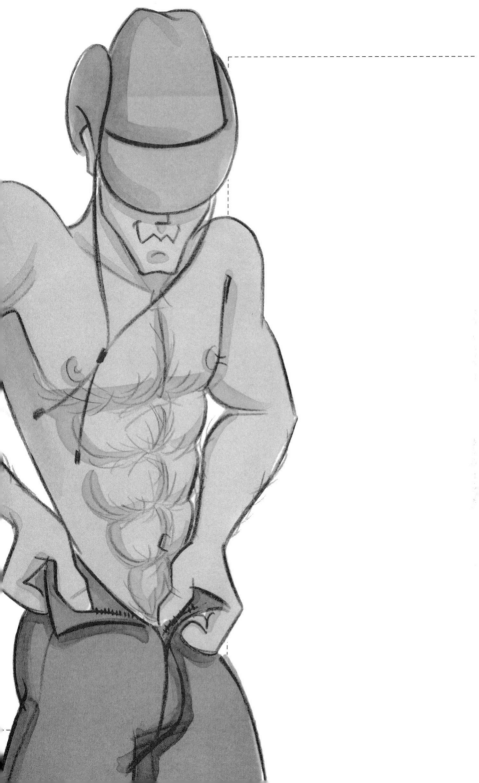

bibliography

101 Gay Sex Secrets Revealed by Jonathan Bass (2004).

Abnormally Happy: A Gay Dictionary by Richard Summerbell (1985).

A Boy's Own Story by Edmund White (1982).

A Single Man by Christopher Isherwood (1964).

City of Night by John Rechy (1963).

Faggots by Larry Kramer (1978).

Fantabulosa: A Dictionary of Polari and Gay Slang by Paul Baker (2002).

Gay Pride: A Celebration of All Things Gay & Lesbian by William J. Mann ((2004).

gay(s)language: a dic(k)tionary of gay slang by H. Max (1988).

Giovanni's Room by James Baldwin (1956).

Outbursts!: A Queer Erotic Thesaurus by Allan Peterkin (2003).

Tales of the City by Armistead Maupin (1978).

The Bear Handbook: A Comprehensive Guide for Those Who Are Husky, Hairy, and Homosexual and Those Who Love 'Em compiled by Ray Kampf (2000).

The City and the Pillar by Gore Vidal (1948).

The Fabulous Sylvester by Joshua Gamson (2005).

The Gay Book of Lists by Leigh W. Rutledge (2003).

The Guild Dictionary of Homosexual Terms by Dr. Albert Ellis (1965).

The Homosexual and His Society: A View from Within by Donald Webster Cory and John P. LeRoy (1963).

The Lord Won't Mind by Gordon Merrick (1970).

The New Gay Teenager by Ritch C. Savin-Williams (2005).

The Queens' Vernacular: A Gay Lexicon by Bruce Rodgers (1972).

The Unofficial Gay Manual: Living the Lifestyle (or at Least Appearing To) by Kevin DiLallo and Jack Krumholtz (1994).

Word's Out: Gay Men's English by William L. Leap (1996).

Innumerable Web sites were consulted, but one in particular, www.glbtq.com, we should all look in on from time to time; The Webster's; an American Heritage and a coupla French dictionaries . . . and finally . . . *Roget's Thesaurus.*

acknowledgments

A book as full of stuff as this one couldn't have become quite the pretty package it is were it not for the help of an amazing assortment of individuals (and institutions). Therefore, the author would like to thank the following for their contributions, help, and support:

My original editor, Michael Connor, who, before going on to new horizons, saw the potential of this dictionary as something more than just words on a page; my knight-in-shining-armor editor, Keith Kahla, who rescued *Gay-2-Zee* from dragons who would set it ablaze; all the "peeps" at St. Martin's Press (Gregory Gestner, Jessie Markland, et al.) who helped bring it to a bookstore (and Web site) near you; and my *fab*-ulous agent, Mitchell Waters, who saw it, loved it, sold it, and endured my typical gay insecurities throughout! Mwah!

And without further ado: A Different Light, Alan A., Jess B., Matt Bell (and a few choice issues of *Genre*), Richard B., Eric B., Paul B., Kim Brinster (Oscar Wilde and Lambda Rising), Mitch B. & Harris, Dan B. & Joe, Charles Busch, David Carter, Terry C., Mike C. & Chris, Rick Coleman (Q Trading), John D. & Bill, Jim D. & Gary, Pat D. & Jerry, Frank D., John Epperson (and his comely cohort, Lypsinka), the GLBT Center in New York (especially Robert Woodworth), Giovanni's Room (in Philly), Kim G., Boze H., Steve H., Jennifer J., Billy J., Kevin Joseph (and his fierce friend, Flotilla DeBarge), Jon K., Lady Bunny, Professor William Leap, Joe M., Miisa M., Lee and the boys, Mark M. & Gary, Neil M., Kevin M., Wayne M. & Kenny, Peter O. & John, Dan O., Darlene O. & John, Pauline Park, Bob Podrasky, David R. & Ben, Philip Rafshoon (Outwrite), Mike R. & Chris, Ray S., all the wonderful people at SAGE (especially Tom Weber, William Falk, and Philip Katz), Mike Sheldon (Sublime), Bill Sherman (and all the other skilled homoeroticists at Ajaxx63), Paul S., Caroline S-G & James, Teresa S. & Ward, Tony T., Unabridged (in Chicago), Garry W., and Wes W. & Steve.

To Red, Treat, and the whole gang of l'il dickens.

Finally, to my partner, Robert, for just being there and for being who he is. There are far better ways to express my gratitude, devotion, and love. But, of all things to have happen, words fail me!

Also by Donald F. Reuter